D1739322

HISTORICAL DICTIONARIES
OF U.S. HISTORICAL ERAS
Jon Woronoff, Series Editor

1. *From the Great War to the Great Depression*, by Neil A. Wynn, 2003.
2. *Civil War and Reconstruction*, by William L. Richter, 2004.
3. *Revolutionary America*, by Terry M. Mays, 2005.
4. *Old South*, by William L. Richter, 2006.
5. *Early American Republic*, by Richard Buel Jr., 2006.
6. *Jacksonian Era and Manifest Destiny*, by Terry Corps, 2006.
7. *Reagan–Bush Era*, by Richard S. Conley, 2007.
8. *Kennedy–Johnson Era*, by Richard Dean Burns and Joseph M. Siracusa, 2008.
9. *Nixon–Ford Era*, by Mitchell K. Hall, 2008.
10. *Roosevelt–Truman Era*, by Neil A. Wynn, 2008.
11. *Eisenhower Era*, by Burton I. Kaufman and Diane Kaufman, 2009.

Historical Dictionary
of the Eisenhower Era

Burton I. Kaufman
Diane Kaufman

Historical Dictionaries of
U.S. Historical Eras, No. 11

The Scarecrow Press, Inc.
Lanham, Maryland • Toronto • Plymouth, UK
2009

SCARECROW PRESS, INC.

Published in the United States of America
by Scarecrow Press, Inc.
A wholly owned subsidiary of
The Rowman & Littlefield Publishing Group, Inc.
4501 Forbes Boulevard, Suite 200, Lanham, Maryland 20706
www.scarecrowpress.com

Estover Road
Plymouth PL6 7PY
United Kingdom

British Library Cataloguing in Publication Information Available

Library of Congress Cataloging-in-Publication Data

Kaufman, Burton Ira.
  Historical dictionary of the Eisenhower era / Burton I. Kaufman, Diane
Kaufman.
      p. cm. — (Historical dictionaries of U.S. historical eras ; no. 11)
  Includes bibliographical references.
  ISBN-13: 978-0-8108-5507-6 (cloth : alk. paper)
  ISBN-10: 0-8108-5507-0 (cloth : alk. paper)
  ISBN-13: 978-0-8108-6284-5 (ebook)
  ISBN-10: 0-8108-6284-0 (ebook)
  1. United States–History–1953–1961–Dictionaries. 2. United States–Politics and
government–1953–1961–Dictionaries. 3. United States–Biography–Dictionaries.
I. Kaufman, Diane. II. Title.
  E835.K37 2009
  973.92–dc22   2008033598

∞ ™ The paper used in this publication meets the minimum requirements of
American National Standard for Information Sciences—Permanence of Paper
for Printed Library Materials, ANSI/NISO Z39.48-1992.
Manufactured in the United States of America.

Contents

Editor's Foreword

Time has an amazing ability to put a glow on the past and create the impression that an earlier era was a golden age, whereas the period itself was more mixed, and occasionally frightening. This applies notably to the presidency of Dwight D. Eisenhower. An outstanding soldier throughout his career, and the primary Allied commander during the final phase of World War II, he was widely admired and respected, enough so that he was easily elected president of the United States in 1952. He remained sufficiently popular that he was reelected in 1956. Much of what he did was positive, and the country passed through a period of relative peace and prosperity, whose tranquility did not quite snuff out movements for reform or the rise of a rather different younger generation. But this was only part of the picture—the other side included racial discrimination against African Americans, two major recessions, and nasty pockets of poverty. Internationally, it was a time of serious—and sometimes extremely dangerous—competition between the United States and the Soviet Union, the two great powers at the end of World War II. With the Cold War periodically heating up in confrontations such as the Korean War, and the Soviet Union catching up on nuclear weapons and pulling ahead in the space race, international concerns impacted domestic politics, as seen in the Red Scare and efforts to root out American communists with rather un-American methods.

This makes the *Historical Dictionary of the Eisenhower Era* one of the more interesting volumes in the series. It deals with a crucial time of transition, and it highlights the good and bad aspects, revealing a clearer overall picture. Just how many significant events occurred in less than a decade is immediately apparent from the chronology. What they added up to, taking the positives and the negatives, is explained more cogently in the introduction. But the dictionary section is the key to a deeper understanding of the 1950s. Its roughly 400 entries look at many important aspects, not only domestic politics and foreign policy but also education, the economy, technological innovations, arts and sciences, and popular culture. Since the period is so fascinating, and the nostalgia for it keeps growing, readers will be pleased to find a substantial bibliography leading to more, sometimes detailed literature on the various relevant topics.

This book was written by Burton and Diane Kaufman, who lived through the Eisenhower era with considerable pleasure and few regrets, to judge by the lively text they give us in what is all too often a rather glum genre, the encyclopedia. They grew up during the 1950s and not long after began their respective careers. Diane initially taught in Kansas, where she was awarded for her leadership in elementary and secondary education, and then worked as a reference librarian and archivist in Kansas, Virginia, and Ohio. Burton had a busy career teaching at the University of New Orleans, Kansas State University, and Virginia Tech, where he headed the history department. He later became, in addition to professor of history, dean of the School of Interdisciplinary Studies at Miami University in Ohio, and he is presently adjunct professor of history at the University of Utah. Both of them have written on the Eisenhower era before, and both are busily working on a forthcoming volume in this series dealing with the Carter era.

Jon Woronoff
Series Editor

Acknowledgments

A number of people helped complete this book. Scott, our son, is owed a special note of gratitude. His knowledge of the Eisenhower era was especially helpful with some entries. Bob Zieger answered questions about labor unions. Al Keithley found nostalgic websites related to the 1950s. Eleanor Sprowl, Debbie and Marty Quitt, Sue and Jack Leglise, Bev and Dick Graves, Sue and Ed Brooks, Carolyn Giles, Sandra Leatham, Sharon Long, and Leta Roberson recalled television shows, movies, fashions, fads, and their years in school. The reference librarians at the University of Utah's Marriott Library deserve a special note of thanks.

Acronyms and Abbreviations

AAU	Amateur Athletic Union
ACLU	American Civil Liberties Union
AEC	Atomic Energy Commission
AFL	American Federation of Labor
AFL	American Football League
AFL-CIO	American Federation of Labor and Congress of Industrial Organizations
ATA	American Tennis Association
BOI	Bureau of Investigation
CAA	Civil Aeronautics Administration
CBS	Columbia Broadcasting System
CCA	Comics Code Authority
CCP	Chinese Communist Party
CEA	Council of Economic Advisors
CIA	Central Intelligence Agency
CIO	Congress of Industrial Organizations
DAR	Daughters of the American Revolution
DNA	deoxyribonucleic acid
EST	Eastern Standard Time
FAA	Federal Aviation Administration
FBI	Federal Bureau of Investigation
FDA	Food and Drug Administration
FORTRAN	Formula Translation system
FSA	Federal Security Administration
FTC	Federal Trade Commission
HEW	Department of Health, Education, and Welfare
HUAC	House Un-American Activities Committee

IADB	Inter-American Development Bank
IAEA	International Atomic Energy Agency
IBM	International Business Machines
ICBMs	intercontinental ballistic missiles
INA	Immigration and Nationality Act
IRBMs	intermediate-range ballistic missiles
LPGA	Ladies Professional Golf Association
MGM	Metro-Goldwyn-Mayer
MIT	Massachusetts Institute of Technology
NAACP	National Association for the Advancement of Colored People
NASA	National Aeronautics and Space Administration
NATO	North Atlantic Treaty Organization
NBA	National Basketball Association
NBC	National Broadcasting Company
NFL	National Football League
NFL	National Front for Liberation of South Vietnam
NOW	National Organization for Women
NSC	National Security Council
OAS	Organization of American States
OEEC	Organization for European Economic Cooperation
OPEC	Organization of Petroleum Exporting Countries
OSS	Office of Strategic Services
PGA	Professional Golf Association
PVDC	polyvinylidene chloride
SAC	Strategic Air Command
SEATO	Southeast Asia Treaty Organization
SCLC	Southern Christian Leadership Conference
SPD	Berlin Social Democratic Party
Todd-A-O	Todd-American-Optical
UAR	United Arab Republic
UFO	unidentified flying object
UN	United Nations
UNAEC	United Nations Atomic Energy Commission
UNICEF	United Nations Children's Fund
UNIVAC	Universal Automatic Computer I
UPI	United Press International

USS	United States Ship
USSR	Union of Soviet Socialist Republics
USWA	United Steelworkers of America
VHF	very high frequency
WAAC	Women's Auxiliary Army Corps
WCC	White Citizens Council
WPA	Works Progress Administration

Chronology

1951 1 January: Chinese Communists break through United Nations forces in Seoul, Korea. **4 January**: UN forces abandon Seoul. **7 January**: General Dwight D. Eisenhower, in Paris to discuss European defense strategies, encounters hostile crowds. **18 January**: French forces hold Hanoi, Indochina, against Viet Minh guerrillas. **1 February**: The United Nations accepts the U.S. resolution condemning Chinese Communist attacks on Korea. General Eisenhower, supreme commander of North Atlantic Treaty Organization (NATO) forces, tells a joint session of Congress that the Cold War will become hotter if American troop numbers and military supplies are limited. **11 February**: UN forces cross the 38th parallel in Korea. **26 February**: 22nd Amendment limiting presidents to two terms is added to the U.S. Constitution. **10 March**: Alger Hiss is found guilty of perjury. **14 March**: UN troops regain control of Seoul. **29 March**: Chinese Communists reject General Douglas MacArthur's offer of a truce. **5 April**: Ethel and Julius Rosenberg are sentenced to death for giving atomic bomb secrets to the Soviet Union. **11 April**: President Harry S. Truman fires General MacArthur for insubordination. **28 April**: Mohammed Mossadegh becomes prime minister of Iran. **12 May**: Tests in the Pacific show the power of the hydrogen bomb. **21 June**: Iran seizes control of British petroleum holdings in Abadan; negotiations fail between Great Britain and Iran. **23 June**: The *New York Times* reports television is changing the lifestyle of Americans; motion picture attendance is down 40 percent in some cities. **16 August**: Egypt demands British troops leave the Suez Canal area. **4 September**: First transcontinental television transmission covers President Truman's discussion of Japanese treaty talks. **8 October**: Egypt announces plans to take control of the Suez Canal and to eject British troops. **16 October**: The Columbia Broadcasting System (CBS) televises first color television program in New York. **28 November**:

Peace talks begin between the Communist Chinese and United Nations negotiators designating the 38th parallel as the dividing line between North and South Korea.

1952 8 February: Elizabeth II crowned queen of the United Kingdom. **8 March**: The first mechanical heart is used on a human patient. **11 April**: Eisenhower asks for his release from NATO command as of 1 June. **15 April**: Peace treaty officially ending World War II is signed by President Truman. **2 May**: British Overseas Airways begins the first commercial jet service. **8 May**: Allied forces bomb North Korea after the Communist Chinese turn down an offer for peace. **2 June**: Supreme Court rules President Truman's seizure of steel mills during a strike was unconstitutional. **14 June**: President Truman announces construction of the first nuclear submarine, the USS *Nautilus*. **27 June**: The McCarran-Walter Act, also known as the Immigration and Nationality Act (INA), is passed over President Truman's veto. **12 July**: Dwight D. Eisenhower officially nominated as Republican Party's candidate for president. Senator Richard M. Nixon nominated for vice president. **14 July**: General Motors introduces air conditioning for the 1953 model cars. **26 July**: Governor Adlai E. Stevenson of Illinois nominated as Democratic Party's candidate for president. **3 August**: Olympics held in Helsinki, Finland; for the first time in 12 years the Soviet Union sends athletes. **24 August**: Vice presidential candidate Nixon appears on television to defend himself in what becomes known as the Checkers speech. **30 September**: Cinerama, a new wide-screen projection system, introduced to an audience of New York moviegoers. **23 October**: Supreme Court rejects the Rosenbergs' appeal. **24 October**: Eisenhower promises that if elected, he will go to Korea to seek an end to the war. **4 November**: John F. Kennedy elected senator from Massachusetts. **5 November**: Eisenhower and Nixon are elected president and vice president of the United States. **20 November**: President-elect Eisenhower names three cabinet members: Secretary of State John Foster Dulles, Secretary of Defense Charles E. Wilson, and Secretary of the Interior Douglas McKay. **17 December**: Eisenhower travels to Korea as promised.

1953 20 January: Eisenhower sworn in as president, delivers his inaugural address. **30 January**: President Eisenhower amends the Agricultural Adjustment Act of 1938. **5 March**: Death of Soviet leader Joseph Stalin announced. **26 March**: Success of the Salk vaccine in preventing polio is announced. **1 April**: Congress creates Department of Health, Education, and Welfare (HEW). **11 April**: HEW officially begins, with Oveta Culp Hobby as first secretary. **26 May**: Armistice negotiations at Panmunjom announced by President Eisenhower. **2 June**: Edmund Hillary becomes first person to reach top of Mt. Everest. **19 June**: President Eisenhower refuses to intervene in Rosenberg case. **8–9 July**: President Eisenhower and Iran's Prime Minister Mossadegh discuss aid to Iran and the Iranian government's seizure of British oil holdings. **28 July**: President Eisenhower announces Korean armistice has been signed. **31 July**: Senator Robert A. Taft, Senate majority leader, dies. **6 August**: The Farm Credit Act of 1953 signed. **14 August**: Soviet Union announces it is capable of building a hydrogen bomb. **22 August**: Mossadegh's government overthrown and the shah of Iran returns to power. **8 September**: Chief Justice Fred M. Vinson dies. **10 September**: Secretary of Labor Martin P. Durkin resigns. **13 September**: Nikita Khrushchev becomes new leader of the Soviet Union. **8 December**: President Eisenhower, British Prime Minister Winston Churchill, and French Prime Minister Joseph Laniel conclude Bermuda Conference. **8 December**: President Eisenhower addresses Congress and calls for "Atoms for Peace."

1954 13 January: Secretary of State John Foster Dulles meets with Soviet ambassador to discuss a limit on the uses of atomic energy. **14 January**: Marilyn Monroe marries baseball great Joe DiMaggio. **21 January**: The first nuclear submarine, USS *Nautilus*, launched. **31 January**: Berlin Conference held to discuss the future of Germany. **17 February**: Scientific proof that smoking leads to lung cancer puts tobacco companies on the defensive; cigarette sales decline. **25 February**: Senator Joseph McCarthy accuses government officials of communist connections. **1 March**: Puerto Rican nationalists open fire in Congress, wounding five. **1 March**: United States' first hydrogen bomb successfully tested in the Pacific Ocean. **12 March**: Edward R. Murrow accuses Senator McCarthy of spreading half-truths about the threat of communism in the United States. **25 March**: Record Company of America (RCA) begins mass production of 12-inch color television sets. **1 April**: Eisenhower establishes the Air Force Academy. **29**

April: Atomic physicist J. Robert Oppenheimer accused of being a security risk. **8 May**: French defeated at Dien Bien Phu in Vietnam. **13 May**: Eisenhower authorizes building St. Lawrence Seaway. **17 May**: Supreme Court rules "separate but equal" doctrine unconstitutional. **24 May**: International Business Machines (IBM) announces its "electronic brain," precursor of the computer. **17 June**: Televised Army-McCarthy hearings end after 36 days of questions. **12 July**: Eisenhower proposes Interstate Highway System. **19 July**: Roy Cohn resigns as Senator McCarthy's chief counsel. **2 August**: Eisenhower signs Housing Act providing 35,000 new homes. **5 August**: Shah of Iran and President Eisenhower announce 25-year agreement between Iran and eight oil companies. **10 August**: Construction of St. Lawrence Seaway begins. **24 August**: Communist Control Act of 1954 is signed. **28 August**: Agricultural Act of 1954 is signed. **30 August**: Atomic Energy Act of 1954 is signed. **11 November**: Eisenhower Museum dedicated in Abilene, Kansas. **27 September**: Mao Zedong reelected as leader of Communist China. **2 October**: West Germany admitted into NATO. **13 November**: Gamal Abdel Nasser becomes leader of Egypt. **2 December**: Senator Joseph McCarthy censured by the Senate.

1955 9 February: The American Federation of Labor and Congress of Industrial Organizations merge, forming AFL-CIO. **28 March**: John Marshall Harlan becomes a Supreme Court justice. **5 April**: Winston Churchill resigns as Britain's prime minister. **6 April**: Anthony Eden appointed prime minister of the United Kingdom. **18 April**: Albert Einstein dies. **14 May**: Warsaw Pact signed. **31 May**: Supreme Court rules that states must integrate their public schools "with all deliberate speed." **13 July**: Oveta Culp Hobby resigns as secretary of health, education, and welfare. **18 July**: Disneyland opens. **23 July**: Geneva Summit ends with the Big Four (France, United Kingdom, United States, and Soviet Union) calling it a success. **24 September**: Eisenhower suffers a heart attack. **2 November**: David Ben-Gurion becomes Israel's prime minister. **26 November**: The Soviet Union successfully tests its first hydrogen bomb. **1 December**: Rosa Parks arrested for refusing to give up her seat on a Montgomery, Alabama, bus. **5 December**: Montgomery Bus Boycott begins under leadership of Martin Luther King Jr.

1956 27 January: Elvis Presley's recording of "Heartbreak Hotel" sells 300,000 copies in its first week. **24 February**: Khrushchev denounces Stalin's leadership and actions. **29 February**: Eisenhower announces he will run for second term. **9 March**: British government deports Archbishop Makarios from Cyprus. **19 April**: Grace Kelly marries Prince Ranier of Monaco. **15 May**: Syngman Rhee elected to third term as leader of South Korea. **28 May**: President Eisenhower signs farm bill that allows the government to store agricultural surpluses. **5 June**: U.S. District Court in *Browder v. Gayle* rules against segregation on buses. **9 June**: Eisenhower undergoes surgery to relieve an intestinal obstruction. **29 June**: Eisenhower signs $33.4 billion Interstate Highway Act. **29 June**: Marilyn Monroe marries playwright Arthur Miller. **30 June**: Some 650,000 United States steelworkers go on strike. **26 July**: Nasser nationalizes Suez Canal. **17 August**: Democrats again nominate Adlai Stevenson for president, Senator Estes Kefauver as running mate. **22 August**: Republicans renominate Eisenhower and Nixon. **27 September**: Babe Zaharias, considered world's greatest female athlete, dies of cancer. **23 October**: Hungarian Revolution begins; Soviet police fire on protestors. **31 October**: United Nations calls emergency meeting after France, Israel, and Great Britain attack Egypt. **6 November**: President Eisenhower elected for second term; UN announces cease-fire in Suez Crisis. **13 November**: U.S. Supreme Court upholds *Browder v. Gayle* decision of lower court. **23 November**: Soviet tanks end the Hungarian Revolution.

1957 10 January: Harold Macmillan replaces Anthony Eden as British prime minister. **21 January**: Eisenhower inaugurated for second term. **9 March**: Eisenhower announces his Mideast doctrine permitting the United States to send military aid to any Mideast country desiring help. **20 March**: Eisenhower and Macmillan meet in Bermuda to end strained relations after Suez Crisis. **25 March**: Western European countries form the Common Market. **2 May**: Senator Joseph McCarthy dies. **3 May**: United States promotes the Baghdad Pact. **29 July**: International Atomic Energy Commission formed to use atomic energy for peaceful purposes. **29 August**: Eisenhower signs Civil Rights Act. **4 September**: Arkansas state militia prevents African American students from entering Central High School; Governor Orval Faubus calls in Arkansas national guard to prevent integration of schools. **25 September**: U.S. Army troops sent by Eisenhower escort nine African American students into Central High School. **4 October**: Soviet Union announces launching of space satellite *Sputnik*. **17 December**: United States launches its first intercontinental ballistic missile.

1958 1 February: United States launches its first satellite. **24 March**: Elvis Presley begins his tour of duty in the U.S. Army. **27 March**: Khrushchev named premier of Soviet Union. **13 April**: Van Cliburn wins Soviet Union's International Tchaikovsky Piano Competition. **7 May**: Vice President Nixon greeted by protestors in Lima, Peru. **14 May**: Nixon cuts short his trip to Latin America due to protests in Venezuela and Peru. **1 June**: Charles de Gaulle becomes premier of France, seeks to quell crisis in Algeria. **4 June**: De Gaulle greeted with cheers in Algeria. **28 June**: Dedication of Michigan's Mackinac Bridge, world's longest suspension bridge. **15 July**: Eisenhower sends U.S. marines to Lebanon to help President Camille Chamoun. **29 July**: National Aeronautics and Space Administration (NASA) created. **7 August**: USS *Nautilus* completes trip under the North Pole begun on 3 August. **17 August**: First U.S. moon shot fails when the rocket explodes at 50,000 feet. **2 September**: National Defense Education Act signed. **5 September**: Civil rights leader Martin Luther King Jr. arrested in Alabama; African American Althea Gibson wins U.S. tennis title at Forest Hills. **12 September**: Arkansas Governor Faubus orders four Little Rock high schools closed rather than integrate them. **22 September**: Sherman Adams resigns after scandal over accepting gifts. **31 October**: Meeting in Geneva, the United States, Soviet Union, and Great Britain reach an agreement on a draft of a nuclear test ban. **4 November**: Nelson Rockefeller elected governor of New York; John F. Kennedy reelected to U.S. Senate. **27 November**: Soviet Union threatens to cut access from East Germany to West Germany if U.S. troops remain in West Germany.

1959 1 January: Fidel Castro seizes control of Cuba's government. **3 January**: Alaska becomes 49th state. **7 January**: United States recognizes new Cuban government. **8 January**: Charles de Gaulle elected president of France. **3 February**: Rock and roll stars Buddy Holly, Richie Valens, and J. P. "the Big Bopper" Richardson die in plane crash in Iowa. **1 March**: Archbishop Makarios returns to Cyprus after three years of exile. **16 April**: Arab nations meet in Cairo for first conference on oil production. **25 April**: St. Lawrence Seaway officially opens. **11**

May: The Big Four (United States, Soviet Union, France, and Great Britain) meet in Geneva to discuss German reunification. **27 May**: Secretary of State John Foster Dulles dies. **12 July**: National Association for the Advancement of Colored People celebrates 50th anniversary at New York convention. **15 July**: Some 500,000 steelworkers strike for a new contract. **25 July**: Khrushchev and Nixon hold "Kitchen Debate" in the American National Exhibition in Moscow. **21 August**: Hawaii becomes 50th state. **15 September**: Khrushchev visits United States for first time. **9 October**: Baghdad Pact ends its first meeting in Washington with a name change, becoming the Central Treaty Organization (CENTO). **16 October**: General George C. Marshall dies. **1 November**: Patrice Lumumba arrested after his involvement in Congo crisis. **7 November**: Supreme Court ends steelworker strike. **1 December**: United States, Soviet Union, and 10 other countries sign treaty stating Antarctica to be used only for scientific research.

1960 9 January: Vice President Nixon announces he will run for president. **24 January**: French citizens in Algeria launch uprising after President de Gaulle promises to grant independence to Algeria. **31 January**: Democratic Senator John F. Kennedy announces he will run for president. **1 February**: Four African Americans stage a sit-in at an all-white lunch counter in Greensboro, North Carolina, sparking sit-ins throughout South to end segregation. **17 February**: Eisenhower approves plan to overthrow Castro. **9 March**: Thousands of African American students gather on steps of Montgomery, Alabama, capitol building to protest segregation. **15 March**: Ten nations, including the United States and Soviet Union, meet in Geneva to discuss disarmament. **28 April**: President Syngman Rhee of South Korea resigns. **29 April**: Disarmament talks end in deadlock. **1 May**: Soviets down U.S. U-2 spy plane; pilot Francis Gary Powers captured. **6 May**: President Eisenhower signs Civil Rights Act of 1960. **9 May**: Food and Drug Administration (FDA) approves first birth control pill. **14 May**: The Big Four meet in Paris. **17 May**: Paris meeting of Big Four ends over U-2 incident. **17 May**: Senator Hubert Humphrey drops out of race for president; Senator John F. Kennedy expected to be the Democratic Party candidate. **19 May**: Nine disc jockeys, including Alan Freed, arrested for payola. **23 May**: Nazi Adolph Eichmann arrested in Argentina. **4 June**: Communist China attacks island of Quemoy. **17 June**:

Congress passes 23rd Amendment, giving District of Columbia citizens the right to vote in presidential elections. **18 June**: Communist China again shells Quemoy. **29 June**: Fidel Castro seizes American oil refineries. **8 July**: Belgian citizens flee the Congo as Congolese army rebels riot; Nikita Khrushchev warns United States to stay out of Cuba and threatens rocket attacks. **12 July**: Democrats adopt strong civil rights platform. **15 July**: Democrats nominate Senator John F. Kennedy for president and Senator Lyndon B. Johnson of Texas for vice president; United Nations forces land in Congo to quell violence. **28 July**: Republicans nominate Richard M. Nixon for president, Henry Cabot Lodge Jr. as his running mate. **7 August**: Castro nationalizes all U.S.-owned property in Cuba. **19 August**: U-2 pilot Francis Gary Powers sentenced to 10 years in Soviet prison. **24 August**: FDA approves use of Sabin polio vaccine. **14 September**: Organization of Petroleum Exporting Countries (OPEC) formed. **26 September**: Kennedy and Nixon meet for first TV debate. **4 October**: United States launches first active telecommunications satellite. **12 October**: Soviet leader Khrushchev shows anger at United Nations by banging his shoe on the desk. **9 November**: John F. Kennedy elected president by narrowest margin in history. **12 December**: Kennedy names Dean Rusk as secretary of state.

1961 17 January: Eisenhower delivers his farewell address, warning the country against a growing "military-industrial complex." **20 January**: John F. Kennedy sworn in as president.

Introduction

After World War II, U.S. armed forces returned from the war, praised for their heroism. Many women who had entered the workforce returned to their prewar positions as wives and mothers. Veterans settled into jobs or took advantage of the G.I. Bill to further their education. The 1950s began with President Harry S. Truman, a Democrat, in office. He had ended World War II by ordering the use of atomic bombs on two major cities in Japan, killing thousands of people. Although the devastation was horrible, Truman believed the use of the atomic bomb brought about Japan's quick surrender, thereby saving American lives. However, the power wielded by the Union of Soviet Socialist Republics (USSR) after World War II created fear in the United States. The Soviet Union had tested its first nuclear weapon in 1949, and the possibility of a nuclear war was on Americans' minds.

In June 1950, North Korea, which was under communist rule, invaded South Korea. Despite opposition by many Americans reluctant to enter into another war, Truman declared a police action in Korea. By mid-July of 1950, U.S. forces were engaged in a conflict in a country many Americans had never heard of.

The 1952 presidential election centered on the Korean War and the worldwide threat of communism. War-weary Americans sought an end to the country's second war in a decade. They also wanted a candidate who was strong enough to confront the spread of communism. The Republican nominee, Dwight D. Eisenhower, promised that if elected, he would go to Korea and broker a peace treaty. He won in November and kept his promise. On 27 July 1953, an armistice was signed at Panmunjom, Korea. During Eisenhower's two terms as president, the United States experienced peace.

The country entered a decade of leisure with an economy affording new luxuries. African Americans, however, were in a struggle for civil rights. Even though blacks and whites had fought alike for their country in World War II and the Korean War, racial tensions continued. As middle-class whites moved from the major cities into the newly developing suburbs, a number of the inner cities became areas of African American poverty. The new demographics led to other changes. New roads had to be built and goods had to be provided to the suburbs. Franchises and chain stores began to populate suburbia. Suburbs grew and prospered while many inner cities crumbled.

The fear of communism infiltrating life in the United States led to a Red Scare in the late 1940s that continued into the 1950s. It was thought that if countries turned to the Soviet Union for aid, they would be lost to communism. To meet this challenge, the president introduced the Eisenhower Doctrine. The United States would extend a hand to help any country desiring it, and many nations accepted the offer. Meanwhile, the Central Intelligence Agency (CIA) used covert operations to overthrow pro-communist leaders in a number of countries.

By the time Eisenhower left office in January 1961, life in the United States had been improved by advances in technology and medicine. Most households had a television. The birth control pill was available. Polio was almost nonexistent in the United States. The civil rights movement brought more equality to African Americans. The women's movement opened up opportunities for many women. However, the problems in Southeast Asia were increasing, and with communism threatening Vietnam, the United States would find itself in another military conflict.

RED SCARE

Fear of the spread of communism created a Red Scare in the United States, which Republican Senator Joseph McCarthy of Wisconsin seized upon. He created havoc with the lives of those in the entertainment industry. The House Un-American Activities Committee (HUAC) summoned people to appear before them and pressured them to testify that colleagues were, or had been, involved in communist groups. Even comic books faced scrutiny by the committee. President Eisenhower ignored McCarthy until the HUAC questioned his administration.

Democrats were angry that Eisenhower took so long to respond to McCarthy's tactics. From 1950 until his censure by the Senate in December 1954, McCarthy's committee especially scrutinized the entertainment industry. Some people named others as communists, accurately or not, simply to save their own careers. Others were hounded until they told the committee whatever it wanted to hear. Some people lost their jobs and were unable to work in Hollywood for years. Some were sentenced to prison for refusing to cooperate with the committee. A few took their own lives. More than 300 people were blacklisted by the HUAC.

CIVIL RIGHTS MOVEMENT

During the Eisenhower era, the civil rights movement was at the forefront of the news. Some of the most important civil rights legislation evolved from the simple acts of a few courageous African Americans. Rights activist Martin Luther King Jr. was introduced to the world, as was Rosa Parks. The word "sit-in" was added to the vocabulary.

In the 1950s, the civil rights movement took its most important steps up to that time to gain equality for African Americans. By its 1954 decision in *Brown v. Board of Education*, the Supreme Court forced the integration of public schools. The president found the Court's ruling tested when Arkansas Governor Orval Faubus stood at the entrance of Central High School in Little Rock and kept African American students from entering the all-white high school. Eisenhower sent troops to the school to protect the students as they entered.

In 1955, an African American woman named Rosa Parks refused to give up her seat on a Montgomery, Alabama, city bus and was arrested. In response, a little-known African American minister named Martin Luther King Jr. led a bus boycott, knowing the majority of bus riders in Montgomery were African American. The economic effect on the city of Montgomery forced it to relent, and African Americans returned to riding city buses, able to sit anywhere they wanted. The boycott's effect rippled throughout the country.

African Americans in many parts of the South were often prevented from voting. By the time Eisenhower left office, two civil rights acts involving voting rights had been passed. African Americans were expected to vote without interference from anyone or any group. Although blacks' voting rights were not as strong as hoped, the stage was set for major civil rights acts in the coming decade.

On 1 February 1960, four young African American men in Greensboro, North Carolina, sat at an all-white lunch counter waiting to be served. Each day they returned with more people, black and white, who continued the sit-in. Other potential customers thus could not be seated or served. This form of protest spread throughout the country, bringing economic woes to segregated businesses. Eateries slowly began to desegregate. In July 1960, when the four young men who began the original sit-in returned to the all-white lunch counter, they were served.

FOREIGN AFFAIRS AND THE ATOMIC AGE

The Cold War dominated Eisenhower's two terms. He tried to promote the use of atomic energy for peaceful purposes. He hoped his policy of "open skies" would allow the superpowers to inspect each other's territory, but the Soviet Union rejected the idea.

After World War II ended, Germany was divided into two parts. The Soviet Union controlled East Germany; the United States, Great Britain, and France oversaw West Germany. The Soviet Union did not want Germany rearmed, and it wanted the Allied occupation of West Germany ended. When its demands were not met, the Soviet Union halted free access between East and West Germany. Many families were separated. In 1961, the Soviet Union built a wall in the middle of Berlin. It took almost three decades before the wall was torn down.

The Soviet Union, under Joseph Stalin, strengthened its hold on eastern Europe. Even the death of Stalin did little to change the Soviet tactics. Nikita Khrushchev, Stalin's successor, continued the government's control of its satellite countries. Eisenhower was determined the United States and pro-Western nations should remain free from communist threats. He used the plan of containment to keep communism in check, but as part of his containment policy, he developed the theory of massive retaliation: a threat to use nuclear weapons in response to aggression. When Lebanon's government faced internal turmoil and turned to

Eisenhower for help, the president sent U.S. marines to restore peace. In October 1956, the people of Hungary revolted against their Soviet-controlled government. But the United States was then involved in the Suez Crisis and was unable to help in their struggle. Soviet troops forced an end to the Hungarians' fight to be free, which Eisenhower lamented after leaving office.

The CIA, with Eisenhower's backing, used a covert operation to overthrow the pro-communist government in Guatemala. In Iran, from which the pro-Western shah was forced to flee, Prime Minister Mohammed Mossadegh nationalized the oil fields and threatened to turn to the Soviet Union for support. The CIA overthrew Mossadegh in 1953 and reinstated the shah. In 1959, the Cuban Revolution ended with Fidel Castro becoming Cuba's new leader. A Marxist-Leninist, Castro nationalized industries and turned to the Soviet Union more and more as time passed.

As the 1950s came to a close, Soviet leader Nikita Khrushchev and President Eisenhower seemed to be on good terms. In September 1959, Khrushchev visited the United States, and the president was planning to visit the Soviet Union the following year. The downing of a U.S. U-2 spy plane over Soviet territory in May 1960 precluded any hope for friendly relations to continue between the countries.

SOCIAL, CULTURAL, AND ECONOMIC CHANGES

Magazines, books, and movies began to change during the 1950s. Morals were easing. Grace Metalious's book *Peyton Place* showed a shocking side of life in a small New England town. It became a best seller. Hugh Hefner introduced *Playboy*, a men's magazine featuring a centerfold of an almost nude playmate each month. Sex symbol Marilyn Monroe was the first centerfold. Movies became more risqué. Words that had been censored before were heard for the first time. Some plots focused on adultery or teenage sex, topics prohibited in the past.

After conducting research about the unhappy state of women in the country, Betty Friedan released her findings in *The Feminine Mystique* (1963), a best seller that contributed to the women's movement and changed lives. The birth control pill allowed women the freedom to become pregnant on their schedule. And the new medium of television followed the real-life pregnancy of Lucille Ball on the popular series *I Love Lucy*.

The U.S. economy boomed after World War II. Automobiles became more elegant now that metals used in the war were available. Chrome shone on new models, and many owners traded in their older cars for new models. Appliances that made life easier were introduced, including clothes dryers, garbage disposals, dishwashers, and blenders. Kitchens had freezers, and frozen foods were available. Air conditioners cooled homes during the warm months. And televisions offered home entertainment that bought families together to watch their favorite programs.

The 1950s changed dramatically when Elvis Presley's recordings became popular. Teenagers suddenly became important to the economy. Businesses began to cater to them. Movies, clothing, and magazines were aimed at teenagers. Teens dressed like the teen idols they saw on television and in films. Drive-in movies and drive-in restaurants became meeting places. Transistor radios allowed teens to carry their music with them. They made record companies and recording artists wealthy. Teenagers continue to play a major role in the economy today, but their importance as a group had its birth in the 1950s.

TECHNICAL AND MEDICAL ADVANCES

World War II necessitated new technologies in order to win the war. Sonar and radar were used extensively, and rudimentary computers were produced. Such materials as synthetic rubber and nylon were developed. Atomic and nuclear energy, vital to ending the war, provided a new energy source for the military and businesses. Nuclear power plants provided electricity. Nuclear-powered submarines and ballistic missiles were introduced. Transistors, integrated circuits, and vacuum tubes were created. These innovations were used in the 1950s to make computers, cameras, copiers, and video recorders. Space exploration began in the United States after the Soviet Union's successful launch of the satellite *Sputnik*.

The polio vaccine wiped out a dreaded disease. The birth control pill helped to prevent unwanted pregnancies. Tuberculosis was cured by streptomycin, and lung cancer was linked to smoking. Ultrasound helped doctors view an unborn child in the womb. Tranquilizers, steroids, and open-heart surgery were medical advances in the 1950s. The discovery of DNA would become a vital tool in the future of medicine, forensics, and the law.

PRESIDENT EISENHOWER'S ERA IN RETROSPECT

By the time President Eisenhower left office on 20 January 1961, the United States had a modern interstate highway system, which made traveling across the lower 48 states easier. Two stars were added to the flag when Alaska and Hawaii became the 49th and 50th states. Leisure time included travel, television, movies, and a variety of new magazines. Families in the suburbs enjoyed relaxing in their backyards.

In the 1950s, women and African Americans made breakthroughs in their quests for equality. More women sought work outside the home and equal opportunities for women and men. African Americans wanted the same rights and advantages promised to all citizens. In both cases, they gradually got what they wanted.

Historians have reassessed the Eisenhower era. During his presidency, Eisenhower was viewed as a grandfather figure who preferred golf to being president. In reality, he was in complete control of his administration. He left behind a country largely at peace, but he also warned of the dangers it faced if the new technological advances for the military were not kept in check. The country soon learned how correct Eisenhower was when his successor chose a different path for his presidency.

The Dictionary

– A –

ACHESON, DEAN (1893–1971). President **Harry S. Truman**'s secretary of state and a vocal critic during the presidency of **Dwight D. Eisenhower**. Dean Gooderham Acheson was born in Connecticut. He received his undergraduate degree from Yale University (1915) and his law degree from Harvard Law School (1918). When **Joseph McCarthy** began to criticize members of the State Department, Acheson spoke out against the senator, which only angered McCarthy even more. Opposed to the use of nuclear weapons, Acheson was outspoken about their use during Eisenhower's administration. When **John F. Kennedy** and **Lyndon B. Johnson** were president, Acheson was a trusted advisor. *See also* ATOMIC AND NUCLEAR ENERGY; COHN, ROY; FOREIGN POLICY; HOUSE UN-AMERICAN ACTIVITIES COMMITTEE (HUAC).

ADAMS, SHERMAN (1899–1986). White House chief of staff 1953–58. Llewelyn Sherman Adams was born in Vermont. He graduated from Dartmouth College (B.A., 1920) and continued to live in New Hampshire. He was a Member of the U.S. House of Representatives in 1945–47 and New Hampshire's governor in 1948–52. As **Dwight D. Eisenhower**'s chief of staff, Adams exercised great power and was considered by some historians to be the most powerful chief of staff in U.S. history. He tightly guarded access to the Oval Office and would not allow Eisenhower to be disturbed by controversies; Adams solved those himself, including comments made by Senator **Joseph McCarthy** about the president. Many people joked that if Adams died, Eisenhower then would be the president. Unfortunately a scandal erupted over an expensive fur coat and oriental rug that

Adams received from Bernard Goldfine, who was being investigated for violations by the Federal Trade Commission. The acceptance of the gifts from Goldfine led to Adams's downfall. After being forced to resign in 1958, he returned to New Hampshire, where he opened a ski resort.

ADENAUER, KONRAD (1876–1967). Chancellor of West **Germany** 1949–63. After graduating college with a degree in law and economics, Adenauer pursued a career in politics. His first political post was as a member of the Cologne city council. After Germany was defeated in World War I, he became lord mayor of Cologne (1917) and served for 16 years in this position. An opponent of the Nazis, in 1933 he was arrested and accused of taking part in a plot to kill Adolf Hitler, for which he was imprisoned. After World War II, he was chosen to help write a constitution for West Germany. In 1949, he rose to the position of chancellor because of his abilities as a leader. By the late 1950s, Adenauer helped West Germany become a major world power. In August 1959, Adenauer and President **Dwight D. Eisenhower** met in Germany to discuss disarmament, German reunification, and the continuing cooperation between West Germany and the United States. Eisenhower reassured Adenauer that the United States and its allies would work together to protect Berlin and West Germany. The **Geneva Conference** was also discussed, with a primary topic being relations between the **Soviet Union** and West Germany. *See also* FOREIGN POLICY.

ADVERTISING. The years following World War II produced a robust American **economy**, more leisure time, and increased consumer power. With the advent of **television**, advertisers had a new and very lucrative medium with which to reach consumers. Very quickly they learned to produce an appealing ad in a small window of 30 seconds.

For the first time, campaign commercials aired on television for the presidential elections. In the **1952 election**, **Democratic** candidate **Adlai Stevenson** and **Republican** candidate **Dwight D. Eisenhower** had to find slogans and ways to market themselves to the public. Eisenhower's campaign slogan and commercials were produced by Rosser Reeves, the man responsible for the M&M's ad "Melts in your mouth, not in your hands." In a departure from traditional practices, Reeves placed his ads between programs, which reduced television costs. He had Eisenhower filmed standing in a bare room so that all viewers saw was the candidate. The camera angle made the audience appear to be asking Eisenhower questions. The slogan used was "Eisenhower Answers America." Although Stevenson believed the commercials insulted voters' intelligence, the idea worked. In the **1956 election**, Stevenson searched for an advertising agency to help him with his television commercials.

Automobiles were no longer a luxury for the majority of Americans, and car manufacturers used television to sell their products, often with a beautiful woman by the car. Popular singer Dinah Shore became famous for singing the jingle "See the USA in Your Chevrolet." She always ended her weekly variety show with the jingle, after which Shore covered her mouth with her hand and then threw a kiss to her audience. When Volkswagen, the German automaker, began to sell its models in the United States, its ad simply stated "Think Small."

Burma Shave, a shaving cream company, used small signs along the highways on which drivers could read clever four-part rhyming commercials which ended with a fifth sign simply saying "Burma Shave."

Cigarettes were a popular product in the 1950s, and advertisers often used **cinema** stars in their commercials. One of the most famous and recognizable icons of television and **magazine** ads was "The Marlboro Man," a cowboy with a Marlboro cigarette in his mouth or perhaps lighting up a Marlboro. Winston cigarettes advertised "Winston tastes good—like a cigarette should."

Many advertisements promoted women's beauty products, and coloring one's hair became popular. Clairol, one manufacturer of home coloring kits, produced the famous ad "Does she, or doesn't she? Only her hairdresser knows for sure."

The addition of fluoride to Crest toothpaste led to ads showing a child coming home from the dentist's office to proclaim, "Look, Ma! No cavities." Pepsodent Toothpaste's ad stated, "You'll wonder where the yellow went." Another substance emphasized in ads was chlorophyll, which was added to toothpaste, gum, deodorants, and even dog food. In 1952, 90 products contained chlorophyll and consumers spent $135 million dollars on them.

Timex had a successful ad in which one of their watches was immersed in a tank of water. The watch was attached to a motor boat's propeller and the water churned. When the commentator took the watch out of the water, he held it to his ear and proclaimed, "Takes a lickin' and keeps on tickin'."

In response to the influence of ads on the consuming public, **Vance Packard** published *The Hidden Persuaders* (1957), in which he explained how the industry and the media manipulated the public to vote for a candidate or to purchase a particular product. The book sold over 1 million copies.

During the 1950s, advertisers began to use demographics to produce advertisements for particular groups. **Arthur C. Nielsen**'s ratings helped advertisers decide ad placements on television. As the 1950s came to an end, advertisers had already learned the basic methods needed to reach a specific audience.

The **Quiz Show Scandals** of the 1950s were perpetrated by unethical advertisers who wanted to increase their viewing audience by giving answers to some of the contestants. When this tactic was exposed, the advertising sponsors were seriously damaged. *See also* SUBLIMINAL ADVERTISING.

AFRICAN AMERICANS. For over 50 years, the **civil rights movement** had been testing the doctrine of "separate but equal" established by the **Supreme Court** in *Plessy v. Ferguson* (1896). In 1954, the Court overturned "separate but equal" in its landmark decision in *Brown v. Board of Education*, which ended segregation in public schools. President **Dwight D. Eisenhower** led the way to more equality. Eisenhower's involvement in the civil rights movement was crucial, for many Americans were not ready to accept the Supreme Court's decision. By the end of Eisenhower's eight years in office, African Americans were attending formerly segregated public institutions from elementary school through higher education. They were also able to sit anywhere on public transportation and to seek employment in areas not opened to them before.

The shift in the public's thinking affected more than simply equality. In 1951, the popular radio program *Amos 'n Andy* moved to **television**. The **National Association for the Advancement of Colored People (NAACP)** protested almost immediately the degrading, stereotypical portrayal of African Americans as lower-class and crude. Within two years, the program was taken off the air. African Americans also became members of national groups, played on major athletic teams, and appeared in major film roles for the first time. *See also* AILEY, ALVIN; *AMERICAN BANDSTAND*; AMERICAN CIVIL LIBERTIES UNION (ACLU); ARMSTRONG, LOUIS; BELAFONTE, HARRY; BERRY, CHUCK; *BROWDER V. GAYLE*; BUNCHE, RALPH; CINEMA; CIVIL RIGHTS ACT OF 1957; CIVIL RIGHTS ACT OF 1960; CIVIL RIGHTS MOVEMENT; DU BOIS, W. E. B.; FAUBUS, ORVAL; GIBSON, ALTHEA; HAMMOND, JOHN; HARLAN, JOHN MARSHALL; HUGHES, LANGSTON; KING, CORETTA SCOTT; KING, MARTIN LUTHER, JR.; MARSHALL, THURGOOD; MATHIS, JOHNNY; MONTGOMERY BUS BOYCOTT; MOTOWN RECORDS; MUSIC; PARKS, GORDON; PARKS, ROSA; POITIER, SIDNEY; POWELL, ADAM CLAYTON, JR.; RACIAL INTEGRATION; RANDOLPH, A. PHILIP; ROCK AND ROLL; RUDOLPH, WILMA; SIT-IN; SOUTHERN CHRISTIAN LEADERSHIP CONFERENCE (SCLC); SPORTS; WHITE CITIZENS COUNCIL.

AGEE, JAMES (1909–1955). Critic and Pulitzer Prize–winning author. James Rufus Agee was born and raised in Tennessee. The loss of his father when Agee was only six years old affected him for the rest of his life. His satire of *Time*, written while at Harvard University (B.A., 1932), netted him a job after graduation with *Fortune*. His first assignment was to report on the plight of tenant farmers in the deep South during the Great Depression. *Fortune* expected a report written in conventional style and not the prose poem that Agee wrote. In it, he expressed the tenant farmers' ability to endure with dignity seemingly impossible odds. Although *Fortune* rejected his unconventional reporting, Agee used his investigative research to write what critics consider his masterpiece, *Let Us Now Praise Famous Men*, a novel that took five years to complete. Agee's book, both autobiographical and philosophical, expressed his concern for the tenant farmers as individuals and not as a societal problem.

Having written insightful reviews of movies for *Time* and the *Nation*, Agee also became a screenwriter. In the 1950s, he wrote the scripts for *The African Queen* and *The Night of the Hunter*. His final novel was *A Death in the Family*, in which a six-year-old boy was faced with the death of his father. His book incorporated many of his childhood memories. Written when Agee was in ill health after several heart attacks, *A Death in the Family* was not published until 1957, two years after a final heart attack ended his life. In 1960, it was made into the stage play *All the Way Home. See also* CINEMA; LITERATURE.

AGRICULTURAL ACT OF 1954. This act had two purposes: it established flexible price supports, and it gave authority in an emergency to the Commodity Credit Corporation to provide aid from its reserves for either domestic or foreign relief. If the Commodity Credit Corporation had to extend aid, the government was to repay the corporation. This legislation was designed and supported by Secretary of Agriculture **Ezra Taft Benson**. *See also* AGRICULTURE; ECONOMY; FOREIGN POLICY.

AGRICULTURAL TRADE DEVELOPMENT AND ASSISTANCE ACT OF 1954 (FOOD FOR PEACE). Also known as Public Law 480, the Agricultural Trade Development and Assistance Act of 1954 established the Food for Peace program that provided overseas food aid from the United States. President **Dwight D. Eisenhower** wanted exports overseas to benefit American farmers and to feed the people of other countries in need of food. Agricultural products sent from the United States to these countries were to be purchased through long-term low-interest loans. Provisions of the act also provided for food donations. *See also* AGRICULTURE; BENSON, EZRA TAFT; ECONOMY; FOREIGN POLICY.

AGRICULTURE. Soon after his inauguration, President **Dwight D. Eisenhower** delivered a special message to Congress concerning farm subsidies. In his view, the practice was outdated. The money for subsidies should be redirected to more timely needs, including school lunches and disaster relief as well as aid to famine-stricken countries. In 1954, Congress passed the **Agricultural Act** and the **Agricultural Trade Development and Assistance Act**. The former provided for both domestic and foreign monetary relief; the latter provided food assistance for other countries and permanently expanded U.S. agricultural exports, benefiting both the United States and the recipients in other countries.

For many years before Eisenhower became president, illegal immigrants provided cheap labor for the American farmer. In 1954, Operation Wetback was established to deport as many illegal immigrants as possible. That meant primarily Mexicans. Many farm owners, in need of farm workers, complained about the practice. Operation Wetback ended in 1958 when Eisenhower vetoed the farm-freeze bill believing it would hurt, not help, America's farmers. In a radio address following his veto, the president explained to the public that passage of the bill would increase farm surpluses and hinder parity practices. Eisenhower wanted to be sure the individual farm family could compete against a growing number of large mechanized farms owned by corporations. For the duration of his presidency, Congress supported Eisenhower's views on agriculture. *See also* BENSON, EZRA TAFT; ECONOMY; FOREIGN POLICY.

AILEY, ALVIN (1931–1989). Dancer, choreographer, and founder of the Alvin Ailey American Dance Theater. Alvin Ailey was born in Texas. After his father abandoned him and his mother, they moved to Los Angeles in 1943. On a junior high school field trip, Ailey attended a production of the Ballet Russe de Monte Carlo. Realizing he wanted to **dance**, he began in 1949 to study dancing with choreographer Lester Horton. The year Horton died (1953) was the same year Ailey debuted on stage in Horton's troupe.

The next year, he appeared in the Broadway production of **Truman Capote**'s *House of Flowers*. Remaining in New York, he studied ballet with Martha Graham. In 1958, he choreographed *Blues Suite*. The production was a critical and financial success. This was the beginning of the Alvin Ailey American Dance Theater. In 1962, the group toured Asia and Australia as part of President **John F. Kennedy**'s "President's Special International Program for Cultural Presentations." Ailey integrated his all-black dance company in 1963.

In 1965, after his company had gained worldwide fame, Ailey concentrated on choreography. In 1966, he choreographed Samuel Barber's opera *Anthony and Cleopatra*, which debuted that year at the Metropolitan Opera. In 1971, he choreographed **Leonard Bernstein**'s *Mass*, which was written for the opening of the Kennedy

Center for the Performing Arts. In 1980, the Alvin Ailey American Dance Theater made its new home in a building on Broadway. After Ailey's death in 1989, the company toured Russia, **France**, and **Cuba**.

Alvin Ailey created over 79 dances for his company, and many of the members also choreographed dances. In 1979, the **National Association for the Advancement of Colored People (NAACP)** awarded Ailey the Spingarn Medal, which recognizes **African Americans** who have achieved distinction in America. *See also* THEATER.

ALASKA. Alaska was a U.S. territory for almost a hundred years before becoming a state. After gold was discovered in Alaska in the late 1890s, fortune seekers flocked to Alaska, and many settled there. The territory's proximity to Asia was vital during World War II. Military bases were built, and after the war ended, some of the bases remained. In the 1940s, the United States used many of Alaska's natural resources without giving much in return. In order to acquire better roads, schools, and other federal entitlements, Alaska began in 1946 to prepare for statehood. A constitution was drawn up.

Because the population of Alaska was small, Congress proposed that much of Alaska be owned by the federal government, thereby allowing Alaskans to use their tax dollars in the few populated areas. In 1958, Congress granted statehood to Alaska. In 1959, it became the 49th state.

AMERICAN BANDSTAND. Beginning as a local **television** program in Philadelphia, Pennsylvania, *American Bandstand* moved in 1957 to ABC. Hosted by Dick Clark, the program was watched by millions of **teenagers** after school. Local teens danced to the Top-40 tunes, showing the latest **dances** and rating the newest songs introduced by Clark. Singers whose records were on the pop charts performed on the show and were interviewed by Clark. *American Bandstand* was on weekday afternoons until August 1963. From August 1963 until its cancellation in 1987, it aired on Saturdays. *See also* BERRY, CHUCK; HAMMOND, JOHN; JAZZ; MATHIS, JOHNNY; MOTOWN RECORDS; MUSIC; PRESLEY, ELVIS; ROCK AND ROLL.

AMERICAN CIVIL LIBERTIES UNION (ACLU). The ACLU expanded more in the 1950s than in the 30 years since its beginning in 1920. The **Cold War, Joseph McCarthy**'s rise to power in the Senate, and the **civil rights movement** elicited outspoken responses from ACLU members. They aided in the publication of *The Judges and the Judged* by Merle Miller, which exposed McCarthy's unethical tactics in claiming that innocent people were communists. The ACLU also played a pivotal role in the integration of public schools through *Brown v. Board of Education* as well as the end of censorship of films and written materials with a communist theme (*Burstyn v. Wilson/McCaffrey*). *See also* AFRICAN AMERICANS; *BROWDER V. GAYLE*; CINEMA; COHN, ROY; HOUSE UN-AMERICAN ACTIVITIES COMMITTEE (HUAC); KING, MARTIN LUTHER, JR.; MARSHALL, THURGOOD; PARKS, ROSA; RACIAL INTEGRATION.

AMERICAN FEDERATION OF LABOR. *See* AMERICAN FEDERATION OF LABOR AND CONGRESS OF INDUSTRIAL ORGANIZATIONS (AFL-CIO).

AMERICAN FEDERATION OF LABOR AND CONGRESS OF INDUSTRIAL ORGANIZATIONS (AFL-CIO). The American Federation of Labor (AFL) merged with the Congress of Industrial Organizations (CIO) in 1955, forming the nation's largest labor organization. The main purpose of the merger was to unify organized labor behind repealing or amending the Taft-Hartley Act. Congressional passage of the Landrum-Griffith Act removed some of the objectionable features of that legislation. In the late 1950s, the Teamsters were expelled from the AFL-CIO for corruption and nondemocratic union governance. The AFL-CIO supported the **Civil Rights Acts of 1957 and 1960**. *See also* ECONOMY; KENNEDY, JOHN F.; LABOR MANAGEMENT REPORTING AND DISCLOSURE ACT; RANDOLPH, A. PHILIP.

ANDERSON, MAXWELL (1888–1959). Playwright James Maxwell Anderson was born in Pennsylvania, but the family moved to North Dakota when he was in high school. He received his B.A. in 1911 from the University of North Dakota and his M.A. from Stanford

University in 1914. Widely regarded as one of the most important American playwrights of the first half of the 20th century, Anderson dominated the **theater** from the 1920s through the 1950s. His plays, some of which were written in verse, explored social and moral problems. His success began in 1924 with *What Price Glory?* considered one of the most sensational plays of the decade. It was followed by *Winterset*, based on the Sacco and Vanzetti case. Of Anderson's many plays, at least 12 were made into movies and many more into televised productions, including *Anne of the Thousand Days*, *Key Largo*, and *The Bad Seed. What Price Glory?* was a silent motion picture (1926) and was remade in 1952 by director John Ford. *See also* CINEMA; LITERATURE.

ANDERSON, MARIAN (1897–1993). Concert singer Marian Anderson was born in Philadelphia, Pennsylvania. Her singing career began with financial support from her church for vocal lessons. After winning a contest in New York, she performed with the New York Philharmonic Orchestra. Although she was signed to a contract, as an **African American** she was given few chances to perform in the United States. As a result, between 1925 and 1933, she performed largely in European opera houses. Although she met racial discrimination within the United States, in 1929 she was the first African American to perform in Carnegie Hall. In 1939, when the Daughters of the American Revolution (DAR) prevented her from performing in Constitution Hall, **Eleanor Roosevelt** arranged to have her sing at the Lincoln Memorial before an estimated 75,000 listeners.

In 1955, Anderson was the first African American to perform at the Metropolitan Opera. President **Dwight D. Eisenhower** invited her to sing at the White House, the first black singer to perform there. In 1958, the president appointed her a delegate to the **United Nations**. She received the Medal of Freedom in 1966. *See also* MUSIC.

ANDERSON, ROBERT B. (1910–1989). Secretary of the navy 1953–54, secretary of the treasury 1957–61. A high school teacher turned lawyer, Robert Bernard Anderson received his law degree from the University of Texas in 1932. He was elected to the Texas State House of Representatives and worked in his native Texas in various political, government, and business positions. During World War II, he was an advisor to the secretary of the navy. In 1953, President **Dwight D. Eisenhower** named him secretary of the navy and then secretary of the treasury. Anderson ended racial discrimination in the U.S. Navy. He also advanced defense **technology**. In 1956, Eisenhower tried unsuccessfully to replace his vice president, **Richard M. Nixon**, with Anderson. After leaving office, Anderson represented President **Lyndon B. Johnson** on diplomatic missions. The last part of his life proved tragic. In the 1980s, he was hospitalized for alcoholism several times and disbarred for illegal activities in banking operations. In 1987, he served a prison term for tax evasion. *See also* INTERCONTINENTAL BALLISTIC MISSILES (ICBMs); INTERMEDIATE-RANGE BALLISTIC MISSILES (IRBMs); USS *NAUTILUS*.

ANN LANDERS AND DEAR ABBY. Twin sisters Esther Pauline Friedman (1918–2002) and Pauline Esther Friedman (1918–) became rival journalists in the 1950s when each was offered the position of writing an advice column at different newspapers. Esther Pauline became "Ann Landers" and Pauline Esther became "Dear Abby." Their competing columns led to a clash in their personal lives, and they did not speak to each other from the mid-1950s until their reconciliation in 1964. Ann Landers published several books giving advice on everything from etiquette to cancer. She died of cancer in 2002. Dear Abby ended in the 1980s when Pauline Esther developed Alzheimer's disease, but her daughter continued the column under the name "Abigail Van Buren."

ANZUS PACT (ANZUS TREATY), 1952. The Pacific Security Treaty, or Anzus Pact, was signed by Australia, New Zealand, and the United States. The three countries agreed to solve problems mutually and to provide aid if one of the three was in harm's way. In the 1980s, New Zealand banned any ships with nuclear weapons from docking in its port. This led the United States to suspend its role in the pact. However, the United States and New Zealand continued their partnership in overseeing the safety of the Pacific region. *See also* ATOMIC AND NUCLEAR ENERGY; FOREIGN POLICY.

ARCHITECTURE. World War II led to many **technological innovations** in construction, and these carried over to architecture in the 1950s. Modern architect Frank Lloyd Wright influenced other architects with homes having smaller rooms, fewer closets, lower ceilings, and fewer walls, thereby making them more open. Wright also designed the Guggenheim Museum in New York City. Among the modern architects influenced by Wright were Ludwig Mies van der Rohe and Le Corbusier (Charles Edouard Jeanneret). Some architects also designed furniture. Their designs might be mass produced using synthetic materials. Accessories could be zany, extreme, or whimsical, with the word "kitsch" added to the dictionary to describe these innovations. One of the most innovative architects of the era was **Morris Lapidus**, responsible for the curved lines of the elegant Fountainbleau Hotel of Miami Beach as well as some of the hotels of Las Vegas. Despised by critics at the time, his hotels were applauded years later. *See also* MUMFORD, LEWIS.

ARENDT, HANNAH (1906–1975). Philosopher and author Hannah Arendt was born in **Germany**, where the rise of Nazism in the 1930s forced many Jews, including Arendt, to flee. She first went to **France** before immigrating to the United States in 1941. In her first major book, *The Origins of Totalitarianism*, she explained the reasons for the rise to power of Adolf Hitler and **Joseph Stalin**. Racism was a thread that ran through both regimes, eventually leading to the extermination with unspeakable cruelty of certain groups. In her various books and articles, Arendt stressed that the individuals who inhabit the earth must share it. Arendt's most controversial book, *Eichmann in Jerusalem: A Report on the Banality of Evil*, painted a picture of former Nazi SS leader **Adolph Eichmann** not as a monster but as a banal bureaucrat, and it was critical of Jews who had collaborated with the Nazi regime. The book caused a storm of anger in the Jewish community.

ARMSTRONG, LOUIS (1901–1971). Jazz musician Louis Armstrong was born in New Orleans. When he was 12, he shot a gun into the air, for which he was convicted of delinquency and sent to a home for **African American** boys for two years. While there, he learned to play the cornet. He played with a number of bands from 1919 until the late 1920s, becoming the star singer for several of them. He also played the trumpet, and in 1947 he formed his own band, which then traveled around the world. His personality was such that he became a goodwill ambassador for the United States. While on a trip to England, he was greeted with the words "Hello, Satchmo," a shortened form of an earlier nickname: "Satchelmouth."

Armstrong's winning smile and personality led to parts in at least 50 movies. He also composed songs, influenced future jazz musicians, and performed in as many as 300 concerts a year. Considered one of the 20th century's great personalities, he entertained dignitaries and heads of state worldwide. In the 1950s, Armstrong spoke out during the crisis in Little Rock, Arkansas, when Governor **Orval Forbus** tried to prevent desegregation of the schools. Scheduled to tour Russia in his role as ambassador, he cancelled in protest when African American students were not allowed to enter Central High School as required by law. *See also* CINEMA; CIVIL RIGHTS MOVEMENT; MUSIC.

ARMY-MCCARTHY HEARINGS. In 1954, Senator **Joseph McCarthy** was accused by the U.S. Army of attempting to gain special treatment for Private **G. David Schine**, who had been on McCarthy's staff. During a televised hearing that lasted over a month, the army's attorney, Joseph Welch, held McCarthy up to public ridicule. While McCarthy attempted to argue that the army was retaliating against his investigations, claiming the army allowed communists and security risks to join the military, Welch revealed McCarthy to be a demagogue who yelled and bullied others to get what he wanted. The hearings led to McCarthy's downfall. In 1954, McCarthy was censured by the Senate; however, the damage he did to many people through his ruthlessness was immeasurable.

For the first time, the American public saw the importance of **television** in a congressional investigation. The 1964 documentary *Point of Order* examines the Army-McCarthy hearings. *See also* COHN, ROY; HOUSE UN-AMERICAN ACTIVITIES COMMITTEE (HUAC).

ARNAZ, DESI (1917–1986). *See* BALL, LUCILLE, AND DESI ARNAZ.

ART. Art styles of the 1950s were reflected in the consumerism of the postwar years. Record labels and **magazines** used a style that came to be known as popular art, or pop art. Pop art was a reaction to the abstract expressionism of artists such as Jackson Pollock. Pop artist Roy Lichtenstein painted comic book panels on a large scale; Robert Indiana used love as a theme in his pop art. Andy Warhol, one of the founders of the pop art movement, used his background in commercial art to paint likenesses of everyday products such as a Campbell's soup can as well as celebrities like **Marilyn Monroe**.

Prior to the launch of *Sputnik* by the **Soviet Union**, art was a strong part of **education** in the United States. In 1958, as a result of a new emphasis on math, science, and foreign languages, art was removed from many public school curriculums, and artists had to fight for the importance of their career choice. *See also* O'KEEFFE, GEORGIA; ROCKWELL, NORMAN.

ASIMOV, ISAAC (1920–1992). Science fiction author Isaac Asimov was born in Russia but moved with his family to New York City in 1923. Educated at Columbia University (B.A., 1939; M.A., 1941; Ph.D., 1948), he became an associate professor in biochemistry at the Boston University School of Medicine (1949). In 1979, he was promoted to professor.

Asimov, however, also enjoyed writing fiction and sold his first story when he was 18. In 1941, he published his first science fiction work, *Nightfall*. He wrote nearly 500 books on various subjects, including science fiction, mystery, history, short stories, and guides to the Bible and the works of Shakespeare. Some of his most popular works are *Foundation*, *Foundation and Empire*, *Second Foundation*, *The Caves of Steel*, and *The End of Eternity*.

Asimov began his association with Hollywood in 1979 as a consultant for the science fiction film *Star Trek: The Motion Picture*. His filmography continued into the 1990s. He was involved in a number of features that were based on his works: *Nightfall*, *Bicentennial Man*, *Alien Love Triangle*, *Light Years*, and *I, Robot*.

Asimov, Robert Heinlein, and Arthur C. Clarke are widely considered the three grand masters of 1950s science fiction. Of the three authors, Asimov was the most prolific. He also used the pseudonym Paul French. *See also* LITERATURE.

ATOMIC AND NUCLEAR ENERGY. General **Dwight D. Eisenhower** opposed the use of the atomic bomb against Japan in 1945, believing the country was already defeated. However, President **Harry S. Truman** ordered atomic bombs to be used on two Japanese cities to end the war quickly. When Eisenhower became president, he inherited an arms race to make nuclear weapons. Eisenhower's concern about the use of nuclear weapons led to his **Atoms for Peace** speech in 1953, in which he stated that atomic power should be used for peaceful purposes. Eisenhower's plea for the peaceful use of atomic energy led to creation of the **International Atomic Energy Agency (IAEA)** in 1957.

In 1955, the United States made the first nuclear-powered submarine, the **USS** *Nautilus*. In the 1950s, the first nuclear power plants were built in the United States. *See also* BARUCH, BERNARD; COLD WAR; FOREIGN POLICY; KHRUSHCHEV, NIKITA; SOVIET UNION, RELATIONS WITH.

ATOMIC ENERGY COMMISSION (AEC). In 1946, the Atomic Energy Act created a commission whose primary goal was to oversee the production of nuclear energy in the United States. In 1953, **Lewis Strauss** succeeded David Lilienthal as head of the AEC. He was followed by **John McCone**. In 1954, the commission included private industries in the production of nuclear technologies, which led to more work for the group. In 1974, Congress dissolved the commission and separated its duties into two new governmental agencies: the Nuclear Regulatory Commission and the Energy Research and Development Administration. *See also* BARUCH, BERNARD; CONANT, JAMES B.

ATOMS FOR PEACE. Speech given by President **Dwight D. Eisenhower** at the **United Nations** 8 December 1953 in which he proposed the peaceful development of **atomic and nuclear energy** and the establishment of an international atomic energy commission. In the speech, Eisenhower proposed that all nations use their knowledge of nuclear power for peaceful purposes. This led to the formation of the **International Atomic Energy Agency (IAEA)** in 1957. *See also* COLD WAR; FOREIGN POLICY; KHRUSHCHEV, NIKITA; MCCONE, JOHN A.; SOVIET UNION, RELATIONS WITH; STRAUSS, LEWIS L.

AUSTRIAN STATE TREATY, 1955. Treaty ending postwar occupation of Austria by Western and Soviet troops. Negotiations for the treaty had begun after the end of World War II. The signing of the treaty on 15 May 1955 meant Austria's prisoners of war could go home. By this treaty, Austria had to remain a neutral country. Austria would also have to repay German assets in the country, which equaled about $150 million dollars. President **Dwight D. Eisenhower** urged the U.S. Senate to accept the treaty, which it did in 1955. *See also* FOREIGN POLICY; GERMANY, RELATIONS WITH.

AUTOMOBILE INDUSTRY. The prosperity of the postwar years made the 1950s Detroit's golden decade. With more money to spend and petroleum in abundance, Americans spent more time on the road. Automobiles were luxurious and fun at the same time. Hood ornaments were prominent, and tail fins added glamour to the back and sides. Fender skirts partially covered the popular white-wall tires. Two-tone sedans were introduced. Chrome gleamed inside and out. Cigarette lighters, air conditioning, arm rests, comfortable seats, power brakes, power steering, and automatic transmission were some of the new innovations introduced in the 1950s. Drive-in restaurants and drive-in movies answered the desire to enjoy one's car without leaving it. Hot rods and drag racing were popular **sports** with **teenagers**, who often spent their paychecks to buy and to improve their cars. Many Americans were trading in their cars every few years for bigger and better models. Besides the Big Three Automakers—General Motors, Ford, and Chrysler—other popular car companies were Nash, Hudson, Studebaker, and Packard. In 1957, the "compact" car was introduced in response to the rise in foreign car sales. In 1960, about 30 percent of cars sold in the United States were compacts. *See also* FRANCHISES, CHAINS, AND SHOPPING CENTERS; SUBURBIA.

– B –

BAGHDAD PACT. *See* MIDDLE EAST TREATY ORGANIZATION.

BALDWIN, JAMES (1924–1987). James Arthur Baldwin was born and raised in Harlem, part of New York City. He experienced racism at an early age, which became a theme in his writings. Upset with the treatment of **African Americans** in the United States, he lived in Europe from 1948 to 1957, where he wrote *Go Tell It on the Mountain*, his autobiography, which became a best seller. *Nobody Knows My Name* and *The Fire Next Time* also attracted large audiences and turned him into one of the leading writers of his generation. The **civil rights movement** in the late 1950s lured Baldwin back to the United States, where he became a leading civil rights activist. For the next three decades, he continued to write novels and plays with a focus on various forms of bigotry in the United States. The novel *Giovanni's Room* studied gay relationships while the novel *Another Country* examined racism and sexuality. His writings continue to be both controversial and influential. *See also* LITERATURE; THEATER.

BALL, LUCILLE (1910–1989), AND DESI ARNAZ (1917–1986). Lucille Ball was born in New York. She was a model and chorus girl before moving to Hollywood, where her movie career began slowly with parts in B-movies. Ball provided the voice of the wife on the popular radio program *My Favorite Husband*. By now she had married Desi Arnaz, a Cuban, who was an actor and a band leader. When *My Favorite Husband* was to become a **television** show in 1951 starring Lucille Ball, she insisted that her husband, Cuban actor and band leader Desi Arnaz, play the part of her husband on the show. Renamed *I Love Lucy* (1951–55), the show became an immediate hit. Her timing as a comedian was impeccable. The predicaments delighted audiences, who could not wait to see the next program. Desi Arnaz proved to be the perfect husband on the show.

While Ball was pregnant with their first child, she continued to star on the program. The episodes that followed were groundbreaking for television as Ball's shape changed. A real pregnant woman had never been seen on any screen, movie or television. Even the word "pregnant" was forbidden to be used by network executives. *I Love Lucy* continues to entertain audiences in syndication because Arnaz insisted the programs be taped, which was not a common practice at that time.

The couple eventually divorced, and Ball starred alone in two other television shows, but neither was as popular as *I Love Lucy*. Ball and Arnaz had formed Desilu Productions, and after their divorce, Arnaz continued to produce television programs. Desilu Productions had several hit television programs, including *Make Room for Daddy*, *Our Miss Brooks*, and *The Untouchables*. The couple had two children, both of whom became actors. *See also* CINEMA.

BANKING. The 1950s were generally a time of prosperity in the United States. By the time President **Dwight D. Eisenhower** left office in 1961, however, inflation had swept the country. The United States followed the terms of the Bretton Woods Agreement of 1944 with respect to monetary problems. But because the agreement effectively pegged exchange rates to the value of the dollar and the United States enjoyed a favorable balance of trade with other countries, most of those countries were unable to settle accounts with the United States at the rate set in 1944.

Two recessions occurred during the 1950s. The recession of 1953–54 was the result of inflation and more money going into funding national security. Also, in 1952, expecting higher inflation, the Federal Reserve reacted with a restrictive monetary policy. In 1957–58, again as a result of poor fiscal policy, a second recession occurred.

The Diner's Club issued the first **credit card** in 1950. In 1958, American Express and the Bank of America (BankAmericard) created credit cards that were accepted in numerous restaurants and stores. *See also* ANDERSON, ROBERT B.; BARUCH, BERNARD; ECONOMY; HUMPHREY, GEORGE M.; IN GOD WE TRUST.

BARBIE DOLL. Co-founders of the Barbie Doll, Ruth and Elliott Handler introduced their new creation to the Mattel Toy Company in the 1950s. Ruth Handler had noticed that her daughter Barbara (for whom Barbie is named) liked to play with dolls that looked like adults. While on a trip in Germany, she saw an adult doll, Bild Lilli, that was enjoyed by both adults and children, who would dress the doll in various fashions. Ruth Handler took the idea to Mattel. Although Mattel was hesitant, the Barbie Doll was introduced at the American International Toy Fair in New York City in 1959. The doll was called a "Teen-age Fashion Model" and came with clothes designed by one of Mattel's fashion designers. Barbie was a sensation, and in 1961, Ken, her boyfriend, was introduced by Mattel. *See also* TOYS AND GAMES.

BARCODE. A product's barcode, the set of lines and numbers seen on most supermarket items today, contains information pertinent to one item. It is a way to manage inventory. The idea of inventory management began in the early 1800s when Charles Babbage invented a mechanical calculator to keep track of inventory. He also tinkered with the idea of punch cards. When the cards were run through a machine, the holes in the cards provided the desired information. Punch cards were first used with success in the 1890 U.S. Census. In 1932, Walter Flint, a Harvard business student, wrote his master's thesis on the use of punch cards for inventory management in grocery stores.

In 1952, Norman Joseph Woodland and Bernard Silver, two Drexel University students, received the first patent for a barcode reader. Their idea originated from a conversation Silver overheard concerning a firm's inability to track inventory. The two students tried using patterns of ink that could be read under an ultraviolet light, but the instability of the ink posed a problem. With the combination of Morse Code and an idea from a movie sound machine created by **Lee de Forest**, Woodland had the winning combination. International Business Machines (IBM) expressed interest in the idea; however, Philco offered more money. Philco and other companies worked to improve the basic idea of a barcode reader. By the 1970s, barcode readers were being used in grocery stores. Now barcodes and simplified readers are used for a variety of purposes. *See also* TECHNOLOGICAL INNOVATIONS.

BARUCH, BERNARD (1870–1965). A self-made multimillionaire and an economic advisor to U.S. presidents, Bernard Mannes Baruch was born in South Carolina but educated in New York City, where his family moved while he was very young. Beginning as a broker on Wall Street, he worked his way up to a seat on the New York Stock Exchange, where he made his fortune. Baruch advised Presidents Woodrow Wilson and Franklin D. Roosevelt and helped draft the National Recovery Act during the 1930s. When **Harry S. Truman** assumed the presidency, Baruch was appointed U.S. representative to the **Atomic Energy Commission**. In 1946, Baruch proposed a plan that would impose restrictions on the use of **atomic energy** by all countries. At the time, the United States was the only country with atomic weapons. Baruch stated that if this plan were followed, the United States would destroy its atomic bombs. When the **Soviet Union** insisted that the United States destroy its nuclear weapons without restrictions, Washington refused. In 1949, the Soviet Union tested its first atomic bomb, which led the United States to revoke Baruch's plan as well as to diminish the importance of the Atomic Energy Commission. *See also* COLD WAR; ECONOMY; FOREIGN POLICY.

BASEBALL. The New York Yankees dominated the World Series during President **Dwight D. Eisenhower**'s administration. Of the 10 World Series during 1951–61, the Yankees played in nine, winning six of them. The 1950s were a decade of change for the game. Ebbets Field, home of the Brooklyn Dodgers, lacked space for parking as well as seating. Dodgers' owner Walter O'Malley wanted a new domed stadium for his team. He met opposition from New York City's building commissioner, who wanted the stadium to be built in Queens. O'Malley, unable to have a new stadium in Brooklyn, not only moved his team to Los Angeles but also was influential enough with the owner of the New York Giants to have that team move to San Francisco. These changes in 1958 brought the first major league baseball teams to the West Coast.

Branch Rickey did more to break the color barrier than anyone else in the sport with the signing of Jackie Robinson to the Dodgers in 1945, the first **African American** to play in the major leagues. Further diversity came to baseball with players such as Roberto Clemente, who was from Puerto Rico. Some of the most remarkable baseball players of all time were on teams in the 1950s, including Ted Williams (Boston Red Sox), Joe DiMaggio (New York Yankees), Mickey Mantle (New York Yankees), Willie Mays (New York Giants), Sandy Koufax (Los Angeles Dodgers), and Stan Musial (St. Louis Cardinals). *See also* RACIAL INTEGRATION; SPORTS.

BASKETBALL. The Boston Celtics were the dominant team in the National Basketball Association (NBA) in the 1950s. In 1950, Red Auerbach, the new Celtics coach, drafted the first **African American**, Charles Cooper, to an NBA team. By the end of the 1950s, two other African Americans were NBA draftees. In 1959, the Basketball Hall of Fame was created in Springfield, Massachusetts, and the following Celtic players were inducted: Bob Cousy, Elgin Baylor, and Bill Russell. Another star of the 1950s, Wilt Chamberlain, began his career with the Harlem Globetrotters and later played for the Philadelphia Warriors. *See also* RACIAL INTEGRATION; SPORTS.

BAY OF PIGS, 1961. The Bay of Pigs invasion was a failed attempt backed by the United States to overthrow Cuban leader **Fidel Castro**. Although the actual invasion was carried out during the presidency of **John F. Kennedy**, the plan to invade **Cuba** and overthrow Castro's government was proposed during the administration of President **Dwight D. Eisenhower**. The plan was to send a brigade of exiled Cubans to the island nation, landing them in an area called the Bay of Pigs. Kennedy and the **Central Intelligence Agency (CIA)** thought the Cubans would welcome their liberation from Castro's communist grip. Plans to send more men to help the invaders never panned out, and most of the brigade was killed, wounded, or captured. The failed Bay of Pigs invasion only made Castro more popular in his country's eyes. The Kennedy administration was embarrassed, and the CIA director and others involved in the plan were forced to resign. *See also* DULLES, ALLEN; FOREIGN POLICY; SOVIET UNION, RELATIONS WITH.

BEAT GENERATION. The 1950s, largely seen as a decade of conformity, spawned a number of nonconformist writers and musicians who came to be known as "beatniks" or "beats." The term "Beat Generation" was coined by **Jack Kerouac**, who drew on the use of the word "beat" by **jazz** musicians. Kerouac believed that his generation was disillusioned and that many did not know how to express themselves except through drugs, drinking, or promiscuity. His work was an incentive for **Allen Ginsberg** and **William S. Burroughs** to express their beliefs and experiences through their writing. *See also* LITERATURE; MAILER, NORMAN.

BEAUTY PAGEANTS. The 1950s was a golden age of beauty pageants. Women contestants were judged on appearance as they paraded in bathing suits across a stage. Sometimes a display of talent, such as singing or baton twirling, was required. The Miss America Pageant was already popular, although it was not **televised** until

1954. In 1951, the Miss World Pageant was created. The next year, it was combined with the Miss Universe Pageant. The America's Junior Miss Pageant began in 1958 as a way to recognize high school seniors; a bathing suit competition was not included in this contest. In 1960, the first Little Miss Universe contest was held, but the pageant was abandoned in 1966. The Miss USA Pageant made history in 1960 when the first **African American** represented a state in a national beauty contest. In 1961, the Miss Teenage America Pageant was created to honor the achievements of young women with scholarships; a swimsuit competition was not included in this contest. *See also* WOMEN'S MOVEMENT.

BELAFONTE, HARRY (1927–). An actor, singer, and rights activist, Harry George Belafonte was born in Harlem, in New York City. His mother, a Jamaican, left her alcoholic husband and returned to Jamaica with her two sons. When he was 13, Belafonte returned to Harlem. Suffering from dyslexia, he dropped out of school.

After being given tickets to attend a play at Harlem's American Negro Theater, he pursued a career in acting. He starred in *Days of Our Youth* at the American Negro Theater. His understudy was **Sidney Poitier**. When Belafonte was unable to perform one evening, Poitier took his place and overwhelmed the audience. Realizing his limits as an actor, Belafonte turned to singing. In 1951, he opened in New York at Gordon's Blue Angel. His singing led to a RCA recording contract. Belafonte introduced calypso **music** to audiences. His recordings of "Matilda," "Banana Boat Song," and "Day-O" were hits during the 1950s. In 1959, he appeared in his first solo **television** special, for which he won an Emmy. He was the first **African American** to receive the award.

In 1956, Belafonte met **Martin Luther King Jr.** and became active in the **civil rights movement**. In 1961, he helped to finance the Freedom Riders, who traveled through the South to test the federal government's ban of segregation on buses within the United States. In 1963, he bailed King out of jail in Birmingham, Alabama. Subsequently, thousands of civil rights protestors were freed from jail with the funds he helped raise. He also helped organize the 1963 March on Washington. For his involvement in the civil rights movement, Belafonte was called before the **House Un-American Activities Committee (HUAC)** and **blacklisted**. Harry Belafonte remains active in rights movements around the world and has served as a goodwill ambassador for the **United Nations** Children's Fund.

In the 1950s, he starred in several movies, including *Bright Road*, *Carmen Jones*, *Island in the Sun*, and *Odds Against Tomorrow*. He has appeared in two movies with Sidney Poitier, *Buck and the Preacher* and *Uptown Saturday Night. See also* CINEMA; COHN, ROY; DANCES; MCCARTHY, JOSEPH; RACIAL INTEGRATION.

BEN-GURION, DAVID (1886–1973). Prime minister of **Israel** 1948–53, 1955–63. Born David Gryn in an area of Russia that is now part of Poland, he left home in 1906 and went to Jaffa, a Palestinian city on the Mediterranean Sea. His arrival prompted him to change his last name to the Hebrew name Ben-Gurion. Hoping to create a Jewish state, the Zionist pioneer began to farm and then to engage in the labor movement. He attempted to organize Jewish workers, but his activities only angered the ruling Turkish government. Exiled during World War I, he went to the United States, where he married. In 1919, after **Great Britain** took control of Palestine, Ben-Gurion returned with his wife, Paula.

Although Ben-Gurion hoped initially that the Arabs and the Jews could co-exist in peace, by the mid-1930s, he changed his mind. Palestine, he concluded, should be strictly a Jewish state. He worked to bring Jews to this new land and to arm the people if they needed to defend their new homeland. Although the British tried to halt the covert activities of Ben-Gurion's underground army in 1948, they could not control the influx of new Jewish citizens. When the **United Nations** voted to establish a Jewish state in Palestine in 1948, Ben-Gurion named it Israel. He became its first prime minister. Although Arab armies invaded the new state, the Israeli army was able to defeat them.

In 1956, during the **Suez Crisis**, President **Dwight D. Eisenhower** wrote Prime Minister Ben-Gurion demanding that he withdraw the Israeli army from Egypt and allow the United Nations to end the crisis. Ben-Gurion responded in 1957 that Israel did not want to occupy any territory, but it needed to be assured of its safety from Egyptian aggression. The Israeli army did withdraw that year, and President Eisenhower sent the prime minister a letter commending him on his action.

When **Adolph Eichmann** was captured and brought to Israel for trial in 1960, Prime Minister Ben-Gurion used the occasion to teach young Israelis about the World War II Holocaust. *See also* FOREIGN POLICY; NASSER, GAMAL ABDEL.

BENNY, JACK (1894–1974). Born Benjamin Kubelsky in Illinois, Jack Benny began his career in vaudeville. He returned to the stage after naval duty during World War I. In the 1920s and 1930s, he had small parts in a few motion pictures, but his popular radio program in the 1930s, *The Jack Benny Show* (1933–41), led to lead roles in several feature films, including *Charley's Aunt* and *To Be or Not To Be*. In 1950–64, he appeared on the CBS **television** series *The Jack Benny Show*. Unique in the 1950s, his television program also starred **African American** actor Eddie Anderson as Rochester, Benny's assistant. Rochester was depicted as an equal to Benny and not subservient, breaking from a harmful stereotype of the era.

A talented violinist, Benny often used his violin comically in his skits. A common theme in the series was Benny's cheapness. In real life, Benny was very charitable. Benny also had impeccable timing and could simply pause, look at the audience, and say his famous "Well!" which generated laughter. *See also* CINEMA.

BENSON, EZRA TAFT (1899–1994). Secretary of agriculture 1953–61. Ezra Taft Benson served as secretary of agriculture in President **Dwight D. Eisenhower**'s administration during both terms. In order to accept the position, Benson, a Mormon, had to receive the permission of the president of the Mormon Church. Both an ardent anticommunist and antisocialist, Benson fit into the **Cold War** era perfectly. As a farmer, he had spoken out against federal mismanagement of farmlands when he was appointed the executive secretary of the National Council of Farmer Cooperatives, and he gained prominence as an outspoken critic of federal policies. He urged fewer controls on farmers as well as lifting subsidies and price supports. When Benson was appointed secretary of agriculture, he immediately set his plans in motion. The **Agricultural Act of 1954**, which he supported against strong congressional opposition, provided for flexible price supports. Benson traveled around the United States, telling farmers that they knew what was better for their farms than Washington did. *See also* AGRICULTURAL TRADE DEVELOPMENT AND ASSISTANCE ACT OF 1954; ECONOMY.

BERLE, MILTON (1908–2002). Born Milton Berlinger in New York, Berle was performing by the age of five in silent films and in vaudeville acts, but he was best known as **television**'s first superstar. "Mr. Television" appeared every Tuesday night on the *Texaco Star Theater* (1948–56). Many people in the 1950s bought a television because of the popularity of Berle's show. He used the same cast each week; however, the skits were so innovative that guests were really unnecessary. The National Broadcasting Company (NBC) gave Berle a contract for 30 years, beginning in 1951, which proved to be very advantageous for NBC. Berle's show set the stage for a number of NBC's comedies for many years. After his career in television waned, he appeared in movies and did guest spots on various television programs. Berle's career in show business spanned about 80 years, and he never lost his ability to make people laugh.

BERLIN CONFERENCE. The foreign ministers of **France**, **Great Britain**, the **Soviet Union**, and the United States met in Berlin from 25 January to 18 February 1954 to discuss European concerns as well as what to do about reunifying **Germany**. Another topic was the future of Austria. At one time, the Soviet Union had proposed it be turned into a demilitarized neutral country. However, during the conference, the Soviet Union decided against its own proposal. In the end, the conference accomplished nothing other than an agreement for the foreign ministers to meet again in Geneva to discuss France's involvement in Vietnam, where the French army was losing its colonial war against the communist Vietnamese led by **Ho Chi Minh**. *See also* AUSTRIAN STATE TREATY; COLD WAR; FOREIGN POLICY; VIETNAM WAR.

BERLIN CRISIS, 1954–1962. The **Soviet Union**'s fear of West Germany's rearmament and obtaining nuclear weapons led to four years of East–West talks and confrontations from 1958 to 1962 involving Berlin. In 1958, Premier **Nikita Khrushchev** of the Soviet Union insisted that **Germany** must be nuclear free and that the four powers who occupied Germany must end their occupation of that country. If his demands were not met, East Germany would control access to Berlin. The downing of the United States' **U-2** spy plane in 1960 damaged the talks between Khrushchev and President **Dwight D. Eisenhower**. The newly elected **John F. Kennedy** inherited the situation; however, his talks with Khrushchev were futile. Khrushchev responded to the failed talks by erecting the Berlin Wall in 1961. *See also* ATOMIC AND NUCLEAR ENERGY; COLD WAR; FOREIGN POLICY.

BERLIN, IRVING (1888–1989). One of the most popular and prolific songwriters of the 20th century, Irving Berlin was born in Russia in 1888 but immigrated to the United States in 1893 with his parents. His father died when Berlin was a young man. Berlin did odd jobs while writing songs on the side. Some of his earliest compositions were sung in vaudeville. "Alexander's Ragtime Band" brought him national prominence. During World War I, he enlisted and wrote **music** and performed in army shows. After the war, he returned to writing songs, a number of which were sung in movies and in hit Broadway musicals, including *Annie Get Your Gun*. He wrote over 3,000 compositions, including "God Bless America," introduced by Kate Smith during World War II, a song many Americans wanted to be the new national anthem. Some of his other famous songs are "There's No Business like Show Business," "Easter Parade," "Always," and the best-selling single for almost 50 years, "White Christmas." A political conservative, Berlin supported President **Dwight D. Eisenhower** and wrote the campaign song "I Like Ike." When music began to change in the 1950s, he realized his compositions were out of date. When his musical *Mr. President* was poorly received, he became a virtual recluse for the remainder of his life. He died of a heart attack in 1989 at the age of 101. *See also* CROSBY, BING; CINEMA; THEATER.

BERMUDA CONFERENCE. President **Dwight D. Eisenhower** and Secretary of State **John Foster Dulles** met with British Prime Minister **Winston Churchill** and **France**'s Prime Minister Joseph Lanier and Foreign Minister George Bidault in Bermuda on 4–8 December 1953 to discuss the relationship between France and **Germany**. Dulles stressed the dangers if France and Germany became enemies again, but no agreements were reached at the conference. *See also* FOREIGN POLICY.

BERNSTEIN, LEONARD (1918–1990). Massachusetts-born Leonard Bernstein was educated at Harvard University (B.A., 1939) and the Curtis Institute of Music (1939–41). In 1943, he was the substitute conductor of the New York Philharmonic Orchestra, displaying an energetic style of conducting. Within two years, he was asked to become director of the New York Symphony. Bernstein was only in his mid-20s at that time. His career spanned compositions, **cinema** scores, Broadway plays, **television** appearances, and recordings. Bernstein's award-winning 1950s Broadway musical *West Side Story* made his name a household word. The musical was unique, for the subject, based on Shakespeare's *Romeo and Juliet*, was gangs in New York City. It became a 1960 Academy Award–winning movie. Bernstein also composed the music for the movies *On the Waterfront* and *On the Town*. His *Young People's Concerts*, which were televised, spanned three decades from the 1950s through the 1970s. *See also* MUSIC; THEATER.

BERRY, CHUCK (1926–). A songwriter and singer of some of the biggest **rock and roll** hits of the 1950s, Charles Edward Anderson Berry was born in St. Louis, Missouri. He began playing in a trio in 1953 and by 1955 had his first hit song, "Maybelline." Some parents were fearful of his **music**, but **teenagers** loved him. He starred in two movies in the 1950s, *Rock, Rock, Rock* (1956) and *Go, Johnny, Go* (1959). In 1959, he was arrested after a 14-year-old hat-check girl he had fired from his club was arrested on a charge of prostitution. His involvement with her was enough to convict him under the Mann Act. In 1963, he was freed from prison and his career rebounded.

Berry's guitar techniques and stage presence, with his unique duck walk, were popular with audiences. In *Hail! Hail! Rock 'n' Roll*, a 1986 documentary celebrating Berry's 60th birthday, many musicians who had been influenced by Berry made appearances. Berry was also one of the first inductees into the Rock and Roll Hall of

Fame and was named as one of the 100 greatest artists of all time by *Rolling Stone*. Some of Berry's other top hits are "Long Tall Sally," "Tutti Frutti," "Johnny B. Goode," "Sweet Little Sixteen," and "Roll Over, Beethoven." *See also AMERICAN BANDSTAND*; CINEMA.

BIRTH CONTROL PILL. With a grant from Planned Parenthood, **Margaret Sanger** solicited the help of Gregory Pincus, a biologist, to create an oral contraceptive for birth control. In 1956, testing on humans began, and the Food and Drug Administration (FDA) approved the birth control pill in clinical use. Women could now have sex without the fear of becoming pregnant. Some historians believe the pill contributed to the sexual revolution of the 1960s. *See also* MEDICAL ADVANCES; WOMEN'S MOVEMENT.

BLACK, HUGO (1886–1971). Associate justice of the **Supreme Court** 1937–71. Hugo Lafayette Black was born in Alabama. He received his law degree in 1906 from the University of Alabama at Tuscaloosa and specialized in personal injury and labor law. In 1926, he won a seat in the U.S. Senate. He served for 10 years before his appointment to the U.S. Supreme Court by President Franklin D. Roosevelt. His appointment was controversial because Black had been a member of the Ku Klux Klan during the 1920s, yet he proved to be a strong supporter of the **civil rights movement**. In his 34 years on the bench, Justice Black ruled on some of the most important cases of the 20th century, including *Brown v. Board of Education*, which declared segregation unconstitutional. Although Black was burned in effigy in his home state of Alabama, he continued to express support for the civil rights movement. *See also BROWDER V. GAYLE*; CIVIL RIGHTS ACT OF 1957; CIVIL RIGHTS ACT OF 1960; RACIAL INTEGRATION.

BLACKLIST. With the start of the **Cold War** after World War II, a **Red Scare** swept across America. The House of Representatives formed the **House Un-American Activities Committee (HUAC)** to investigate all forms of mass media that might spread communist propaganda. Filmmakers, actors in **cinema** and **theater**, authors, and journalists suspected of being communists were blacklisted. Over 320 people were found on HUAC's blacklist. Some lost their livelihoods. Only 10 percent of those in the movie industry who were blacklisted were able to return to work in Hollywood. Others worked under pseudonyms or found work in other countries. A few were driven to suicide.

One of the active anticommunists groups in Hollywood was the Motion Picture Alliance for the Preservation of American Ideals. **John Wayne**, a member of the group, and other well-known performers willingly named alleged communists in the entertainment industry. They believed it was their patriotic duty to name names, not worrying about the possible lasting effect on other members of the film community. Anyone who refused to testify before HUAC, or asserted the Fifth Amendment right not to testify, was added to the blacklist. *See also* BELAFONTE, HARRY; COHN, ROY; HELLMAN, LILLIAN; HORNE, LENA; KAZAN, ELIA; MCCARTHY, JOSEPH; PARKER, DOROTHY; ROBESON, PAUL; SCHINE, G. DAVID.

BOONE, PAT (1934–). Born Charles Eugene Boone in Jacksonville, Florida, Pat Boone began his career while attending North Texas State College in Denton, Texas. In 1954, he appeared on **Arthur Godfrey**'s **television** program, after which he was awarded a contract with Republic Records. A year later, he changed to the Dot label. In 1955–62, he was on the top 40 charts every year, often singing a rhythm and blues song in his smooth, slow manner. Boone's signature white shoes (white bucks) became popular, and his clean-cut image appealed to mainstream audiences. When his popularity began to wane in the 1960s, he turned to singing gospel songs.

Boone starred in several movies, singing the popular title song for two of them: *April Love* and *Bernardine*. Some of his other hit songs are "Moody River," "I Almost Lost My Mind," "Love Letters in the Sand," and "Tutti Frutti." Even while recording and having his own television program (1957–60), Boone completed his college degree, graduating from Columbia University in 1958. *See also AMERICAN BANDSTAND*; CINEMA; MUSIC; TEENAGERS.

BOXING. Television brought boxing into American homes in the 1950s. The small screen was perfect for boxing, and in the 1950s one could watch as many as four or five boxing shows a week on network television. The *Gillette Cavalcade of Sports*, which featured boxing, was one of the most popular television shows of the decade. When jet planes made traveling easier, boxers from around the world appeared on TV. Some of the greatest boxers in the 1950s were Rocky Marciano, Sugar Ray Robinson, Archie Moore, Joe Louis, and Floyd Patterson. *See also* SPORTS.

BRANDO, MARLON (1924–2004). Actor Marlon Brando, who was born in Nebraska, had a difficult upbringing. His mother, an alcoholic, was involved in local **theater**, which led to Brando's interest in acting. He first performed on Broadway in 1944 in *I Remember Mama* but became famous for his starring role in *A Streetcar Named Desire*.

Brando influenced a whole school of method actors in the 1950s, including **James Dean**. Although Dean became a cultural icon after his untimely death in 1955, his clothing and acting style were copied from Brando, who was the first to wear **T-shirts** as outerwear. Rebellious and a nonconformist, Brando practiced a form of acting that was unique.

In 1950, he had his first screen role in *The Men*, but he achieved film stardom in *The Wild One*, in which he played a rebel motorcyclist. Wearing jeans and a motorcycle jacket and riding a motorcycle became popular among **teenagers** in part because of Brando's character in *The Wild One*. **Elvis Presley** used Brando as a model for his role in *Jailhouse Rock*. Every year from 1952 through 1955, Brando was nominated for an Academy Award. He won in 1955 for his performance in *On the Waterfront*. Although Brando's career declined in the 1960s, he won an Academy Award in 1973 for his performance in *The Godfather*, making him a star once more. He turned down the award, however, in protest against the treatment of Native Americans by the film industry.

After the death of **Martin Luther King Jr.**, Brando used his money and influence in the **civil rights movement**, giving large contributions to the **Southern Christian Leadership Conference (SCLC)** during the 1960s. *See also* CINEMA.

BRANDT, WILLY (1913–1992). Mayor of West Berlin 1957–66, chancellor of West Germany 1969–74. Born Herbert Ernst Frahm, he changed his name to Willy Brandt in 1933 to avoid capture by the Nazis and fled to Norway, where he became a journalist. Following the 1940 occupation of Norway by the Nazis, he fled to Sweden, continuing his career as a journalist. After World War II, Brandt returned to **Germany**. He became active in the Berlin Social Democratic Party (SPD), which led to his election as mayor of West Berlin (1957–66). During the **Berlin Crisis** of 1958–61, Brandt was an important participant when the **Soviet Union** wanted to force the Allies out of Berlin. The building of the Berlin Wall in 1961 meant families in Berlin were often forced apart. Brandt was able to devise a plan accepted by the East Berlin government that allowed visitation of families from West Berlin to East Berlin.

In August 1959, Brandt met with President **Dwight D. Eisenhower** prior to speaking at the 150th celebration of Abraham Lincoln's birthday in Springfield, Illinois. Brandt wanted to reinforce the importance of the mutual dependence of the United States and Berliners. In 1961 and again in 1965, Brandt campaigned for the chancellorship of West Germany, a position he finally achieved in 1969. In 1971, he was awarded the Nobel Peace Prize. He was forced to resign as chancellor in 1974 when a report disclosed that his close aide, Gunther Guillaume, was actually a spy for East Germany. *See also* COLD WAR; FOREIGN POLICY; KHRUSHCHEV, NIKITA.

BRENNAN, WILLIAM J., JR. (1906–1997). Associate justice of the **Supreme Court** 1956–90. William Joseph Brennan Jr. was born in New Jersey and was educated in both parochial and public schools. He received his undergraduate degree from the Wharton School at the University of Pennsylvania (B.A., 1928) and his law degree from Harvard University in 1931. After graduation from Harvard, he practiced labor law in one of New Jersey's most prestigious law firms.

After serving in World War II, Brennan returned to the New Jersey law firm. Although he became a partner in the firm, he left it in 1949 to become a superior court judge. In 1952, he was appointed to the state supreme court. Brennan's appointment to the U.S. Supreme Court was a political one by President **Dwight D. Eisenhower**. With the **1956 election** in the offing, Eisenhower believed the appointment of a liberal northeastern Catholic would help him win a second term.

Justice Brennan was one of the most liberal of the nine justices on the Supreme Court. He opposed the death penalty and took a pro-choice position on abortion. Brennan had the gift of persuasion and was able to coax his fellow justices to follow his opinions. In his many years on the bench, he listened to some of the most important cases in U.S. history, including issues such as free speech (*Roth v. United States*, 1957), abortion (*Rowe v. Wade*, 1973), voting (*Baker v. Carr*, 1962), and **civil rights** (*Green v. New Kent County*, 1968). *See also* CIVIL RIGHTS ACT OF 1957; CIVIL RIGHTS ACT OF 1960; EDUCATION; RACIAL INTEGRATION.

BRINKER AMENDMENT. Introduced in 1951 by Senator John W. Brinker of Ohio, the Brinker Amendment sought to prohibit a president from reaching agreements or signing treaties without Congress's consent. Brinker worried about the increasing power of the executive branch. When **Dwight D. Eisenhower** became president, the Brinker Amendment had not been passed, and Eisenhower used his persuasive skills to diffuse Brinker's attempt to inhibit the power of the presidency. *See also* FOREIGN POLICY.

BRINKSMANSHIP. A policy formulated during the **Cold War** by Secretary of State **John Foster Dulles**, brinksmanship referred to the practice of threatening to go to the brink of a nuclear war in a crisis. Both Dulles and President **Dwight D. Eisenhower** used brinksmanship against the **Soviet Union**. Since both the Soviet Union and the United States had nuclear weapons, the danger of one nation attacking the other was always a concern. **Adlai Stevenson**, Eisenhower's opponent in two presidential elections, disapproved of the use of brinksmanship, fearing that it could backfire. Some historians, however, believe the use of brinksmanship helped end both the **Korean War** and the **Quemoy and Matsu crises** in 1954–55 and 1958. *See also* ATOMIC AND NUCLEAR ENERGY; FOREIGN POLICY; MASSIVE RETALIATION.

BROADWAY. *See* THEATER.

BROWDER V. GAYLE, 1956. Soon after the **Montgomery Bus Boycott** began in 1955, which followed the arrest of **Rosa Parks** for refusing to give up her seat on a bus, **African American** rights activists helped to develop a lawsuit that would challenge segregation on buses in Alabama. Aurelia Browder was one of four plaintiffs in the case who had refused to give up her seat on a Montgomery city bus to a white rider and had been taken to jail. The suit was filed against the city of Montgomery and the mayor, W. A. Gayle.

Fred S. Gray, a prominent Tuskegee **civil rights** lawyer, consulted with **Thurgood Marshall** and Robert Carter, legal counsels to the **National Association for the Advancement of Colored People (NAACP)**. Gray represented the four plaintiffs when the case of *Browder v. Gayle* reached the U.S. District Court for the Middle District of Alabama. On 5 June 1956, the court ruled that segregated city buses were in violation of the Fourteenth Amendment.

The U.S. District Court's decision in *Browder* was upheld by the U.S. Supreme Court on 13 November 1956. *See also* RACIAL INTEGRATION.

BROWN V. BOARD OF EDUCATION, 1954. Linda Brown, an **African American** third grader in Topeka, Kansas, had to walk a mile to school by way of a train switchyard. Although an elementary school was only seven blocks away, the principal would not enroll the African American student. After Brown's father turned to the **National Association for the Advancement of Colored People (NAACP)**, it brought suit to test the constitutionality of segregation. *Brown v. Board of Education of Topeka, Kansas* resulted in a unanimous decision by the U.S. **Supreme Court** in 1954. The Court overturned *Plessy v. Ferguson* (1896), which had upheld the constitutionality of separate but equal facilities. The *Brown* decision paved the way for integration of public schools. *See also* CIVIL RIGHTS MOVEMENT; EDUCATION; FAUBUS, ORVAL; MARSHALL, THURGOOD; RACIAL INTEGRATION.

BROWNELL, HERBERT, JR. (1904–1996). Attorney general of the United States 1953–57. Born in Nebraska, Herbert Brownell Jr. graduated from Yale University Law School in 1927 and practiced law in New York. After serving in the New York Assembly, he managed Thomas E. Dewey's campaigns for New York governor (1938 and 1942) and for president (1944 and 1948). In 1944, he was made national chair of the **Republican Party**. He held that position for two years and played a leading role in **Dwight D. Eisenhower**'s successful campaign for president. In 1952, Eisenhower appointed Brownell attorney general. In this position, he played a crucial role in the execution of **Ethel and Julius Rosenberg**, who had been found guilty of spying for the **Soviet Union**, and in the desegregation of Little Rock High School. He resigned his post in 1957 to return to his former law firm. *See also* ELECTION, 1952; FEDERAL BUREAU OF INVESTIGATION (FBI).

BRUCE, LENNY (1925–1966). Comedian and satirist Lenny Bruce was born Leonard Alfred Schneider in 1925. His parents divorced when he was five, and he was shuffled from one relative to another until he was a teenager. After holding several jobs and serving in the navy, he began his nightclub career as a comedian in Baltimore, Maryland. His act was improvised and often obscene; however, his intellectual observations about life attracted large audiences. He even appeared on national **television** with Steve Allen. Bruce was arrested a number of times for illegal possession of drugs. He died from a drug overdose in 1966.

BUCKLEY, WILLIAM F., JR. (1925–2008). Author, talk-show host, editor, and founder of the *National Review*, William Frank Buckley Jr. was born into a wealthy New York family. In 1950, he graduated from Yale University, where he had excelled as a debater. His 1951 book *God and Man at Yale: The Superstitions of "Academic Freedom"* criticized Yale for, in his opinion, losing its traditional values. He paid his publisher, Regnery, $10,000 to advertise his book.

Buckley worked for a year with the **Central Intelligence Agency**. From 1952 until he founded the *National Review*, he was a freelance writer. In his 1954 book *McCarthy and His Enemies*, he defended Senator **Joseph McCarthy**. In the 1950s, Buckley believed **African Americans** were inferior, and therefore whites should impose their ideas on blacks. His views upset many conservatives, and Buckley refined his comments by saying both uneducated whites and blacks should not have the right to vote. In the **1952 election**, the *National Review* reluctantly endorsed **Dwight D. Eisenhower** for president by simply stating, "We prefer Ike." Although usually associated with **Republican** politics, Buckley unsuccessfully attempted to capture the office of mayor of New York City in 1965 as a Conservative Party candidate.

Considered one of the founders of the modern conservative movement, Buckley became a popular figure on **television** hosting the talk show *Firing Line* (1966–99), which ran longer than any other television program hosted by one person. One of the great intellects of the second part of the 20th century, he held his own with political figures, writers, and people in the news. With his boyish looks, gregarious personality, and wit, he had a commanding presence.

In 1990, Buckley retired as editor but remained editor-at-large of the *National Review*. He continued to make appearances on radio and television shows and on the lecture circuit. In addition to his political books, he wrote 11 spy novels. Blackford Oakes, a CIA agent, was the main character in each one. **Elvis Presley** was one character in a historical novel. He also wrote a novel about the Nuremberg trials. Buckley died peacefully at his desk in 2008. *See also* LITERATURE; MAGAZINES.

BUNCHE, RALPH (1904–1971). First **African American** to hold a major position in the **United Nations**; 1950 recipient of the Nobel Peace Prize. Ralph Johnson Bunche was born in Detroit, Michigan. His parents' health required a move to a drier area, and the family moved to New Mexico when Bunche was 10. Unfortunately, the move did not improve his parents' health, and within two years, both died. His grandmother, who had moved to New Mexico with them, raised Bunche and his siblings.

Bunche won prizes in history and English while in elementary school, and he was valedictorian of his high school graduating class. At the University of California, Los Angeles, which he attended on an athletic scholarship, he majored in international relations and was valedictorian of his college graduating class (1927). He continued his education at Howard University (M.A., 1928) and received his doctorate from Harvard University (1934), after a year in Africa (1932–33) doing research for his dissertation. Bunche did postgraduate research with various institutions of higher learning, including Northwestern University and the London School of Economics.

Bunche was active in the **civil rights movement** throughout his life. He spoke out against segregation and worked closely with groups that fought for the rights of African Americans. He also held positions in the State Department, which led to his most valuable contribution: an armistice between **Israel** and the Arab States, signed in 1949, for which Bunche was awarded the 1950 Nobel Peace Prize. He continued his career at the United Nations. In 1960, he was sent to oversee UN activities during the **Congo Crisis**. *See also* FOREIGN POLICY; NATIONAL ASSOCIATION FOR THE ADVANCEMENT OF COLORED PEOPLE (NAACP).

BUREAU OF INVESTIGATION. *See* FEDERAL BUREAU OF INVESTIGATION.

BURNS, ARTHUR F. (1904–1987). Chair of **Council of Economic Advisors** 1953–56. Born in Austria, Arthur Frank Burns immigrated with his family to the United States, settling in New Jersey. He received degrees from Columbia University (B.A., 1921; M.A., 1925; Ph.D., 1934). After graduation, he taught at Columbia. Burns's economic expertise led to his appointment as chair of President **Dwight D. Eisenhower**'s Council of Economic Advisors. President **Richard M. Nixon** appointed Burns chair of the Federal Reserve System (1970–78). In 1981–85, Burns was U.S. ambassador to the Federal Republic of **Germany**. *See also* BANKING; ECONOMY; FOREIGN POLICY.

BURROUGHS, WILLIAM S. (1914–1997). Beat Generation novelist William Seward Burroughs was born in St. Louis. His grandfather invented an adding machine and established the Burroughs Corporation to make the machine. As a child, Burroughs had nightmares and was told by a nurse that smoking opium would help overcome them, advice he was determined to follow as an adult.

He graduated from Harvard University (B.A., 1936) with a degree in English literature and worked for an advertising agency. In 1944, he began to use drugs, including opium and heroin. In 1951, he accidentally killed his common-law wife but was not tried for her death. *Junkie*, published in 1953, told of his drug use.

In 1957, writers **Allen Ginsberg** and **Jack Kerouac**, whom he had met in the mid-1940s, visited Burroughs in Tangiers, where he was living. In 1957, with Ginsberg's help, Burroughs published *The Naked Lunch*. The novel was semiautobiographical, involving his experiences as a drug addict. Although the book won praise, its homosexual themes led to the United States' last major obscenity trial. Burroughs lived abroad, in London, Paris, and Mexico City, and he continued to publish novels, including *Exterminator*, *The Soft Machine*, *Nova Express*, and *The Ticket That Exploded*. *See also* LITERATURE; MAILER, NORMAN.

BURTON, HAROLD H. (1888–1964). Mayor of Cleveland 1936–40, U.S. senator 1941–45, and **Supreme Court** justice 1945–58. Harold Hitz Burton was born in Massachusetts but settled in Ohio after graduating from Harvard University Law School (1912). His political career began as mayor of Cleveland. Rising quickly in politics, he was elected to the U.S. Senate in 1941. During World War II, President **Harry S. Truman** and Burton worked closely on the Senate investigative committee overseeing the country's war effort. After Truman became president, he named Burton to the U.S. **Supreme Court**. Burton played a major role in *Brown v. Board of Education*. He also championed U.S. membership in the **United Nations**. His ability to bring the justices together when opinions caused tempers to flare was one of his great attributes on the bench. He objected to the federal government's interference in states' rights unless a person suffered from a state's laws. *See also BROWDER V. GAYLE*; CIVIL RIGHTS MOVEMENT; RACIAL INTEGRATION.

– C –

CAESAR, SID (1922–), AND IMOGENE COCA (1908–2001). Sid Caesar and Imogene Coca, along with **Milton Berle**, **Lucille Ball**, and **Red Skelton**, were major **television** celebrities of the 1950s. The duo starred in *Your Show of Shows* (1950–54), a Saturday-night fixture. Both Caesar and Coca appeared on Broadway before they were paired to star on television. Caesar was born in Yonkers and graduated from Yonkers High School in 1939 before going into show business. Coca was born in Philadelphia and was performing alone on stage by the age of 11. She appeared on Broadway for the first time in 1934. Caesar's Broadway debut was in 1948. *Your Show of Shows* introduced other comedians who would continue in the entertainment industry for years, including Carl Reiner, Mel Brooks, Neil Simon, and Howard Morris. Although *Your Show of Shows* lasted only four years with Caesar and Coca as the headliners, the skits they did were innovative and so entertaining that the program dominated Saturday nights for the four years it was on. The duo then decided to pursue opportunities on their own. Caesar had his own productions throughout the 1950s; Coca's show lasted one season. Both made numerous guest appearances on other programs. *See also* THEATER.

CAPOTE, TRUMAN (1924–1984). Author Truman Capote, born in 1924 in New Orleans, was one of the leading literary figures of the 1950s and 1960s. Capote won several literary prizes while in school, but he gained notoriety with his novels *The Glass Harp* (1951) and *Breakfast at Tiffany's* (1958). In the early 1960s, Capote traveled to Kansas to research his first nonfiction work, *In Cold Blood*, based on the murder of the Clutter family. Both *Breakfast at Tiffany's* and *In Cold Blood* were successful as motion pictures. Capote wrote numerous articles and novels, many of which are considered literary classics and some of which became **television** programs. Diminutive in stature, with a high-pitched drawl and a talent for story-telling, Capote was an entertaining guest on television talk shows. *See also* CINEMA; LITERATURE; THEATER.

CARACAS CONFERENCE (TENTH INTERNATIONAL CONFERENCE OF AMERICAN STATES). In the Caracas Conference held 1–28 March 1954, **Dwight D. Eisenhower**'s secretary of state, **John Foster Dulles**, met with representatives of Latin American countries to discuss growing communist intervention in those countries. The conference ended with passage of a resolution in which the representatives agreed to work together against communism. Only **Guatemala** refused to go along with the conference's decision. Later, the leader of Guatemala, Jacobo Arbenz Guzman, was ousted from power by a covert operation led by the **Central Intelligence Agency (CIA)**. The move met little opposition from the other Latin American countries. *See also* FOREIGN POLICY.

CARSON, RACHEL (1907–1964). A marine biologist and environmentalist, Rachel Carson was born in Pennsylvania and taught zoology at Johns Hopkins University, where she had earned her master's degree (1932). From 1936 to 1949, she worked for the U.S. Fish and Wildlife Service as a marine biologist. Although she wrote scientific articles as part of her position with the government, she was a gifted writer who could appeal to a popular audience. Her first book, *Under the Sea-Wind* (1941), became a best seller. Other books and articles followed, including *The Sea Around Us*, which won the 1952 National Book Award and was made into an Oscar-winning documentary.

Carson is best known, however, for her campaign against the use of the pesticide DDT. As she learned more about this pesticide, she became concerned about its effects on the environment. In 1962, she turned her concerns into a new book, *Silent Spring*, which became a sweeping best seller. In 1963, she appeared on **television** to debate a chemical company executive on the toxic effects of DDT. Following the debate, Carson received more awards, speaking engagements, and honors. Above all, however, her work made the United States aware of the serious harm to the environment caused by indiscriminate use of pesticides. DDT was eventually banned. Many people consider Carson the spark that ignited the global environmental movement.

CASTRO, FIDEL (1926–). President of **Cuba** 1959–2008. Fidel Alejandro Castro Ruz, who was born in Cuba, earned a law degree in 1950. In 1959, he led a successful revolution against the American-supported and corrupt government of Fulgencio Batista. After taking control of the government, Castro prohibited foreign-owned property, signed an agreement to purchase oil from the **Soviet Union**, and took control of American oil refineries. The latter act led to President **Dwight D. Eisenhower**'s decision to break diplomatic relations with Cuba. Castro then declared he was a communist. In 1961, the failed **Bay of Pigs** invasion only solidified Castro's position in Cuba and his ties with the Soviet Union. As the leader of Cuba for almost 50 years, Castro ruled longer than any other head of state. In 2008, he resigned as president due to ill health, and his younger brother Raul became the new president of Cuba. *See also* FOREIGN POLICY; KENNEDY, JOHN F.; KHRUSHCHEV, NIKITA.

CENTRAL INTELLIGENCE AGENCY (CIA). Established in 1947, the Central Intelligence Agency was originally named the

Office of Strategic Services (OSS). Part of the National Security Council (NSC), the CIA is responsible for gathering information deemed pertinent to the safety of the United States. President **Dwight D. Eisenhower** used the CIA to engage in covert operations abroad. In 1953, it helped overthrow the Iranian government of **Mohammed Mossadegh** and reinstate the shah of **Iran**. In 1954, it was responsible for overthrowing **Guatemala**'s President Jacobo Arbenz Guzman. Another covert operation led by the CIA was the **Bay of Pigs** invasion of **Cuba** in 1961. The CIA uses sophisticated **technology**, installing satellites as well as spies on the ground to gather foreign intelligence. During the Eisenhower presidency, the head of the CIA was **Allen Dulles**. *See also* DULLES, JOHN FOSTER; FOREIGN POLICY; KENNEDY, JOHN F.; MCCONE, JOHN A.; PAHLAVI, MOHAMMED REZA.

CENTRAL TREATY ORGANIZATION (CENTO). *See* MIDDLE EAST TREATY ORGANIZATION.

CHAMOUN, CAMILLE (1900–1987). President of **Lebanon** 1952–58. Born in Deir el-Qamar to a Maronite Christian family, Camille Nimr Chamoun was educated in France. He received his law degree in 1923 and entered Lebanese politics in 1929. Controlled by the French government, the country was divided at the end of World War II into three sections along religious lines. Each section was represented in the Lebanese parliament. Chamoun had been a member in the 1930s. In 1943, he was arrested for championing independence from France but was released after 11 days. In 1947–51, he was again a member of parliament. He then served as the ambassador to **Great Britain** (1944–46). In 1952, President Bishara el-Khoury, who was accused of corruption, was forced to resign and Chamoun was elected to replace him.

In 1958, a civil war almost began when Muslims, backed by **Gamal Abdel Nasser**, attempted to overthrow Chamoun's government. Chamoun pleaded for help from the United States based on the **Eisenhower Doctrine**. President **Dwight D. Eisenhower** sent U.S. marines to end the revolt. Under pressure from Eisenhower and in order to appease the Muslims, Chamoun resigned and was replaced by General Faud Chehab, who was popular in the Muslim community.

Chamoun continued to play a part in Lebanese politics until his death at age 87. *See also* FOREIGN POLICY.

CHECKERS SPEECH. Soon after becoming the **Republican** vice-presidential candidate in 1952, **Richard M. Nixon** was accused of taking money illegally from a slush fund. A brilliant politician, Nixon went on **television** on 23 September 1952 and took his case to the American people. With his wife near him, Nixon explained that he was not a crook and had not done anything illegal. He added that his daughters had been given a dog named Checkers by an admirer and they would not give the dog back. The television audience responded with such overwhelming support of Nixon that presidential candidate **Dwight D. Eisenhower** decided to keep Nixon as his running mate. Eisenhower won the **1952 election** decisively.

CHIANG KAI-SHEK (1887–1975). Leader of the Chinese Nationalists, Chiang Kai-shek received his military training in Japan. In 1928, he had reunified **China**. However, left-wing splinter groups were a constant problem. The most powerful of these were the Chinese Communists led by **Mao Zedong**. After World War II, they drove the corrupt Chiang government from power. Chiang was forced to retreat to the island of Formosa (Taiwan).

Chiang controlled islands off the coast of China, among them **Quemoy and Matsu**, which he used as staging grounds to launch raids on the Chinese mainland. This appears to have been one reason for the decision by Communist China to launch an August 1954 artillery attack on the islands, which prompted the first of two Taiwan Strait crises. Believing China's plan was to take Quemoy and Matsu, and then Taiwan, the U.S. Senate passed the **Formosa Resolution**, giving President **Dwight D. Eisenhower** the power to take whatever military action was necessary to protect Formosa. Meanwhile, administration officials issued vague threats of force, including the possible use of nuclear weapons, to prevent an invasion of those two islands. In 1955, the Chinese Communists stopped the shelling.

In 1958, again apparently in part because of Chiang's harassment of the mainland, the shelling of the islands resumed. The United States once more threatened the use of force and sent warships to the area. Later that year, for reasons that are unclear, the bombardment stopped. *See also* BRINKSMANSHIP; MASSIVE RETALIATION.

CHINA LOBBY. After World War II, during the height of the **Red Scare** in the United States, many powerful right-wing groups joined together as the **China** Lobby. Supporters of **Chiang Kai-shek**, they were angered that the United States had allowed communists to take over China. The group worked closely with Senator **Joseph McCarthy**'s Senate Permanent Subcommittee on Investigations. *See also* FOREIGN POLICY; HOUSE UN-AMERICAN ACTIVITIES COMMITTEE (HUAC).

CHINA, RELATIONS WITH. After World War II, fighting resumed in China between the communists led by **Mao Zedong** and the Nationalists led by **Chiang Kai-shek**. In 1949, the communists forced Chiang and his followers to flee to Formosa (Taiwan). The United States thereafter began to give economic and military aid to the Nationalist government while imposing a trade embargo on the Chinese Communists. President **Dwight D. Eisenhower** continued those policies. In 1954–55 and again in 1958, Chinese Communist artillery batteries began to hit the Nationalist-controlled islands **Quemoy and Matsu**, located just off mainland China. The Eisenhower administration believed that the communists' intention was to capture those islands and then Taiwan. To deter the Chinese during the first Taiwan Strait crisis, the United States signed a defense pact with the Nationalist government, approved the **Formosa Resolution**, and kept the Chinese Communists guessing as to whether the United States might use military force if they tried to capture the two islands. During the second Taiwan Strait Crisis, the U.S. response included renewed statements about the possible use of force as well as sending warships to the strait. Though it is not entirely clear why, the Chinese communists both times ended their bombardment, and Quemoy and Matsu remained in Nationalist hands. *See also* BRINKSMANSHIP; FOREIGN POLICY; MASSIVE RETALIATION.

CHURCHILL, WINSTON (1874–1965). Prime minister of **Great Britain** 1940–45 and 1951–55. Winston Leonard Spencer Churchill was born and educated in England, where he was elected to Parliament in 1900. As First Lord of the Admiralty during World War I, he took the blame for the disastrous defeat at Gallipoli. He resigned from the government in 1915 and reenlisted in the army. But in 1917, he was appointed to the position of minister of munitions.

Prior to Great Britain's entrance into World War II, Churchill feared his country was not ready to defend itself. Prime Minister Neville Chamberlain dismissed Churchill's warnings. In 1940, shortly after the outbreak of World War II, Churchill was named prime minister, succeeding Chamberlain. Churchill gave his country the hope it needed to resist **Germany**'s threat during the war. After the war, Churchill's Conservative Party was defeated in a general election by the Labour Party, which chose Clement Atlee to be prime minister.

In 1951, the Conservatives and Churchill were returned to power. He helped the country rebuild from the war, and he pressed the government to invest in the development of nuclear weapons. In December 1953, Churchill met with President **Dwight D. Eisenhower** and **France**'s Prime Minister Joseph Laniel in the **Bermuda Conference** to discuss relations with **Germany**. Churchill also faced crises in several of Great Britain's colonies, including Malaya and Kenya, which required sending British troops. In 1955, Churchill resigned as prime minister. *See also* EDEN, ANTHONY; FOREIGN POLICY; GENEVA CONFERENCE AND ACCORDS; ISRAEL, RELATIONS WITH; NASSER, GAMAL ABDEL; SUEZ CRISIS.

CINEMA. The challenges of the postwar years were reflected in many of the films produced during the 1950s. *The Day the World Stood Still* warned of the destruction of the world by **atomic** bombs in the wrong hands. The Japanese movie *Godzilla* featured a dinosaur-like creature created by the effects of radiation, a way for Japan to deal with the horrors of the atomic bombs used against two of its cities during World War II. In the United States, **science fiction** was a way to respond to the threats of communism and nuclear war. *Invasion of the Body Snatchers* centered around strange pods that became clones of the citizens of a small town, taking away their individualism. *Invisible Invaders* used a similar theme, the destruction of the American way of life. The film reflected President **Dwight D. Eisenhower**'s **Atoms for Peace** speech when one of the characters stated that all nuclear powers must work together.

God and the Bible were other themes to confront communism. In *The Next Voice You Hear*, God's voice is heard around the world at the same time but in each country's respective language. God's message is not to fear believing in God. The movie was nominated for a Golden Globe for promoting international understanding. Biblical movies included *The Robe*, *Quo Vadis*, *Barabbas*, *The Silver Chalice*, and *The Ten Commandments*. The latter, an epic, had unusual special effects for the 1950s, including the parting of the Red Sea.

The **House Un-American Activities Committee (HUAC)** subpoenaed writers, directors, actors, and others in the industry to appear before the committee, often falsely accusing them of being communists. For some of those subpoenaed, it was the end of their careers, for they were **blacklisted**. Senator **Joseph McCarthy** held similar hearings as chair of the Senate Permanent Subcommittee on Investigations, focusing on communists in the government and elsewhere. Until McCarthy's power waned in 1954, many lived in fear of being called before these committees.

Musicals also were popular in the 1950s, although they lost their popularity by the end of the decade. *Singin' in the Rain* and *American in Paris* are considered two of the finest musicals ever made.

The censoring of movies began to change as the 1950s progressed. Postwar morals began to loosen and conformity was questioned. *The Moon Is Blue* (1952) included the words "seduce" and "virgin," which shocked many movie-goers. *Picnic* (1955) featured an erotic dance between the two stars of the film and was considered daring in the 1950s. *A Summer Place* (1959) dealt with adultery, divorce, and teenage sex. *The Man with the Golden Arm* (1955) showed a drug addict going "cold turkey."

As the 1950s progressed, **teenagers** became a larger audience in movie theaters as many older Americans opted to stay home and watch **television**. Hollywood began to produce more teen-oriented films. **Pat Boone** and **Elvis Presley**, both popular singers, became male leads. Films with and about teenagers became common, often discussing the problems they faced. *Rebel Without a Cause*, *Blackboard Jungle*, and *High School Confidential* dealt with juvenile delinquency, drugs at school, and parent–teenager confrontations. Some films revolved around **rock and roll**, with popular singers in the cast. *The Girl Can't Help It* starred blonde bombshell Jayne Mansfield and some of the 1950s top singers, including the Platters, Fats Domino, Little Richard, and Eddie Cochran. *Rock Around the Clock* and *April Love* were two very popular teen movies.

Some of the movie stars of the 1940s found television a more lucrative medium than films. **Lucille Ball**, **Bob Hope**, **Jack Benny**, and **Red Skelton** were a few of the cinema stars who gained popularity on television.

Cinemascope and Todd-A-O were new film techniques using more than one camera, which allowed for wider screens in theaters. With another technique, 3-D, movie-goers wore glasses with special lenses, one red and one blue, which caused objects to appear three-dimensional, and sometimes to jump off the screen.

In 1960, *Psycho*, directed by Alfred Hitchcock, featured graphic violence not seen before on screen. Westerns were still popular in the 1950s. Some of the most memorable were *High Noon*, *The Searchers*, *She Wore a Yellow Ribbon*, *Rio Bravo*, *The Gunfighter*, and *Shane*. Some of the most bankable movie stars were **Marilyn Monroe**, **Elvis Presley**, **John Wayne**, Gary Cooper, Humphrey Bogart, **Jimmy Stewart**, **Doris Day**, **Marlon Brando**, and **James Dean**.

Hollywood had always been a draw for tourists. In 1958, city leaders asked artist Oliver Weismuller to revitalize the city. He came up with the idea of the Walk of Fame as a way to immortalize the stars of stage, screen, and television. Stars have their names cemented into the walk along with a symbol relating to their roles in entertainment: a microphone for radio personalities, a motion picture camera denoting films, a phonograph record for the recording industry, a television set for TV personalities, and the masks of comedy and drama for theater. One of the city's major tourist attractions, the Walk of Fame now has more than 2,300 stars. *See also* AGEE, JAMES; ANDERSON, MAXWELL; ARMSTRONG, LOUIS; ASIMOV, ISAAC; BELAFONTE, HARRY; BERLIN, IRVING; BERRY, CHUCK; BERNSTEIN, LEONARD; CAPOTE, TRUMAN; CROSBY, BING; DISNEY, WALT; DRURY, ALLEN; FAULKNER, WILLIAM; FORD, JOHN; FORESTER, C. S.; GLEASON, JACKIE; HANSBERRY, LORRAINE; HELLMAN, LILLIAN; HEMINGWAY, ERNEST; HITCHCOCK, ALFRED;

HORNE, LENA; INGE, WILLIAM; JONES, JAMES; KAYE, DANNY; KAZAN, ELIA; KELLY, GRACE; LUCE, CLARE BOOTH; MARTIN, DEAN, AND JERRY LEWIS; MARTIN, MARY; MERMAN, ETHEL; METALIOUS, GRACE; MILLER, ARTHUR; MOTOWN RECORDS; PARKER, DOROTHY; PARKS, GORDON; POITIER, SIDNEY; *RAISIN IN THE SUN, A*; RAND, AYN; ROBBINS, HAROLD; ROBBINS, JEROME; ROBESON, PAUL; RODGERS AND HAMMERSTEIN; SALINGER, J. D.; WARREN, ROBERT PENN; WILLIAMS, ESTHER; WILLIAMS, TENNESSEE; WOUK, HERMAN.

CIVIL RIGHTS ACT OF 1957. The **Supreme Court**'s ruling in *Brown v. Board of Education* (1954) added impetus to the **civil rights movement** during the 1950s. Civil rights groups pressured President **Dwight D. Eisenhower** to protect the voting rights of **African Americans**. Eisenhower, who knew the **1956 election** could be affected if he did not submit some form of legislation to Congress by the end of 1956, sent a watered-down civil rights bill to Congress. Eisenhower blamed the **Democrats** for their failure to pass the legislation, while Democrats accused the president of sending it to Congress when passage was impossible. After Eisenhower's reelection in 1956, he sent the Civil Rights Act of 1957 to Capitol Hill. It was still a watered-down bill. No penalties awaited anyone who attempted to keep others from voting. In the Senate, Majority Leader **Lyndon B. Johnson** was caught between trying to appease his fellow southerners as well as African American voters, since he hoped to run for president in 1960. The Civil Rights Act of 1957 passed, but with little hope of helping African Americans to register and vote. *See also* AMERICAN CIVIL LIBERTIES UNION (ACLU); *BROWDER V. GAYLE*; BUNCHE, RALPH; CIVIL RIGHTS ACT OF 1960; DU BOIS, W. E. B.; FAUBUS, ORVAL; HUGHES, LANGSTON; KING, CORETTA SCOTT; KING, MARTIN LUTHER, JR.; MARSHALL, THURGOOD; MONTGOMERY BUS BOYCOTT; NATIONAL ASSOCIATION FOR THE ADVANCEMENT OF COLORED PEOPLE (NAACP); PARKS, ROSA; POITIER, SIDNEY; POWELL, ADAM CLAYTON, JR.; RACIAL INTEGRATION; RANDOLPH, A. PHILIP; SOUTHERN CHRISTIAN LEADERSHIP CONFERENCE (SCLC).

CIVIL RIGHTS ACT OF 1960. This measure was an outgrowth of the **Civil Rights Act of 1957**. When violence broke out in the South after the passage of the 1957 legislation, which provided few penalties for those keeping **African Americans** from registering to vote, President **Dwight D. Eisenhower** knew more had be done. The Civil Rights Act of 1960 added provisions for the federal government to investigate any case in which African Americans were not allowed to vote. The main concern for both **Republicans** and **Democrats** was the African American vote in the **1960 election**. Many feared the wording of the act would do little to strengthen the Civil Rights Act of 1957; however, others were relieved to know an existing problem was finally coming to the public's attention. The Civil Rights Acts of 1957 and 1960 paved the way for more important voting rights acts that were passed in the 1960s. *See also* AMERICAN CIVIL LIBERTIES UNION (ACLU); BELAFONTE, HARRY; *BROWDER V. GAYLE*; BUNCHE, RALPH; DU BOIS, W. E. B.; FAUBUS, ORVAL; HUGHES, LANGSTON; KING, CORETTA SCOTT; KING, MARTIN LUTHER, JR.; MARSHALL, THURGOOD; MONTGOMERY BUS BOYCOTT; NATIONAL ASSOCIATION FOR THE ADVANCEMENT OF COLORED PEOPLE (NAACP); PARKS, ROSA; POITIER, SIDNEY; POWELL, ADAM CLAYTON, JR.; RACIAL INTEGRATION; RANDOLPH, A. PHILIP; SIT-IN; SOUTHERN CHRISTIAN LEADERSHIP CONFERENCE (SCLC); SUPREME COURT.

CIVIL RIGHTS MOVEMENT. After World War II, **African American** members of the armed forces wanted equal rights, including the end of segregation in the South. President **Harry S. Truman** had ordered complete integration of the military in 1948, but Congress would not extend this policy to the civilian population. When **Dwight D. Eisenhower** became president, he realized many southern members of Congress would resist integration. However, the events of the 1950s forced his hand. In May 1954, the **Supreme Court**'s decision in *Brown v. Board of Education* was the first major step to integrate public schools. This was followed by the **Montgomery Bus Boycott** in 1955, when **Rosa Parks** refused to give up her seat on a bus and was arrested. **Martin Luther King Jr.** led a boycott of the Montgomery, Alabama, bus system, since the majority of riders were African American. For 381 days, African Americans avoided riding the buses, thereby greatly affecting Montgomery's economy. The boycott resulted in the integration of the city bus system. In 1956, the U.S. Supreme Court ruled that all public transportation had to be integrated. Martin Luther King Jr. became the most important civil rights leader.

In 1957, the integration of Little Rock's Central High School was met with opposition when Arkansas Governor **Orval Faubus** stood in the doorway of the school and refused to allow the African American students to enter the building. President Eisenhower responded by sending troops to Little Rock to escort the students into the building.

During Eisenhower's administration, two civil rights acts were passed, one in 1957 and the other in 1960. The **Civil Rights Act of 1957** guaranteed voting rights for African Americans. Referees, appointed by federal district judges, oversaw voting and made sure no one was to be restrained from voting. No penalties were included in the legislation, however, for those preventing African Americans from voting. The **Civil Rights Act of 1960** did include penalties for anyone who kept African Americans from voting. *See also* AMERICAN CIVIL LIBERTIES UNION (ACLU); BELAFONTE, HARRY; *BROWDER V. GAYLE*; BUNCHE, RALPH; DU BOIS, W. E. B.; HUGHES, LANGSTON; KING, CORETTA SCOTT; MARSHALL, THURGOOD; NATIONAL ASSOCIATION FOR THE ADVANCEMENT OF COLORED PEOPLE (NAACP); POITIER, SIDNEY; POWELL, ADAM CLAYTON, JR.; RACIAL INTEGRATION; RANDOLPH, A. PHILIP; SIT-IN; SOUTHERN CHRISTIAN LEADERSHIP CONFERENCE (SCLC).

CLARK, TOM C. (1899–1977). Associate justice of the **Supreme Court** 1949–67. Tom Campbell Clark was born in Texas and graduated from the University of Texas Law School in 1922. In 1937, he joined the Justice Department and served as one of the coordinators who moved Japanese Americans into internment camps during World War II. In 1945, President **Harry S. Truman** named Clark attorney general. Four years later, Truman appointed Clark to the Supreme Court. A conservative justice, Clark believed strongly in individual rights. In *Mapp v. Ohio*, a landmark case in 1961, Clark wrote the majority opinion. It upheld the Fourth Amendment after Mapp's home had been forcibly entered into by Cleveland police without a warrant. When in 1967 President **Lyndon B. Johnson** named Clark's son, Ramsey Clark, attorney general, Clark resigned from the Court in order to avoid a conflict of interest. *See also* *BROWDER V. GAYLE*; *BROWN V. BOARD OF EDUCATION*; RACIAL INTEGRATION.

CLIBURN, VAN (1934–). In 1958, at the height of the **Cold War**, Harvey Lavan (Van) Cliburn Jr. won the First International Tchaikovsky Piano Competition in Moscow. The judges had to ask Premier **Nikita Khrushchev**'s permission to award the prize to the young American. Upon his return to the United States, Van Cliburn was honored with a ticker-tape parade in New York City. Born in Louisiana and raised in Texas, Cliburn began playing the piano at age three. The Van Cliburn International Piano Competition began in Fort Worth, Texas, in 1962, and Cliburn is still an advisor. In 2003, he was awarded the Medal of Freedom. *See also* MUSIC.

CLOTHING AND FASHION. In the 1950s, women wore hats and gloves when they dressed up. Men wore hats. However, changes began to take place. **James Dean** inspired many of the fashion trends for **teenage** boys, such as blue jeans, collars turned up, **T-shirts**, and hair combed into ducktails. They also wore long sideburns. Brylcreem, a hair product for men, gave hair a shine and kept it in place. Socks and dress shirts were white.

Teenage girls wore ponytails, skirts with a felt poodle on them, lots of petticoats under their skirts, and slipover sweaters. Button-down sweaters were often draped over the shoulders, and sometimes a chain attached to each side of the sweater kept it in place. Pedal pushers and short shorts were also in style. A scarf and a poodle pin were common accessories when wearing a sweater. Pierced ears were not acceptable for "good girls," so clip-on earrings were the style. Ankle bracelets and charm bracelets were also very popular. Charms could be added in celebration of various occasions or events. If one wore glasses, the frames were decorated with sparkles.

Prom time meant tuxedos and strapless dresses. Some dresses had very thin straps known as spaghetti straps. Halter tops, which tied at the back of the neck, were also popular. Some skirts were very straight, with a slit at the hem for easier walking. Shoes for teenage girls were normally flats or saddle shoes. Dressing up meant wearing 3-inch heels. Stockings had a seam at the back that had to be straight, not crooked. Penny loafers, worn with an actual penny in the front of the loafer, and saddle shoes were popular for men and boys.

Women's swimsuits were changing with the growing popularity of the two-piece swimsuit and the introduction of the first bikinis; however, the navel was never shown. Accessories to swimwear became important, with hats, sunglasses, beach bags, and footwear to coordinate with one's swimsuit. *See also* FADS; HAIRSTYLES.

COCA, IMOGENE. *See* CAESAR, SID, AND IMOGENE COCA.

COHN, ROY (1927–1986). Controversial lawyer Roy Marcus Cohn was born in New York, graduating from Columbia University Law School at the age of 20 (1947). Working in the U.S. attorney's Manhattan office, he won several important cases against alleged communists. Two of his most notable cases were the trial of Alger Hiss in 1949 and the 1951 trial of **Ethel and Julius Rosenberg** for espionage. His zeal against communists was noticed by **Federal Bureau of Investigation (FBI)** director **J. Edgar Hoover**. Hoover suggested to Senator **Joseph McCarthy** that he employ the young attorney. Cohn and McCarthy worked closely as a team during the hearings conducted by the Senate Permanent Subcommittee on Investigations, which McCarthy chaired. Cohn was its chief counsel.

In 1952, **G. David Schine** published the pamphlet *Definition of Communism*. Schine's family, which owned many hotels, put his pamphlet in each of its hotel rooms. This anticommunist publication brought Schine to Cohn's attention. In 1953, soon after joining Cohn and McCarthy, Schine was drafted into the military. Cohn attempted to get special privileges for the draftee, which became a major point in the 1954 **Army-McCarthy Hearings**. Cohn resigned from McCarthy's staff after the hearings and continued his career as an attorney in New York.

After he left McCarthy's staff, Cohn's life began to spiral out of control. In 1959, he was one of a group of investors who gained control of Lionel Trains. Serving as the company's chief executive, he almost bankrupted it by 1963 and resigned. During federal investigations in the 1970s and 1980s, Cohn was charged on three occasions with witness tampering and perjury. In 1986, he was disbarred by the New York Supreme Court. *See also* BELAFONTE, HARRY; CINEMA; COLD WAR; HELLMAN, LILLIAN; HORNE, LENA; HOUSE UN-AMERICAN ACTIVITIES COMMITTEE (HUAC); KAZAN, ELIA; MILLER, ARTHUR; PARKER, DOROTHY; RED SCARE; ROBESON, PAUL; SEEGER, PETE; THEATER; WEAVERS, THE.

COLD WAR. By 1947, the United States and the **Soviet Union** had entered the era known as the Cold War. This meant such intense international rivalry between the two nations that it could even lead to military conflict. Each superpower sought to align other nations on its side. After the Soviet Union tested its first nuclear bomb in 1949, the rivalry between the two nations escalated. President **Dwight D. Eisenhower**'s administration instituted various ways to combat the fear of nuclear attack, including Conelrad, an emergency broadcast system to alert the country of impending danger. In schools, children learned to "duck and cover," which meant children ducked under their desks and covered their heads with their arms. Supposedly this would protect them from nuclear fallout. The U.S. military developed the Titan rocket, Polaris missile, and **intercontinental ballistic missiles (ICBMs)** to combat the communist threat. Some families built fallout shelters and stocked them with foods with a long shelf life, in case of a nuclear attack.

One result of the Cold War was the **Red Scare**, the fear of communist subversion within the United States. Taking advantage of this fear, Senator **Joseph McCarthy** chaired the Senate Permanent Subcommittee on Investigations, which proceeded to accuse many Americans, often without proof, of being communists. In the U.S. House of Representatives, the **House Un-American Activities Committee (HUAC)** held hearings to root out communists in the entertainment industry, placing many people on a **blacklist** that destroyed their careers. *See also* ATOMIC AND NUCLEAR WEAPONS; ATOMS FOR PEACE; BAY OF PIGS; BRINKSMANSHIP; CASTRO, FIDEL; CENTRAL INTELLIGENCE AGENCY (CIA); COHN, ROY; CONGO CRISIS; CONTAINMENT; CUBA, RELATIONS WITH; DIEN BIEN PHU, BATTLE OF; DOMINO THEORY; DULLES, ALLEN; DULLES, JOHN FOSTER;

KENNAN, GEORGE F.; KENNEDY, JOHN F.; KHRUSHCHEV, NIKITA; KOREAN WAR; MASSIVE RETALIATION; MIDDLE EAST TREATY ORGANIZATION; MURROW, EDWARD R.; NORTH ATLANTIC TREATY ORGANIZATION (NATO); POWERS, FRANCIS GARY; ROSENBERG, ETHEL AND JULIUS; SCIENCE FICTION; SOUTHEAST ASIA TREATY ORGANIZATION (SEATO); STALIN, JOSEPH; TRUMAN, HARRY S.; U-2 INCIDENT; VIETNAM WAR.

COLTRANE, JOHN (1926–1967). **Jazz** great John William Coltrane was born in North Carolina. When he was 13, he began to play the clarinet but switched to the saxophone in high school. After graduating from high school in 1943, he moved to Philadelphia, Pennsylvania. Until he was drafted into the navy in 1945, he studied the saxophone at the Ornstein School of Music. Stationed in Hawaii for two years, Coltrane played in a navy band.

After his service, Coltrane returned to the United States and began to play with various jazz bands, including Dizzy Gillespie's. In 1955, when he teamed with Miles Davis, his reputation as a saxophonist gained worldwide appeal. His musical improvisations and free style delighted audiences.

In 1960, Coltrane formed his own quartet. The interaction of Coltrane with pianist McCoy Tyner, drummer Elvin Jones, and Jimmy Garrison on bass produced intense and complicated jazz sounds. Coltrane became famous for playing saxophone solos, ranging from 20 to 45 minutes, that other musicians found difficult to duplicate. His 1963 recording "A Love Supreme" is still considered his best and the most important of his numerous recordings.

From 1955 until his death in 1967, Coltrane's **music** was constantly changing and evolving. For the last 12 years of his life, he performed almost daily, and often into the early hours of the morning. Coltrane played several instruments, including the tenor and soprano saxophones and the clarinet. Jazz critics consider Coltrane one of the most influential jazz performers of the 1950s.

COMIC BOOKS. In 1938, Action Comics began publishing Superman comic books. This inspired the creation of other comic book superheroes, including Wonder Woman, Batman, Green Lantern, and

Captain America. Some historians consider 1939–54 the "Golden Age of Comic Books," when comic books were extremely popular. During World War II, soldiers enjoyed reading comic books as a relief from stress. After the war, they continued to enjoy many of the same titles.

In 1952, social critics became concerned when EC Comics published *Tales from the Crypt* and *Adventures in Terror*, which told stories of cannibalism, torture, and gore with terrifying drawings. One of the leading social critics was Frederic Wertham, author of the highly influential and controversial book *Seduction of the Innocent* (1954). The early 1950s were the time of **McCarthyism**, the **Cold War**, a rise in juvenile delinquency, and a breakdown in morals. Senator **Estes Kefauver** was investigating organized crime. Wertham's book theorized that EC Comics promoted ideas that led to a rise in juvenile crimes. He added that some of the main characters in the comics were corrupting the morals of young readers. He argued that Robin, Batman's friend, was a homosexual, and that the behavior of Wonder Woman was in direct opposition to the accepted behavior for girls.

The social criticisms of comic books led to a Senate investigation into the relationship between comic books and juvenile crimes. The investigation resulted in the creation of the Comic Magazine Association of America (CMAA), which established the Comics Code Authority (CCA). In 1955, the Senate approved the guidelines of the CCA. Although the committee never completely accepted Wertham's theories, comic books were published with a prominent emblem on the cover signifying they met the code of the CMAA.

The Senate investigation did affect the comic book industry. Many titles were eliminated, including all of the titles of EC Comics except *Mad*. *Mad* responded to the demise of the many comic book titles and the unfounded fears of the decade by using satire and cartoons. *Mad* continues to satirize world events and is published in numerous countries besides the United States. *See also* MAGAZINES.

COMMUNIST CONTROL ACT, 1954. Under the Communist Control Act of 1954, which was signed into law by President **Dwight D. Eisenhower**, the Communist Party was outlawed in the United States. Support of or membership in the Communist Party was a federal offense. The act amended the 1950 Subversive Activities

Control Act, which prohibited communists from holding an office in any labor organization. *See also* BLACKLIST; COHN, ROY; HOUSE UN-AMERICAN ACTIVITIES COMMITTEE (HUAC); MCCARTHY, JOSEPH; RED SCARE.

COMPUTERS. As early as the 1930s, scientists were trying to invent a way to store information; however, no company did more to advance the research for and building of computers than International Business Machines (IBM). In 1951, the first commercial computer (UNIVAC) was manufactured. It had the ability to predict the winner in the 1952 presidential race. In 1954, IBM created FORTRAN, the first programmable computer language. Gene Myron Amdahl created the first computer operating system in 1954, and IBM developed the first hard disk drive in 1956. That same year, silicon became the standard material in the production of semiconductors. Using silicon, the integrated circuit was created in 1958 by **Jack Kilby**, and the computer revolution began. In 1959, Bank of America was the first bank to use a computer to read checks. John Diebold, a pioneer in computers, stressed the use of computers in automation and technology. *See also* TECHNOLOGICAL INNOVATIONS.

CONANT, JAMES B. (1893–1978). An educator and president of Harvard, James Bryant Conant was born in Massachusetts and received his B.A. in 1913 and Ph.D. in 1916 from Harvard University. He then taught at Harvard, rising to become the university's president in 1933. During World War II, he served as chair of the National Defense Research Committee, which was involved in the creation of the **atomic** bomb. After the war, Conant held posts in both the National Science Foundation and the **Atomic Energy Commission**. Under President **Dwight D. Eisenhower**, he served for two years as ambassador to West **Germany**. Conant published several books on **education**, including *Education in a Divided World*, *Modern Science and Modern Man*, and *Slums and Suburbs*. In 1970, he published his autobiography, *My Several Lives*.

CONGO CRISIS. On 30 June 1960, Belgium granted independence to the Congo with the stipulation that within six months it had to show that it could govern itself. Patrice Lumumba was elected prime minister of the Democratic Republic of the Congo and Joseph Kasavubu its president. Almost immediately, however, violence erupted and there was friction between Lumumba and Kasavubu.

On 10 July 1960, Belgium, fearing for the safety of Belgian nationals living in the Congo, sent heavily armed troops to quell the violence. One area of the Congo, Katanga, was rich in copper. Moise Kapenda Tshombe, supported by Belgian business interests, declared the region independent of the rest of the Congo and made himself president. Civil war broke out between those loyal to Tshombe and Lumumba's followers. The war was denounced by other countries worldwide. On 12 July 1960, the **United Nations (UN)** Security Council met to discuss the crisis in the Congo. A resolution was passed in which UN troops replaced troops from Belgium. On 15 July 1960, the first UN troops arrived.

Lumumba decided to invade Katanga with his own troops and asked the United States for help, but President **Dwight D. Eisenhower** refused. Lumumba turned to the **Soviet Union**, but its aid was too little too late. Lumumba was caught by the forces of Joseph Mobutu, a rival for power. He was executed in January 1961 by Mobutu, who was supported by the United States.

The secretary-general of the UN, **Dag Hammarskjold**, traveled to the Congo four times while UN troops were in the country. On his fourth trip in September 1961, he died in a plane crash. The Soviet Union was angered by Hammarskjold's leadership during the Congo crisis. In 1964, the UN troops left the Congo. Their presence helped Katanga remain a province in the Congo. In 1965, Mobutu, who had eliminated both Tshombe and Kasavubu, established dictatorial rule over the Congo. *See also* FOREIGN POLICY.

CONGRESS OF INDUSTRIAL ORGANIZATIONS (CIO). *See* AMERICAN FEDERATION OF LABOR AND CONGRESS OF INDUSTRIAL ORGANIZATIONS (AFL-CIO).

CONTAINMENT. The diplomatic strategy of containment was created by **George F. Kennan** after World War II. Kennan had studied the **Soviet Union** for years prior to the outbreak of World War II, and his knowledge was invaluable after the war. Kennan believed the Soviet Union had to be contained or it would expand its influence throughout the world. The theory of containment was behind the formation of two major alliances whose purpose was to limit Soviet expansion: the **North Atlantic Treaty Organization (NATO)** and the **Southeast Asia Treaty Organization (SEATO)**. During his presidency, **Dwight D. Eisenhower** adopted a form of containment known as **massive retaliation**, using the threat of nuclear weapons to deter communist expansion. *See also* BRINKSMANSHIP; COLD WAR; FOREIGN POLICY.

COPLAND, AARON (1900–1990). While a teenager, Aaron Copland decided he wanted to compose **music**. He played the piano, which he had learned from his older sister. When he was 21, he enrolled at a music school for American students in Paris. After three years, he returned to the United States and played his first composition in Carnegie Hall. At a time when American composers were not highly regarded in the world of classical music, Copland changed the landscape of music. He composed ballets and was commissioned to write for films as well as for orchestras. During World War II, the Cincinnati Symphony commissioned Copland to compose patriotic music. One of the most famous Copland compositions was *Fanfare for the Common Man*. Some of Copland's other most recognizable pieces are *Appalachian Spring*, *Billy the Kid*, and *Rodeo*. Copeland turned to lecturing rather than composing in his later years. He died at the age of 90.

COUNCIL OF ECONOMIC ADVISORS (CEA). The Council of Economic Advisors was formed during the presidency of **Harry S. Truman**. The members of the council are economists who advise the president on economic policies. During the presidency of **Dwight D. Eisenhower**, **Arthur F. Burns** served as its chair.

In 1946, Congress was concerned the United States might return to the depressed **economy** prior to World War II; thus, legislation was passed to provide the president with a three-member council of economic advisors to help stimulate the economy. The first three members of the council had equal authority; however, they had major policy disagreements. One member resigned. After Eisenhower was elected, he believed the council was important but needed restructuring. He changed its makeup to include four members, with one of the four as chair who controlled the CEA. *See also* BANKING.

COUNTRY MUSIC. Country **music**, also referred to as country western music, was first popular in the South. The *Grand Ole Opry*, a country music program, has been broadcast from Nashville, Tennessee, since 1925, making it the longest-running radio program in U.S. history. During the 1950s, country music began to make its presence felt on popular radio stations. Some of the most important country singers of the 1950s were Hank Williams Sr., Johnny Cash, Patsy Cline, Eddy Arnold, and Loretta Lynn. **Elvis Presley** sang his first songs on the *Grand Ole Opry*. Hank Williams Sr. is widely acknowledged as one of the most important singer/songwriters of the 20th century. His honky-tonk style of singing has been emulated by many others in country music. Between 1945 and 1983, Eddy Arnold had 145 songs on the charts; 28 became number one songs. He had more hits on the charts than any other singer. One of his most famous songs was "Make the World Go Away." Johnny Cash's "I Walk the Line" was a top hit on both popular and country music stations, as was Patsy Cline's "I Fall to Pieces." In 1957, *Billboard Magazine* combined its charts of top-selling records into one chart covering both country and popular music. In 1961, the Country Music Hall of Fame was created by the Country Music Association.

CREDIT CARD. Although department stores and some hotel and gasoline companies issued a type of credit card as early as the 1920s, the first universal credit card was issued in 1950 by the Diner's Club. In 1958, American Express issued its card, and in 1959 Bank of America's BankAmericard was introduced. Consumers received a monthly statement that they could pay in full or in monthly installments. Businesses pay credit card companies a fee in order to use their services. *See also* BANKING; ECONOMY; TECHNOLOGICAL INNOVATIONS.

CROSBY, BING (1903–1977). At the end of World War II, U.S. soldiers were asked in a poll who had been the most popular person during the war. The poll found that Bing Crosby was more important to their morale than even General **Dwight D. Eisenhower**. Crosby was an easygoing crooner whose record sales topped both **Elvis Presley** and the Beatles the year he died. The majority of popular singers who followed him credited Crosby with influencing their careers and singing style. Throughout his career, Crosby was a top box office draw, often appearing in movies with **Bob Hope**.

Born in Tacoma, Washington, Harry Lillis Crosby attended Gonzaga University, where he studied law, but he enjoyed entertaining people by singing and playing the drums. Accordingly, he left Washington in 1925 and headed for Los Angeles. His brother, Everett, sent one of his records, "I Surrender, Dear," to the president of the Continental Broadcasting Company. Its success on the radio led to a contract with Paramount Pictures. His first feature film was *King of Jazz* (1930). In *Holiday Inn* (1942), he introduced **Irving Berlin**'s classic "White Christmas," which sold more singles than any other record from the mid-1940s until the mid-1990s. In 1944, he received an Academy Award for his portrayal of a priest in *Going My Way* and won again the following year for starring in the same role in *The Bells of St. Mary's*.

Crosby provided funding for an electronics laboratory to develop both audio and video tape recorders, which he used to tape his own radio and later **television** broadcasts. A star entertainer for five decades (1930s–70s), he was also part owner of the Pittsburgh Pirates baseball team. At the time of his death, he had sold more records than any other recording artist. *See also* CINEMA; MUSIC; SPORTS; TECHNOLOGICAL INNOVATIONS.

CUBA, RELATIONS WITH. Prior to **Fidel Castro**'s revolution in 1959, the United States and Cuba had enjoyed close relations. In 1902, Cuba was given its independence by the United States, which had gained control of the island after the end of the Spanish-American War. Much of the island's sugar and tobacco plantations belonged to Americans. Americans also controlled its gambling and tourist industries. American business and political leaders worked closely with Cuba's leader in the 1950s, Fulgencio Batista. After Castro took control of Cuba, however, his government seized control of all American enterprises. President **Dwight D. Eisenhower** was angered by Castro's actions and knew Cuba had established ties with the **Soviet Union**. When the United States broke diplomatic relations with Cuba in 1961, the Soviet Union stepped in to help Cuba economically and militarily. When Soviet missiles were moved into Cuba in 1962, the worst crisis of the **Cold War** developed. For nearly two weeks the world remained on the brink of a nuclear war. Fortunately, President **John F. Kennedy**'s negotiations with Soviet leader **Nikita Khrushchev** ended the crisis. *See also* BAY OF PIGS; CENTRAL INTELLIGENCE AGENCY (CIA); CONTAINMENT; DULLES, ALLEN; DULLES, JOHN FOSTER; KENNAN, GEORGE F.; RED SCARE.

CUMMINGS, E. E. (1894–1962). Poet and novelist Edward Estlin Cummings was born in Massachusetts and attended Harvard University (B.A., 1915; M.A., 1916). After graduating from Harvard, he began to paint and write to support himself. During the 1920s, he traveled to Paris, where many other American artists, writers, and nonconformists were living. He wrote one novel, *The Enormous Room*, about his experiences in World War I. His books of poetry, all of which showcase an eccentric form of writing that avoids capital letters and uses odd punctuation, include *Tulips and Chimneys*, *Is 5*, *No Title*, and *No Thanks*. Cummings also wrote the play *Him*. *See also* LITERATURE.

CUTLER, ROBERT (1895–1974). National security advisor 1953–55 and 1957–58. Educated at Harvard University Law School, Robert Cutler was a bank executive before becoming the nation's first national security advisor during the presidency of **Dwight D. Eisenhower**. As the national security advisor, Cutler was a member of the National Security Council, a host to foreign officials, and a key member of Eisenhower's **foreign policy** committee.

CYPRUS, RELATIONS WITH. After World War II, **Great Britain** gave independence to the island of Cyprus. However, Cyprus was composed of Greek and Turk populations. As a result, both Greece and Turkey became involved in the governance of Cyprus, where tensions threatened a civil war. Also Great Britain wanted to continue its influence in Cyprus, which meant it had a strategically placed military base in the Middle East. President **Dwight D.**

Eisenhower became annoyed with British Prime Minister **Anthony Eden**, since he was encouraging Turkey to play a dominant role in Cyprus's future. Complicating matters even more was the popularity of the Greek Orthodox Archbishop Makarios III, whom the British colonial government had forced into exile because he wanted to unite Cyprus with Greece. In 1959, Makarios was allowed to return to Cyprus, where in elections for Cyprus's first president, he won in a landslide. He led the Cyprus government in 1959–77. *See also* FOREIGN POLICY.

– D –

DANCE. The 1950s produced popular and unique dance styles, such as the bunny hop and the stroll, in which dance partners did not touch each other. Jitterbugging, a holdover from the 1940s, was still popular, as was the lindy, a form of the jitterbug. The hand jive was done with the hands. In 1961, the twist, a dance in which one moved one's hips as if using a Hula Hoop, became the rage. The mashed potato, the shimmy, and the madison were other popular dances. Many of these dances were introduced to **teenagers** on *American Bandstand*, a very popular **television** program that began in the 1950s. *See also* MUSIC.

DAY, DORIS (1924–). Doris Day was one of the most popular and highest-paid singers in the 1950s. Born in Cincinnati, Doris Mary Anne Von Kapelhoff always wanted to be a dancer; however, her right leg was injured in an automobile accident, ending her dreams of dancing. Instead she turned to singing. By the age of 17, she was performing with Bob Crosby's band. During World War II, her rendition of "Sentimental Journey" was a hit with soldiers stationed overseas. In 1948, she was the leading lady in her first film, *Romance on the High Seas*. During the 1950s, she made some of her most popular movies, including *Calamity Jane*, *Love Me or Leave Me*, *Teacher's Pet*, and *Pillow Talk*. In the 1956 **Alfred Hitchcock** film *The Man Who Knew Too Much*, she sang the Academy Award–winning "Que Sera, Sera," which became one of her most popular songs. In the 1960s, she entered the world of **television** with her own program, *The*

Doris Day Show. In the 1970s, she became an outspoken advocate of animal rights. *See also* CINEMA.

DE FOREST, LEE (1873–1961). An inventor and expert in electronic **technology**, Lee de Forest was born in Iowa but raised in Alabama. His father hoped he would follow him into the ministry; however, de Forest was more interested in inventing new devices, particularly ones powered by electricity. At Yale University, his dissertation described what is now radio. Through his work, de Forest acquired more than 300 patents. He invented the amplifier, the radio telephone (radio receiver), and the vacuum tube. He created the first sounds on film, which led to talking movies. Although Warner Brothers used Vitaphone to produce its talking movies, the process would not have been possible without de Forest's earlier invention. Unfortunately, de Forest was a poor businessman, and his poor judgment and unscrupulous partners caused him many problems. He lost as much money on his inventions as he made as a result of fighting lawsuits involving his inventions. However, they earned Lee de Forest a star on the Hollywood Walk of Fame. *See also* CINEMA.

DE GAULLE, CHARLES (1890–1970). President of **France** 1958–69. Charles de Gaulle wanted to serve in the military even as a young man. He served in both world wars. In 1940, he warned that France was not safe from **Germany**'s leader, Adolf Hitler. When Hitler's panzers invaded France, de Gaulle fled to London and was a leader of the French resistance. During World War II, he insisted he was the acting chief of France and an equal Allied leader. In August 1944, de Gaulle returned to France as a hero. He became president of the postwar government and helped write a new constitution. His opinion that a powerful presidency was necessary was ignored and he resigned. In 1953, he attempted to create a new political party, which failed. De Gaulle retired from public life.

In 1958, France incurred two major problems: instability within the country and a crisis in French-held Algeria. De Gaulle was again asked to lead the country. As prime minister, he proposed a change in the parliamentary form of government to strengthen the presidency. With the acceptance of his proposal, de Gaulle became France's president in 1958. He sought to strengthen France both militarily and financially. He also showed his leadership by creating ties with the Eastern bloc in the **Cold War** and by extending the hand of friendship to Communist China. In protest against the entrance of **Great Britain** into the Common Market, he withdrew France from the **North Atlantic Treaty Organization (NATO)** in 1958.

In 1962, de Gaulle granted Algeria its independence. His decision created anger within France and from French residents in Algeria. In May 1968, university students and workers demonstrated against the de Gaulle government. In 1969, strikes followed. Even with the internal problems, de Gaulle was reelected, and the strikes ended. However, in April 1969, he lost a referendum on government reforms. On 28 April 1969, he resigned as president. He died the following year. *See also* FOREIGN POLICY.

DEAN, JAMES (1931–1955). Born in Indiana, James Byron Dean moved to California after graduating from high school. He wanted to be an actor and was accepted to the prestigious Actors Studio in New York City. While studying in New York, he obtained small **television** roles. His character in most of his television appearances was similar to the one he would play in his movies, that of a misunderstood young man. In both *East of Eden* and *Rebel Without a Cause*, he had to contend with a father much like his real-life father. In *Giant*, which was released after his death, Dean played an older character but still one fighting against the rules. Following in the footsteps of actor **Marlon Brando**, Dean usually wore a **T-shirt**, setting a trend that **teenagers** and others have followed to the present day. He housed cigarettes in a rolled-up sleeve. When he wore a regular shirt, his collar was up. Often his sideburns were long and his hair was combed in the back into a ducktail. He was the picture of "cool" in the eyes of teenagers in the 1950s. James Dean was one with whom they could relate. He died tragically in an automobile accident at the age of 24 but remains a cultural icon. *See also* CINEMA; CLOTHING AND FASHION; FADS.

DEAR ABBY. *See* ANN LANDERS AND DEAR ABBY.

DEMOCRATIC PARTY. For two decades (1932–52), the Democrats won every presidential election, as Americans chose Franklin D.

Roosevelt for four terms, followed by **Harry S. Truman**. But Truman's **Korean War** policies led to a landslide for the **Republican Party** in the **1952 election**. A popular figure, **Dwight D. Eisenhower** was reelected by an even bigger margin in the **1956 election**. In 1952, the Democrats were in the minority in Congress; however, factions within the Republican majority led to the Democrats regaining control of both houses in the 1954 election. With Eisenhower's ability to work well with Congress, many legislative landmark issues were achieved, including **civil rights** legislation, building the **Interstate Highway System**, and building the **St. Lawrence Seaway**. *See also* JOHNSON, LYNDON B.; KENNEDY, JOHN F.; ROOSEVELT, ELEANOR; STEVENSON, ADLAI E.

DEPARTMENT OF HEALTH, EDUCATION, AND WELFARE (HEW). When **Dwight D. Eisenhower** became president in 1953, the Federal Security Administration (FSA) was responsible for health, **education**, and **social security**, but the FSA was not a cabinet-level department. Eisenhower realized these three areas deserved higher federal priority, and he wanted them combined into a new cabinet position. He noted that as far back as President Warren G. Harding's administration, discussions were held about combining the health, education, and welfare systems. But it was not until 1939 that they were combined into the Federal Security Agency. Eisenhower stressed the need for funding for research in cancer and heart disease. The federal government was putting demands on public schools that were burdensome for educators. Citizens who were blind, handicapped, or unable to care for themselves needed financial help from the government. The creation of the Department of Health, Education, and Welfare in 1953 elevated the importance of these public issues. *See also* FLEMMING, ARTHUR; FOLSOM, MARION BAYARD; HOBBY, OVETA CULP.

DIEN BIEN PHU, BATTLE OF. After World War II, **Vietnam** entered a period of war as nationalists joined with the communists to establish independence from **France**. By 1953, the forces of **Ho Chi Minh**, the leader of the communists, had the French on the defensive. With financial aid from the United States, the French fortified the town of Dien Bien Phu and built an airfield. When the Viet Minh surrounded the airfield, supplies were cut off to the French, while Soviet trucks carrying arms from **China** guaranteed ample supplies for the Viet Minh. After a two-month battle, Dien Bien Phu fell. In 1954, the war ended with the **Geneva Accords** and the division of Vietnam into two parts, the north to be governed by the communists and the south to remain under French control. *See also* FOREIGN POLICY; VIETNAM WAR.

DILLON, DOUGLAS (1909–2003). Born in Switzerland, Clarence Douglas Dillon was educated at Harvard University. His graduation gift in 1931 was $185,000 from his father, who headed a Wall Street firm, to purchase a seat on the New York Stock Exchange. By 1938, he was vice president of his father's firm, Dillon, Read and Company. After serving in World War II, Dillon returned to the firm as chair. A staunch **Republican**, he was one of the major contributors to **Dwight D. Eisenhower**'s presidential campaign. The newly elected Eisenhower appointed Dillon ambassador to **France**, a position he held until 1959, when he was named undersecretary of state for economic affairs. In 1961, President **John F. Kennedy** appointed Dillon secretary of the treasury. In 1965, Dillon left politics to use his time and wealth for various causes, including support for the New York Metropolitan Museum and the Republican Party. *See also* ECONOMY; FOREIGN AFFAIRS.

DIRKSEN, EVERETT (1896–1969). U.S. senator 1951–69; Senate minority leader 1959–69. Born in Illinois to German immigrants, Everett McKinley Dirksen grew up on a farm near Peoria. After his election to the Senate in 1950, Dirksen supported legislation for **civil rights**, equal rights for women, the nuclear test ban treaty, and the **St. Lawrence Seaway**. A close friend of Senators **Robert A. Taft** and **Joseph McCarthy**, he did not want the Senate to censure McCarthy, although Dirksen realized his friend had crossed the line with his demagoguery against alleged communist sympathizers. Prior to the 1952 presidential election, he supported Thomas E. Dewey as the **Republican** candidate; however, he threw his support behind **Dwight D. Eisenhower** in both of Eisenhower's bids for the presidency. In 1959, Dirksen replaced **Bill Knowland** as Republican minority leader. He supported the **Vietnam War**. One of President

Eisenhower's strongest supporters, Dirksen was regarded by many as the voice of the Republican Party. *See also* ATOMIC AND NUCLEAR ENERGY; CIVIL RIGHTS ACT OF 1957; CIVIL RIGHTS ACT OF 1960; EDUCATION; FOREIGN POLICY; RACIAL INTEGRATION.

DISNEY, WALT (1901–1966). Animator and producer Walt Elias Disney began his career as a commercial artist. In the 1920s, he opened a small studio in Hollywood, where he created animated film cartoons. In 1928, he introduced Mickey Mouse in his first big screen cartoon. Walt Disney continued to create full-length cartoons that were extremely successful. Some of his most famous animated films were based on children's fairy tales, including *Cinderella*, *Sleeping Beauty*, *Bambi*, and *Snow White and the Seven Dwarfs*. In 1955, Disney opened the Disneyland theme park in Anaheim, California. With the advent of **television**, Disney began to produce television programs aimed at children, including *Davy Crockett*, *Mickey Mouse Club*, and *Disneyland*. Two years before his death, Disney purchased land in Orlando, Florida, where he planned to open another theme park that would be larger than Disneyland. After his death, his brother Roy continued to head the Disney empire and celebrated the opening of the theme park in Florida: Walt Disney World Resort. *See also* CINEMA.

DIXON-YATES CONTRACT. President **Dwight D. Eisenhower** came under fire when he proposed a plan to allow private companies to sell electricity to government properties. In 1954, the Tennessee Valley Authority was in debt. Edgar Dixon and Eugene Yates, both private utility company presidents, submitted a plan to the Bureau of the Budget that would allow private utility companies to construct a $107 million steam plant in Memphis, Tennessee. It was later found that one of the officials was also an executive with the First Boston Corporation, which would financially back the contract. Eisenhower stated he had no knowledge of this conflict of interest, but he had to retract his statement when proof surfaced that he was aware of the problem. *See also* ECONOMY.

DOMINICAN REPUBLIC. *See* TRUJILLO, RAFAEL.

DOMINO THEORY. Although the term was first used by President **Harry S. Truman**, it was President **Dwight D. Eisenhower** who popularized the domino theory during the **Cold War**. The domino theory rested on the assumption that if one country fell to the communists, neighboring countries would fall like a row of dominoes. The administration used the domino theory to support U.S. intervention abroad. The decision to send U.S. troops to **Korea** and to **Vietnam** was based, in part, on the domino theory. *See also* CONTAINMENT; FOREIGN POLICY.

DOS PASSOS, JOHN (1896–1970). Author John Dos Passos was born into a wealthy family and educated at Harvard University (B.A., 1916). Able to travel the world, he went to Europe during World War I and drove an ambulance. Upon his return from the war, he wrote his first novel, *One Man's Intuition*. This was followed by *Three Soldiers*. Like his friend **Ernest Hemingway**, Dos Passos wrote novels reflecting his antiwar sentiments. During the Spanish Civil War, he and Hemingway went to Spain; however, Dos Passos became more conservative politically than Hemingway, and they parted ways. During the 1940s and 1950s, his trilogy *USA*, written in the 1930s, became a popular indictment of the myth of prosperity. In addition to writing 42 novels, Dos Passos was also a painter who created 400 pieces of **art**. *See also* LITERATURE.

DOUGLAS, PAUL H. (1892–1976). U.S. senator 1949–67. Born in Massachusetts, Paul Howard Douglas was educated at Bowdoin College (B.A., 1913) and Columbia University (M.A., 1915; Ph.D., 1921). Prior to his years in the Senate, he spent almost 30 years as a professor of economics at the University of Chicago (1920–49). His first political office was as a member of the city council of Chicago. After serving in World War II, he returned to Chicago and was elected to the U.S. Senate. A **Democrat** who was a staunch anticommunist and **civil rights** activist, he was often critical of President **Harry S. Truman**. Many political experts expected him to be the Democratic nominee in the 1952 presidential election. Douglas hoped, however, that **Dwight D. Eisenhower** would be the Democratic candidate. His hopes were dashed when Eisenhower declared himself a **Republican** and won the Republican nomination. *See also* CIVIL RIGHTS

MOVEMENT; CIVIL RIGHTS ACT OF 1957; CIVIL RIGHTS ACT OF 1960; EDUCATION; FOREIGN POLICY; RACIAL INTEGRATION; STEVENSON, ADLAI E.

DOUGLAS, WILLIAM O. (1898–1980). Associate justice of the **Supreme Court** 1939–75. Born in Minnesota and educated at Columbia University Law School (1925), William Orville Douglas worked for a prestigious New York law firm. He also taught at Columbia University. In 1934, Douglas became a law professor at Yale University, where he was an expert on commercial litigation and bankruptcy. For two years (1937–39), he was chair of the Securities and Exchange Commission. An enthusiastic supporter of the New Deal, he was appointed to the Supreme Court in 1939 by President Franklin D. Roosevelt. He was also a strong supporter of **civil rights**, freedom of speech, and freedom of the press. In the 1950s, Douglas often sided with Justice **Hugo Black** against Justice **Felix Frankfurter**. Douglas wrote several books, including his autobiography. *See also BROWDER V. GAYLE; BROWN V. BOARD OF EDUCATION;* CIVIL RIGHTS ACT OF 1957; CIVIL RIGHTS ACT OF 1960; RACIAL INTEGRATION.

DRURY, ALLEN (1918–1998). Author Allen Drury was born in Texas and graduated from Stanford University in 1939. In 1943, he was hired as a Senate correspondent for United Press International (UPI). In 1959, he published his first novel, *Advise and Consent,* which was based on a journal he kept of Senate proceedings. It not only won a Pulitzer Prize but was a successful Broadway play and a 1962 motion picture. Drury wrote other novels about politics, including *A Shade of Difference, Capable of Honor, Preserve and Protect, A Thing of State,* and *Public Men.* The **Cold War** and the **Soviet Union**'s attempt to undermine life in the United States were common themes in many of his novels. *See also* CINEMA; LITERATURE; THEATER.

DU BOIS, W. E. B. (1868–1963). Born in Great Barrington, Massachusetts, William Edward Burghardt Du Bois was the first **African American** to receive a Ph.D. from Harvard University (1895). He also co-founded the **National Association for the Advancement of**

Colored People (NAACP) in 1908 and was editor of their **magazine** *Crisis* (1910–34).

Du Bois supported the suffragist movement, believing women were in a struggle comparable to African Americans. In 1934, his views were opposite those of the conservative NAACP, which led to his breaking with the association. He expressed his views in several books, including *The Negro, Black Reconstruction, Color and Democracy*, and *The Dark Princess*. He was investigated as early as the 1940s by the **Federal Bureau of Investigation (FBI)** for his socialist writings. In 1961, he published his final book, *Worlds of Color*, joined the Communist Party, and left the United States to live out his life in Ghana. *See also* CIVIL RIGHTS MOVEMENT; HOOVER, J. EDGAR; LITERATURE.

DULLES, ALLEN (1893–1969). Director of the **Central Intelligence Agency (CIA)** 1953–61. The brother of **John Foster Dulles**, Allen Welsh Dulles was born in New York and educated at Princeton University (B.A., 1914; M.A., 1916). He worked in the diplomatic service, then earned a law degree from George Washington University (1926). The Dulles brothers worked together in their law firm.

During World War II, Dulles worked in the Office of Strategic Services (OSS), whose purpose was to gain information about the Nazis. In 1948, he was an advisor to **Republican** presidential candidate Thomas E. Dewey, who lost to **Harry S. Truman**. President **Dwight D. Eisenhower** named Dulles director of the CIA in 1953. During Dulles's tenure, the CIA was involved in various covert operations, including overthrowing the governments of Jacobo Arbenz Guzman in **Guatemala** and Mohammed Mossadegh in **Iran**. Dulles was blamed for the failed **Bay of Pigs** operation during the administration of President **John F. Kennedy**, and he resigned under pressure in 1961. *See also* COLD WAR; PAHLAVI, MOHAMMAD REZA.

DULLES, JOHN FOSTER (1888–1959). Secretary of state 1953–59. John Foster Dulles was born in Washington, D.C., and educated at Princeton University (B.A., 1908) and the Sorbonne in Paris. He joined Sullivan and Cromwell, the foremost New York law firm, after completing his law degree in 1911 at George Washington University. Unable to serve in World War I due to poor eyesight, he was appointed by President Woodrow Wilson as the legal counsel to the U.S. delegation to the Versailles Peace Conference. After the war, he was on the War Reparations Committee. A close friend of Thomas E. Dewey, the 1944 **Republican** presidential candidate, Dulles served as Dewey's **foreign policy** advisor. During the 1940s, he was appointed to serve out the last six months of Senator Robert F. Wagner's term after Wagner, a **Democrat**, resigned because of ill health. Dulles subsequently ran for the seat but was defeated. He continued, however, to serve as a delegate to the **United Nations** General Assembly.

A critic of President **Harry S. Truman**'s foreign policy, Dulles was appointed secretary of state by newly elected President **Dwight D. Eisenhower** in 1953. One of the first major decisions Dulles made was to overthrow **Mohammed Mossadegh**, the prime minister of **Iran**, who had nationalized Iran's oil fields. Through a covert operation carried out in 1953, Mossadegh was overthrown and the pro-Western shah of Iran was returned to power.

A staunch anticommunist, Dulles believed the United States must show strength through the threat of **massive retaliation** as a deterrence to communism. He was also the force behind the creation of the **Southeast Asia Treaty Organization (SEATO)**, an organization whose purpose was to thwart communist aggression in the region. In addition, he set up the **North Atlantic Treaty Organization (NATO)** to counter the **Soviet Union**'s expansionism in Europe. Dulles angered President **Gamal Abdel Nasser** of Egypt in 1956 when Nasser's control of the Suez Canal led to the U.S. decision not to send military arms to Egypt. As a result, Nasser turned to the Soviet Union for military assistance. Dulles resigned in 1959 due to poor health. *See also* BERMUDA CONFERENCE; CARACAS CONFERENCE (TENTH INTERNATIONAL CONFERENCE OF AMERICAN STATES); CENTRAL INTELLIGENCE AGENCY (CIA); DULLES, ALLEN; GUATEMALA, RELATIONS WITH.

DURKIN, MARTIN P. (1894–1955). Secretary of labor January–September 1953. No other secretary of labor served as short a term as Martin Patrick Durkin, who resigned after only eight months in office. Born and educated in Illinois, Durkin became a member of the plumbers' and pipe fitters' union, rising through the ranks to become the union president. The only Democrat in President **Dwight D. Eisenhower**'s cabinet, Durkin expected the new administration to loosen the Taft-Hartley Act, which limited union activities, including the right to strike. When this did not happen, Durkin resigned. He was succeeded by **James Paul Mitchell**. *See also* AMERICAN FEDERATION OF LABOR AND CONGRESS OF INDUSTRIAL ORGANIZATIONS (AFL-CIO).

– E –

ECONOMY. The **1952 election** brought significant changes to the economy. The housing boom, which began with the end of World War II, was still strong, but voters were ready for changes in the federal government. Profits on Wall Street rose in response to **Dwight D. Eisenhower**'s election, an upswing not seen since the 1920s. During Eisenhower's first term, **Republicans**, who now controlled both houses of Congress, began to cut the federal budget. Consumers had money to invest in corporate and municipal bonds, rather than war bonds. The growth of **suburbia** was aided by the availability of more municipal bonds. Americans were learning about and investing in the stock market. Popular and influential radio personality **Walter Winchell** stressed the importance of investing in stocks. Americans used their money to purchase the increasingly large number of affordable consumer products available to them. **Television** advertised time-saving innovations, giving families more time to enjoy their new homes in the suburbs.

Farmers were encouraged to produce goods for the United States as well as for overseas markets. Congress passed the **Agricultural Act of 1954** and the **Agricultural Trade Development and Assistance Act of 1954** to aid farm production, making money available to produce farm products for school lunches, disaster relief, and countries facing famine.

On 24 September 1955, President Eisenhower suffered a heart attack, and the stock market responded two days later with a loss of over $14 billion, a record drop. With the president ill, the economy began to slump, causing a recession. Exports declined and industrial competition increased. In 1959, half a million steel workers went on strike after managers tried to change work rules that could have allowed the companies to cut jobs or hours. A paralyzed steel industry caused **automobile** and appliance production to plummet. The country fell into another recession. The cost of clothing, health care, housing, and transportation rose, while 4 million people found themselves unemployed.

Overall, the 1950s saw the number of **credit** and **bank** loans increase dramatically. Inflation also rose, largely as a result of the removal of controls on prices. Concerned that banks might loan too much money, the Federal Reserve Board increased the amount of funds banks had to keep in reserve. The Board also increased the interest rates on loans, which would serve to curtail inflation. Rates rose from 2.25 percent in 1950 to 5 percent in 1959, the highest in 29 years. *See also* BURNS, ARTHUR F.; COUNCIL OF ECONOMIC ADVISORS; STEEL INDUSTRY; UNEMPLOYMENT.

EDEN, ANTHONY (1897–1977). Prime Minister of **Great Britain** 1955–57. Educated at Eton and Oxford University (1922), Robert Anthony Eden served as British foreign undersecretary in 1931 and foreign secretary in 1935; however, he resigned because of differences with Prime Minister Neville Chamberlain. When **Winston Churchill** became prime minister, Eden again served as foreign secretary. He led the British delegation to the San Francisco Conference, which created the **United Nations**. In 1955, he succeeded Churchill as prime minister. The following year, he infuriated President **Dwight D. Eisenhower** when he sent troops to Egypt during the **Suez Crisis**. Under pressure from Eisenhower, Eden withdrew the troops. His decision continued to haunt him, and he resigned in 1957. He was succeeded by **Harold Macmillan**. Even after his resignation, Eden was widely viewed as one of the world's most knowledgeable statesmen who tried to follow the law to gain world peace. *See also* FOREIGN POLICY.

EDUCATION. During the 1950s, some of the most sweeping changes in education occurred in the United States. President **Dwight D. Eisenhower** had been president for only two years when the U.S. **Supreme Court** declared that the doctrine of "separate but equal" was unconstitutional. The Court's decision in ***Brown v. Board of***

Education (1954) meant that **African American** students could attend formerly all-white schools. In 1957, Eisenhower had to send federal troops to Little Rock, Arkansas, when Governor **Orval Faubus** would not allow African American students to enter Central High School.

When the **Soviet Union** sent an unmanned satellite, *Sputnik*, into orbit in 1957, the **space** race began. Reacting to the Soviet's great **technological** achievement, Congress passed the **National Defense Education Act**, which stressed education in math, science, and foreign languages at the expense of subjects such as **art** and **music**. Fear of a nuclear attack from the Soviet Union led schools to drill students in a tactic called "duck and cover." Students would duck under their desks and cover their heads with their arms as protection from an **atomic** bomb's effects. One of the most influential books detailing the failures in the U.S. education system was *Why Johnny Can't Read* by Rudolph Flesch (1955), which advocated the use of phonics. *See also* CIVIL RIGHTS MOVEMENT; CONANT, JAMES B.; RACIAL INTEGRATION.

EICHMANN, ADOLPH (1906–1962). Adolph Eichmann, a poor student who became a traveling salesman, joined the Austrian Nazi party in 1932 and became a part of the SS, or secret police. Eichmann rose through the ranks. As head of the Nazi government's department for Jewish affairs, Adolph Eichmann oversaw the deportation and extermination of Jews during World War II. With the war's end, Eichmann fled to Argentina, a haven for Nazis. In 1960, Mossad, the Israeli Secret Service, located Eichmann. He was taken to **Israel**, tried for his war crimes, convicted, and hanged. *See also* ARENDT, HANNAH; BEN-GURION, DAVID.

EINSTEIN, ALBERT (1879–1955). Physicist Albert Einstein was born in **Germany** and in 1888 entered the Luitpold school in Munich. He remained in Munich in 1894 although his family settled in Italy. In 1896, he renounced his German citizenship and moved to Zurich, Switzerland, where he entered the Swiss Federal Polytechnical School (1896–1900). He studied physics and mathematics but, after graduation, was unable to find a teaching position. Now a Swiss citizen, he began working at the patent office in Bern. In his spare time, he wrote articles, six of which were published. One, published in 1905, explained his special theory of relativity.

Einstein's ideas were so astonishing that, in 1909, he was given a professorship at the University of Zurich. He worked on quantum theory and in 1911, he was hired as a full professor at the University of Prague. In 1914, he became the director of the Kaiser Wilhelm Institute at the University of Berlin. In 1915, he published his revolutionary general theory of relativity, which changed the world of physics. In 1921, Einstein visited the United States for the first time. That same year, he received the Nobel Prize in Physics.

Einstein was Jewish. In 1933, after the Nazis came to power in Germany, he settled in the United States, doing research at the Institute for Advanced Study at Princeton University. Having worked on **atomic** theory while living in Germany, Einstein feared that Germany would make a nuclear bomb. He encouraged the United States to be the first to build an atomic bomb. Although a pacifist, in 1938 he joined the team of scientists working on the atomic bomb (the Manhattan Project). In 1939, however, he wrote a letter to President Franklin D. Roosevelt stating his concerns about the future of nuclear weapons. In 1945, President **Harry S. Truman** dropped two atomic bombs on Japan, stating this would spare American lives by quickly ending World War II.

In the 1950s, Senator **Joseph McCarthy** became suspicious of Einstein's communist leanings when Einstein pleaded for leniency for **Ethel and Julius Rosenberg**, convicted of spying for the **Soviet Union**. **J. Edgar Hoover** believed uncorroborated stories that Einstein had ties to a scientist who was convicted in 1950 of passing atomic secrets to the Soviet Union.

An ardent Zionist, Einstein believed in the creation of **Israel** and supported the new country. Having met anti-Semitism while living in Europe, he helped Jews flee from Germany. He was offered the presidency of Israel in 1952 but declined. Instead he remained at Princeton University. He died on 18 April 1955. His name is still equated with being a genius: a brilliant person is "an Einstein."

EISENHOWER, DAVID JACOB (1863–1942). Father of President **Dwight D. Eisenhower**. David Jacob Eisenhower was born in Elizabethville, Pennsylvania, but the family moved to Abilene, Kansas, and farmed. He entered Lane University to study engineering but dropped out to marry Ida Elizabeth Stover in 1885. The couple moved to Hope, Kansas, and soon Eisenhower became a partner in a general store. Three years later, his partner disappeared with the store's profits, leaving Eisenhower in financial trouble. The family moved to Texas, where Eisenhower worked for the Missouri, Kansas, and Texas Railroad. In time, he was able to recoup his losses and the family returned to Abilene, where he worked as a mechanic and later held a managerial position in a gas company. Eisenhower died in 1942 while his son Dwight D. Eisenhower was serving as deputy to General **George C. Marshall** during World War II. *See also* EISENHOWER, JOHN; EISENHOWER, MAMIE; EISENHOWER, MILTON.

EISENHOWER, DWIGHT D. (1890–1969). President of the United States 1953–61. Born in Texas and raised in Abilene, Kansas, Dwight David Eisenhower was football and baseball player in high school. Eisenhower was only a mediocre student, but he won appointments to both Annapolis and West Point. At West Point, he preferred football to academics and was well on his way to becoming a star athlete when a knee injury ended his athletic career.

After graduation, Eisenhower was stationed at Fort Sam Houston, Texas, where he met Mamie Doud, whose family had a winter home in San Antonio. Dwight and **Mamie Eisenhower** were married in 1916 in Denver, at the Doud family's home.

Eisenhower received further military training at the Command and General Staff School in Fort Leavenworth, Kansas (1925–26), and the Army War College (1928–29), graduating at the top of his class. In 1932, he became part of General **Douglas MacArthur**'s staff. He accompanied MacArthur to the Philippines in 1935. The next year, he was promoted to lieutenant colonel. In 1939, he returned to the United States. A series of rapid promotions followed. In 1940, he was promoted to chief of staff of the Third Infantry Division at Fort Lewis, which was followed by chief of staff of the new the IX Corps. In 1941, he was promoted to the Third Army Headquarters in San Antonio, Texas, as chief of staff to Lt. General Walter Krueger.

Five days after the 1941 Japanese attack on Pearl Harbor, Eisenhower was told to report to General **George C. Marshall**'s office in

Washington, D.C., where he was made assistant chief of staff of war plans. Eisenhower, known for his ability to assume responsibility, met every challenge handed to him. In 1942, Marshall asked Eisenhower to draw up plans for the next three years of war, which became a model followed by other military planners. In 1943, President Franklin D. Roosevelt named him supreme commander of the Allied forces in Europe. In 1944, Eisenhower oversaw Operation Overlord, the invasion of Europe, which began on 6 June 1944 (D-Day), when the Allied forces landed in Normandy. The success of the plan made Eisenhower a world figure.

After Eisenhower ended his military service in 1948, both political parties wanted him to run for president; however, Eisenhower voted for Thomas E. Dewey, the **Republican** candidate for president in 1948. In 1950, President **Harry S. Truman**, a **Democrat**, named Eisenhower supreme commander of the **North Atlantic Treaty Organization (NATO)**. Eisenhower resigned in 1952 when he decided to run for president. He was nominated as the Republican candidate against Democratic nominee **Adlai Stevenson**. Two issues haunted the Democrats in the election: the **Korean War** and the belief that President Truman was weak against communists. Eisenhower won in 1952 and was reelected in 1956, when his Democratic opponent was again Adlai Stevenson.

During his two terms as president, Eisenhower was confronted with major **civil rights** issues, including the desegregation of the public schools. Communism remained a threat, and Senator **Joseph McCarthy** led a crusade against supposed communists. McCarthy was finally stopped when he began to question the integrity of people in Eisenhower's cabinet. During Eisenhower's term, **Ethel and Julius Rosenberg** were executed for passing plans to the **Soviet Union** for building an **atomic** bomb.

The most embarrassing event during the Eisenhower presidency was the downing of a **U-2** spy plane in 1960 over the **Soviet Union** and the capture of the American pilot. The president attempted to downplay the event, but he only made it worse.

Eisenhower was always looked upon as a grandfatherly figure who preferred golf to being president; however, he was very much in command of his administration. By the end of Eisenhower's two terms, the Korean War had ended. The public schools were integrated, and the United States was in the process of building the **Interstate Highway System**. Many historians place Eisenhower among the nation's best presidents. He is buried in Abilene, Kansas. *See also* ANDERSON, ROBERT B.; BENSON, EZRA TAFT; BRENNAN, WILLIAM J.; BROWNELL, HERBERT, JR.; DOMINO THEORY; DULLES, JOHN FOSTER; DURKIN, MARTIN P.; EISENHOWER DOCTRINE; ELECTION, 1952; ELECTION, 1956; ELECTION, 1960; FAREWELL ADDRESS; FLEMMING, ARTHUR; FOLSOM, MARION BAYARD; GATES, THOMAS S.; HARLAN, JOHN MARSHALL; HERTER, CHRISTIAN A.; HOBBY, OVETA CULP; HUMPHREY, GEORGE M.; MCELROY, NEIL H.; MCKAY, DOUGLAS; MISSION 66; MITCHELL, JAMES P.; MUELLER, FREDERICK H.; NIXON, RICHARD M.; ROGERS, WILLIAM P.; SEATON, FREDERICK A.; STEWART, POTTER; STRAUSS, LEWIS L.; SUMMERFIELD, ARTHUR ELLSWORTH; WARREN, EARL; WEEKS, CHARLES S.; WHITTAKER, CHARLES E.; WILSON, CHARLES E.

EISENHOWER, IDA ELIZABETH STOVER (1862–1946). Mother of President **Dwight D. Eisenhower**. Ida Elizabeth Stover was born in Virginia and met her future husband, **David Jacob Eisenhower**, in Topeka, Kansas, while visiting her brother. Two years later she married. The couple had seven sons, including the future president. Five of Eisenhower's brothers lived to maturity. All were college graduates and had successful careers. Ida Eisenhower was a pacifist and became a Jehovah's Witness later in her life. *See also* EISENHOWER, JOHN; EISENHOWER, MAMIE; EISENHOWER, MILTON.

EISENHOWER, JOHN (1922–). Son of President **Dwight D. Eisenhower**. John Sheldon Doud Eisenhower was born in Denver, Colorado. Like his father, he pursued a military career. After graduating from West Point (1944), he received his M.A. in English literature from Columbia University (1950). At the end of World War II, he was stationed in Europe. He remained there during the **Korean War**. He retired from the army in 1963 but served in the Army Reserves until 1974, attaining the rank of brigadier general.

After his father left office, Eisenhower helped him write his presidential memoirs. An author in his own right, his books include *The Bitter Woods: The Battle of the Bulge, Letters to Mamie by Dwight D. Eisenhower,* and *General Ike: A Personal Reminiscence.* In 1968, he campaigned for **Richard M. Nixon** and served as his ambassador to Belgium (1969–71). *See also* EISENHOWER, DAVID JACOB; EISENHOWER, IDA ELIZABETH STOVER; EISENHOWER, MAMIE; EISENHOWER, MILTON.

EISENHOWER, MAMIE (1896–1979). Mamie Eisenhower, the wife of **Dwight D. Eisenhower**, was born Marie Geneva Doud in Iowa; however, her family moved to Denver, Colorado, when she was seven. The Doud family was wealthy enough to afford a winter home in San Antonio, Texas, where Mamie met Eisenhower, who was stationed at Fort Sam Houston. They were married soon after they met, and like many military couples, they moved numerous times.

When her husband became president, Mamie had little problem running the White House, which she expected to be kept immaculate. She believed women were superior to men in decisions pertaining to real estate and investments, as well as ways to save money. She believed in purchasing food items in bulk even as the first lady and scanned newspaper ads for purchases not only for her family but for state dinners. She personally answered each letter she received. Although she was held back from commenting on some subjects, such as public **television**, she did express her support for the military and the **United Nations**.

The Eisenhowers had two sons; however, their first child died at the age of three from scarlet fever; their second son, **John Eisenhower**, had a military career and also was a writer. Mamie Eisenhower is buried next to her husband in Abilene, Kansas. *See also* EISENHOWER, DAVID JACOB; EISENHOWER, IDA ELIZABETH STOVER; EISENHOWER, MILTON.

EISENHOWER, MILTON (1899–1985). Youngest brother of **Dwight D. Eisenhower**. Born and educated in Kansas, Milton Stover Eisenhower received an undergraduate degree in 1924 from Kansas State College of Agriculture and Applied Science. During World War II, he directed the forced internment of Japanese Americans. After the war, he served as president of Kansas State University, Pennsylvania State University, and Johns Hopkins University. Milton was his brother's closest advisor. His expertise was Latin American affairs, about which he later wrote the book *The Wine Is Bitter*. He also wrote *The President Is Calling*, which gave his perceptions about being a political leader. *See also* EISENHOWER, DAVID JACOB; EISENHOWER, IDA ELIZABETH STOVER; EISENHOWER, JOHN; EISENHOWER, MAMIE.

EISENHOWER DOCTRINE, 1957. Following the 1956 **Suez Crisis**, during which the United States had criticized a joint attack by French, British, and Israeli forces against Egypt, President **Dwight D. Eisenhower** decided he needed the authority to take action in the Middle East should another crisis break out. The **domino theory** argued that if one nation fell to communism, others might follow. Using the argument that without the authority he requested, the dominoes might fall in the strategically important Middle East, Congress granted it to him. The resulting Eisenhower Doctrine permitted the president to use economic and military aid, as well as military force if necessary, to protect a region from communism.

The United States employed the Eisenhower Doctrine when King Hussein of Jordan was nearly overthrown by leftist opponents. The United States sent naval forces to the eastern Mediterranean and offered Hussein economic aid. But the doctrine's biggest test came in July 1958. After the pro-Western government of Iraq was overthrown, officials in **Lebanon**, fearing they might suffer the same fate since Lebanon was facing internal turmoil, asked for U.S. help. Eisenhower sent 5,000 American troops as a demonstration of support for the Lebanese government. Not long thereafter, the vying factions in Lebanon came to an accord, and the troops withdrew. *See also* MIDDLE EAST TREATY ORGANIZATION.

ELECTION, 1952. In 1952, **Dwight D. Eisenhower** defeated Senator **Robert Taft** of Ohio for the nomination for president by the **Republican Party**. His biggest supporter was Thomas E. Dewey of New York, the presidential candidate in two prior elections. Dewey's suggestion for vice president was Senator **Richard M. Nixon** of

California, who became Eisenhower's running mate. The Republican platform condemned President **Harry S. Truman**'s policies toward communism. Eisenhower promised to lower taxes, increase the national defense, balance the budget, and reorganize the government. Many people thought his **Democratic** opponent would be Senator **Paul Douglas** of Illinois, but Douglas's criticisms of Truman threw the Democratic nomination to Governor **Adlai Stevenson**, also of Illinois. Republican Senator **Joseph McCarthy** of Wisconsin argued that the Democrats were soft on communism.

During the election, Eisenhower was the first presidential candidate to campaign on **television**, a medium Stevenson was not able to use to good effect. Television portrayed Eisenhower as genuine and likeable, while Stevenson appeared aloof and intellectual. With the campaign slogan "I Like Ike" and his promise to go to **Korea** to end the war, Eisenhower won in a landslide.

ELECTION, 1956. In 1956, President **Dwight D. Eisenhower** ran for reelection as the **Republican** candidate against **Democratic** candidate **Adlai Stevenson**. Stevenson had an uphill fight against the very popular president. Although Eisenhower tried to discourage **Richard M. Nixon** from continuing as his vice president, Nixon announced he wanted to be on the ticket. Stevenson's campaign called for the end of the draft, a view in opposition to most voters. Before the election, the president of Egypt, **Gamal Abdel Nasser**, had seized the Suez Canal and then faced a joint attack from British, French, and Israeli forces over its control. Eisenhower criticized the attack. Although Eisenhower would almost certainly have been reelected without the **Suez Crisis**, it probably increased his margin of victory. The voters wanted an experienced man in the presidency. In November, he won by a greater landslide than in 1952. *See also* FOREIGN POLICY.

ELECTION, 1960. As President **Dwight D. Eisenhower**'s second term ended, Vice President **Richard M. Nixon** was the **Republican Party**'s presidential candidate, although for a while, New York Governor **Nelson Rockefeller** had been intent on seeking the nomination. With Rockefeller's announcement that he would not be a candidate, Nixon had no other opponents. He chose **Henry Cabot Lodge Jr.** as his running mate.

The **Democratic Party** did not have an easy time choosing a candidate. Well-known Democrats announced their candidacy, including Massachusetts Senator **John F. Kennedy**, Texas Senator **Lyndon B. Johnson**, Minnesota Senator **Hubert H. Humphrey**, and **Adlai Stevenson**, who had lost the previous two elections to Eisenhower. Kennedy's campaign was well financed, and his brother, Robert F. Kennedy, was a savvy campaign manager. When Kennedy's Catholic **religion** became a liability, he met with a group of Baptist ministers in Houston to assure them that he would not be influenced as president by his religion. In time, many voters who had been concerned about Kennedy's religion began to realize his messages of hope for the country in a time of recession were too important to ignore. Kennedy and his wife, Jacqueline, were a handsome couple, young and energetic. By the time the Democratic convention was over, Kennedy was the nominee, with Lyndon B. Johnson as his running mate.

Television played a vital role in the 1960 election, and the debates between the two candidates became a major factor in the victory of Kennedy over Nixon. Kennedy looked handsome and fit, answering questions with confidence. Nixon, on the other hand, looked haggard and angry. His answers showed a determination to continue on the path of President Eisenhower.

Both Nixon and Eisenhower made major mistakes during the campaign. Nixon promised to visit all 50 states, which led to his spending time in a number of Republican strongholds that had few electoral votes. During one lengthy press conference, President Eisenhower was asked what Nixon had done in his years as vice president. Tired and not thinking through his answer, the president stated that he needed a week to think about that question. Eisenhower's comment made voters wonder about Nixon's ability to lead the country.

In October, **Martin Luther King Jr.**, a major **civil rights** activist, was arrested in Atlanta during a **sit-in**. Kennedy helped to secure King's release, and King threw his support to Kennedy. With King's endorsement, **African American** voters gave their votes to Kennedy. He won the election by about 111,000 votes, the closest margin in history.

ELIOT, T. S. (1888–1965). Poet and playwright Thomas Stearns Eliot was born in Missouri and educated at Milton Academy (1905) and

Harvard University (B.A., 1910; M.A., 1914). After winning a fellowship to study in England, he settled there, working in a bank and teaching, all the time writing poetry. *The Waste Land* (1922) led to Eliot's success in London's literary society. He became the literary editor of Faber and Faber, a publishing house, as well as editor of *Criterion* (1922–39), a literary journal he founded. Eliot become a British citizen in 1927.

Raised in the Unitarian Church, Eliot converted to the Anglican Church. His **religion** was evident in his poetry and plays, such as *Ash Wednesday*, *Murder in the Cathedral*, and *The Family Reunion*. Eliot's influence extends beyond modern poetry to popular culture. The highly popular Broadway musical *Cats* is based on *Old Possum's Book of Practical Cats*, originally aimed at children and one of his most popular works. *See also* LITERATURE; THEATER.

– F –

FADS. The 1950s were a time of leisure and fun fads for many Americans. The introduction of the small Volkswagen Beetle in the United States enticed **teenagers** and college students to attempt to fit as many people into the car as possible. Cramming became fun to do in anything small, whether it was a car, a dorm room, or a telephone booth. Some members of the **Beat Generation** sported beards and wore sandals. Coffee houses where poetry was read sprang up on college campuses. The addition of **Hawaii** as a state raised the popularity of the relaxed muumuu dress and the Hula Hoop. Fear of an **atomic** bomb attack led some families to build underground bomb shelters and to store food. *See also* CINEMA; CLOTHING AND FASHION; DANCE.

FAREWELL ADDRESS, 1961. After serving as president for two terms (1953–61), **Dwight D. Eisenhower** delivered his farewell address, in which he warned Americans that after World War II, a new and threatening relationship had developed between weapons manufacturers and the military. To describe this relationship, he coined the term **military-industrial complex**. He also stressed that the world had changed since the end of World War II and new threats were possible He realized that nuclear weapons were available to other nations and that something would be needed to keep them in check. He was worried about the spread of communism, which he considered the cause of the **Cold War**, but he was proud that America remained largely at peace during his presidency. *See also* ATOMIC AND NUCLEAR ENERGY; DOMINO THEORY; EISENHOWER DOCTRINE; FOREIGN POLICY.

FAUBUS, ORVAL (1910–1994). Governor of Arkansas 1955–67. Governor Orval Faubus and Little Rock Central High School will forever be synonymous with the desegregation of public schools. Orval Faubus was born in Arkansas. His family was so poor, they did not own the log cabin in which they lived. While a child, he watched his father form the Socialist Party in Madison County. This peaked Faubus's interest in politics. After serving in World War II, he returned home and began to make friends in the **Democratic Party**. In 1954, he ran for governor and won the first of six terms. After the **Supreme Court**'s decision in *Brown v. Board of Education* (1954), Central High School in Little Rock made international news in 1957 when Faubus refused to allow the school to be integrated. He called in the Arkansas National Guard to prohibit **African American** students from entering the school. In October, President **Dwight D. Eisenhower** ordered the guard members to return to their armories. Eisenhower sent members of the 101st Airborne Division of Arkansas to assist the students. The president showed Faubus and the country that the law would be enforced.

During the school year, the nine black students endured ongoing harassment. In May of the following year, only one of the nine original black students graduated with the white seniors. When George Wallace announced his candidacy for president in 1968, Faubus was one of five men considered for his running mate. Faubus, however, could never escape the Central High episode during his political life.

After 1967, Faubus managed the Li'l Abner theme park in the Ozarks. He attempted unsuccessfully to become governor in 1970, 1974, and 1986 but lost each time. *See also* CIVIL RIGHTS MOVEMENT; HARLAN, JOHN MARSHALL; RACIAL INTEGRATION.

FAULKNER, WILLIAM (1897–1962). A novelist, playwright, and screenwriter, William Faulkner was influenced by his southern roots. Born in Mississippi, he trained as a pilot in Canada at the end of World War I. Failing to see action, he returned home to attend the University of Mississippi. A year after entering the university, he left for Paris, a popular place for writers following the war. In his works, he focused on southern changes in lifestyle after the Civil War and women who had to deal with suicidal men who made their lives unbearable.

In the 1930s, Faulkner moved to California, where he became a screenwriter. He developed a close friendship with director Howard Hawks, who directed *The Big Sleep* and *To Have and Have Not*. Both screenplays were written by Faulkner. After a few more years in Hollywood, he decided to return to Mississippi to continue his literary career.

Unable at first to get his books published, Faulkner saw his fortunes change in 1946 when Viking Press published *The Portable Faulkner*, with a preface by noted critic Malcolm Cowley. Critics gave the volume rave reviews. In 1949, Faulkner was elected to the National Academy of Arts and Letters and received the Nobel Prize in literature. From 1957 until his death, he was a writer in residence at the University of Virginia. Some critics have called Faulkner the greatest American writer of the 20th century. Some of his most celebrated novels are *Absalom, Absalom!*, *A Fable*, *The Sound and the Fury*, *Go Down Moses*, *Requiem for a Nun*, and *The Reivers*. See also CINEMA; LITERATURE.

FEDERAL-AID HIGHWAY ACT, 1956. *See* INTERSTATE HIGHWAY SYSTEM.

FEDERAL AVIATION ACT, 1958. The 1950s witnessed an increase in both the number of commercial airliners and the types of aircrafts used for passenger flights. In 1956, two commercial planes collided over the Grand Canyon. In 1958, a military plane and a commercial airliner collided in Maryland. These two disasters showed that the existing Civil Aeronautics Administration (CAA) was ineffective and that Congress should take action. The Federal Aviation Act of 1958 created the Federal Aviation Administration (FAA), a subsidiary of the Civil Aeronautics Board. The FAA had authority over all flights over the United States, whether military or civilian, including airline safety regulations and investigation of accidents.

FEDERAL BUREAU OF INVESTIGATION (FBI). The Federal Bureau of Investigation began as the **Bureau of Investigation (BOI)** in 1908. It was renamed the Federal Bureau of Investigation in 1935. **J. Edgar Hoover** was the longest-serving director of the Bureau, holding that position from 1924 until 1972. Established to protect and defend the United States from foreign aggressors, the FBI was called into action in 1946 after **Joseph Stalin**, leader of the **Soviet Union**, announced that he believed communism was going to replace capitalism. Americans and Europeans feared his prediction, especially after Stalin's ability to secure more territory after the war, including part of **Germany**. Many Americans believed communist infiltrators were already in the United States. At first, the United States was the only nation to have an **atomic** bomb. When the Soviet Union detonated its first atomic bomb, many Americans believed someone had revealed the secrets of this weapon to the Soviets.

During the presidency of **Dwight D. Eisenhower**, the FBI used its power to counteract the spread of communism. The FBI began to scrutinize Americans in the private sector as well as federal employees. In July 1950, the FBI arrested **Ethel and Julius Rosenberg** for spying for the Soviet Union. They were tried and found guilty of espionage; they were executed in 1953.

When the **House Un-American Activities Committee (HUAC)** began to investigate Americans, the FBI became involved. Hoover began to use his power as FBI director to extend his investigations beyond suspected communists. The **Southern Christian Leadership Conference (SCLC), Albert Einstein, Paul Robeson, Alfred C. Kinsey, Allen Ginsberg**, and **Martin Luther King Jr.** were a handful of famous writers, scientists, entertainers, and **civil rights** leaders investigated by the FBI in the 1950s. **Cinema** star **Lena Horne** was investigated because of her friendship with Paul Robeson. Prior to his appointment in 1949 to the **Supreme Court**, **Tom C. Clark** was investigated by the FBI on suspicion of taking a bribe. Hoover and Senator **Joseph McCarthy** of HUAC communicated with each other. Eisenhower's U.S. attorney general, **Herbert**

Brownell, authorized the FBI to install surveillance devices in the homes or offices of some suspects.

After Eisenhower left office in 1961, Hoover still headed the FBI. Until his death in 1972, Hoover directed the bureau with a firm hand. Although the **Red Scare** ended in the 1950s, the FBI continued to investigate many people using questionable tactics.

FISCHER, BOBBY (1943–2008). Robert James Fischer was born in Chicago, Illinois, but raised in Brooklyn, New York. Introduced to the game of chess at the age of six, he was a competitive player by the age of eight. Between 1956 and 1959, Fischer won both the U.S. Junior and the U.S. Open championships. However, his greatest achievement came in 1972, during the **Cold War**, when he won the international chess crown. His opponent was chess champion Boris Spassky of the **Soviet Union**. In 1975, he lost his title to Anatoly Karpov of the Soviet Union. After his loss to Karpov, Fischer became a recluse. In 1992, he played a rematch with Spassky and won. The match, played in Yugoslavia, was in violation of **United Nations** sanctions against Yugoslavia. He fled to Japan, which was on the verge of extraditing him to the United States when Iceland provided refuge. Fearing he would be imprisoned, Fischer moved to Iceland and renounced his U.S. citizenship.

Fischer became more eccentric as he aged. He accused the chess establishment of deciding the outcome of games before they were played, and although his mother was Jewish, he became an anti-Semite. Always a man of mystery, Fischer died of kidney failure in Iceland, which had granted him citizenship in 2004.

FLEMMING, ARTHUR (1905–1996). Secretary of health, education, and welfare 1958–61. Born in New York State, Arthur Sherwood Flemming graduated from Ohio Wesleyan University in 1927. He continued his education at American University (M.A., 1928) and earned a law degree from George Washington University (1933). He was a reporter for *U.S. News and World Report*, taught at Ohio Wesleyan University, and served as the university's president (1948–53 and 1957–58), as well as being engaged in public service.

Although a lifelong **Republican**, Flemming was appointed by **Democratic** President Franklin D. Roosevelt to the Civil Service

Commission (1939–48). His work on the commission was outstanding and led to the establishment of an award in his honor, given annually to a public employee. Eisenhower appointed Flemming to be secretary of health, education, and welfare after **Marion Bayard Folsom** left the cabinet post in 1958. While secretary, Flemming established the Office on Aging, a governmental office whose importance led to Flemming's influence in other matters having to do with **social security**.

After Flemming left government service, he was appointed president of the University of Oregon (1961–66) and then Macalaster College (1968–71), and he was president of the National Council of Churches USA (1966–69). *See also* DEPARTMENT OF HEATH, EDUCATION, AND WELFARE (HEW); HOBBY, OVETA CULP.

FLYING THE FLAG AT HALF-STAFF. Lowering the flag to half-staff is a long-held tradition to honor a fallen hero or dignitary; however, there were no written rules for this tradition until President **Dwight D. Eisenhower** established them in 1954. The rules are as follows: the flag shall fly at half-staff for 30 days after the death of a president; 10 days for the vice president, chief justice of the **Supreme Court** (whether retired or not), and speaker of the House of Representatives. When an associate justice of the Supreme Court or a cabinet member dies, the flag will fly at half-staff from the day of death until internment. The same rule applies to former vice presidents, majority leaders of the Senate and the House, presidents pro tempore of the Senate, and minority leaders of the House.

FOLSOM, MARION BAYARD (1922–1968). Secretary of health, education, and welfare 1955–58. Born in Georgia, Marion Bayard Folsom received degrees from the University of Georgia (1912) and Harvard University Business School (1914). Much of Folsom's career, which began in 1914, was associated with the Eastman Kodak Company. With his knowledge of statistics, he organized the company's first statistical department and created one of the first life insurance, disability, and retirement plans for employees financed by a company. His accomplishment earned him a position on President Franklin D. Roosevelt's President's Advisory Board of the Committee on Economic Security in 1934. He also helped draft the **Social Security** Act of 1935.

Dividing his time between the public and the private sectors, Folsom became director in 1947 of Eastman Kodak's Unemployment Benefit Plan. In 1953 he was named undersecretary of the treasury by President **Dwight D. Eisenhower**. During his tenure in the treasury, Folsom undertook a complete revision of the tax law, a project no one had attempted since 1874. Folsom also spearheaded all social security legislation changed during the Eisenhower administration. He replaced **Oveta Culp Hobby**, the first secretary of health, education, and welfare, when she resigned in 1955 to care for her ailing husband. In 1958, Folsom left the cabinet to serve on the board of trustees of the Eastman Kodak Company. He also continued to work on various social and health issues in the city of Rochester. *See also* DEPARTMENT OF HEALTH, EDUCATION, AND WELFARE (HEW); ECONOMY.

FOOTBALL. One of the most important changes in professional football in the 1950s was the creation of the American Football League (AFL) by Texas millionaire Lamar Hunt. He wanted a professional football team in Dallas but found that the National Football League (NFL) would not agree to the addition of more teams. Like baseball, football was able to take advantage of the growth of **television** and more leisure time for most Americans.

The Detroit Lions and the Cleveland Browns won more NFL championships in the 1950s than any other teams. Some Football Hall of Fame inductees from the 1950s were Jim Brown, Frank Gifford, Len Dawson, Bart Starr, Johnny Unitas, and Elroy (Crazylegs) Hirsch. Two of the most famous coaches in the NFL were Vince Lombardi of the Green Bay Packers (1959–67) and Washington Redskins (1969) and Weeb Ewbank of the Baltimore Colts (1954–62) and New York Jets (1963–73). The AFL merged with the NFL in 1970. *See also* SPORTS.

FORD, JOHN (1895–1973). Film critics consider John Ford one of Hollywood's best directors. Although many of his movies focused on American history or on his Irish roots, he was most famous for his westerns. For over 50 years, he directed some of the finest westerns, often filming in Monument Valley in Utah and New Mexico. He is credited with discovering **John Wayne** and making him one of Hollywood's favorite actors for four decades.

Born John Martin Feeney in Maine, he followed his brother to Hollywood in 1913, working as a stuntman and actor. In 1917, he directed his first movie *The Tornado*, which was the beginning of a career that included four Academy Awards for best director. Some of his movies during the 1950s were *The Last Hurrah*, *The Searchers*, *Mister Roberts*, *The Long Gray Line*, *What Price Glory*, and *The Quiet Man*, for which he won an Academy Award in 1952. His other award-winning films were *Stagecoach* (1939), *The Grapes of Wrath* (1940), and *How Green Was My Valley* (1941). *See also* CINEMA.

FOREIGN POLICY. In 1952, the **Republican** presidential nominee, **Dwight D. Eisenhower**, set his foreign policy in motion even before he was elected. He promised to travel to Korea if elected, to end the **Korean War**. President Eisenhower kept his promise, and in 1953 an armistice was achieved through diplomatic channels.

Eisenhower announced changes in the military budget. He reduced the size of the military and focused on the production of **atomic** weapons. These changes were soon referred to as the "new look." Not only were nuclear weapons cheaper to build and maintain than conventional forces, but their power, it was believed, would deter the **Soviet Union** from engaging in aggression abroad. **Massive retaliation**, the threat of using America's nuclear might against the communists, became the focal point of the new policy. Eisenhower reportedly sent a message to the Chinese Communists that if they did not agree to end the Korean War, he would launch a nuclear strike.

In **Vietnam**, where **France** was attempting to regain power from communist leader **Ho Chi Minh**, the White House offered large amounts of military aid. When the French found themselves pinned down by the Viet Minh at **Dien Bien Phu**, members of Eisenhower's administration considered the use of nuclear weapons to help the French. Although he believed in the **domino theory**, the president rejected the idea. During the **Quemoy and Matsu Crises** of 1954–55 and 1958, the White House issued warnings that it might use America's atomic capabilities against Communist **China**.

The public in the United States and elsewhere widely condemned the idea of using nuclear weapons, fearing that their use could lead to another world war. It was thus clear to the Eisenhower administration that it had to have other means to stop communist aggression. One was the **Central Intelligence Agency**. In 1953, the White House used the CIA to overthrow **Iran**'s prime minister, **Mohammed Mossadegh**, whom the United States believed was prepared to become a Soviet ally. The following year, the agency overthrew Jacobo Arbenz Guzman in **Guatemala**, for similar reasons.

Though the Eisenhower administration could argue that in its first term it had successfully defended South Korea, Taiwan, Iran, and Guatemala from communism, its second term brought renewed crises. In the summer of 1956, the **Suez Crisis** erupted after Egyptian President **Gamal Abdel Nasser** nationalized the Suez Canal. British, French, and Israeli troops invaded Egypt. Having to choose between its allies and a **United Nations** Charter, which at its heart was anti-imperialist, Eisenhower selected the latter. This meant that the United States found itself siding with the Soviet Union. When the United States threatened embargoes if its allies did not withdraw, Britain, France, and Israel withdrew their troops. Eisenhower later regretted that the Suez Crisis had kept him from issuing a stronger response to the Soviet decision in October 1956 to invade Hungary and crush the **Hungarian Revolution**. In September 1957, the Soviet Union launched the world's first **intercontinental ballistic missile (ICBM)**. This meant that the Soviets could now strike the United States with the push of a button. The following month, Moscow launched *Sputnik*, the world's first unmanned satellite. It appeared to American officials that the United States was losing the arms race, the **space** race, and the **Cold War**.

In 1958, the Middle East came center stage once again. Following the Suez Crisis, Congress had authorized what became known as the **Eisenhower Doctrine**, which allowed the president to use economic and military aid, and if necessary, military force, to defend the Middle East from communism. That doctrine was put to the test when Iraq's pro-Western government was ousted in a coup and replaced by a leftist regime; there were reports that Nasser and the Soviets had a hand in the coup. The government of **Lebanon**, wracked by internal turmoil and fearful that it too might become a target of Egypt and the Soviet Union, turned to the United States for help. Eisenhower sent 5,000 troops to Lebanon. The soldiers withdrew later that year following an agreement among the contending Lebanese factions.

Attention then turned to Europe and Latin America. In November 1958, Soviet General Secretary **Nikita Khrushchev** announced that he was going to give East **Germany** control of East Berlin and the air routes into West Berlin. In 1948–49, the Soviet Union had blockaded West Berlin, and the White House feared that if Khrushchev went through with his plans, another blockade might ensue. In January 1959, revolutionary leader **Fidel Castro** seized control of **Cuba**. Now, the United States had a communist government only 90 miles from its shores. The White House began planning a CIA operation to get rid of Castro, which led to the Bay of Pigs fiasco that took place under President **John F. Kennedy**.

Despite the problems in Europe and Latin America, Eisenhower hoped to end his administration by improving relations with the Soviet Union, including reaching an arms agreement between the superpowers. He invited Khrushchev to come to the United States; the Soviet general secretary accepted and arrived in the United States in September 1959. Khrushchev dropped his threat regarding East Berlin, and it seemed that the two nations might be well on their way to a significant change in their relationship. However, in May 1960, the Soviet Union shot down an American **U-2** spy plane flying over Soviet airspace and captured the pilot. The U-2 Incident soured superpower relations.

The U-2 Incident played its part in the 1960 election. **Democrats** charged that the incident was proof the administration had poorly managed the nation's foreign policy. Both **Richard M. Nixon**, who ran as the **Republican** candidate, and John F. Kennedy, the Democratic candidate, vied over who would be toughest against the communists. In one of the closest elections in U.S. history, Kennedy won. *See also* ANZUS PACT; AUSTRIAN STATE TREATY; BAGHDAD PACT; BERLIN CONFERENCE; BERLIN CRISIS; BRINKSMANSHIP; CARACAS CONFERENCE; CONGO CRISIS; CONTAINMENT; CYPRUS, RELATIONS WITH; FORMOSA RESOLUTION; GENEVA CONFERENCE AND ACCORDS; GENEVA SUMMIT CONFERENCE; INDIA, RELATIONS WITH; JAPANESE PEACE

TREATY; LEBANON CRISIS; MANILA PACT; MARSHALL PLAN; MIDDLE EAST TREATY ORGANIZATION; MUTUAL DEFENSE ASSISTANCE AGREEMENT; ORGANIZATION OF PETROLEUM EXPORTING COUNTRIES (OPEC); NORTH ATLANTIC TREATY ORGANIZATION (NATO); ORGANIZATION OF AMERICAN STATES (OAS); PARIS CONFERENCE; QUEMOY AND MATSU CRISES; SOUTHEAST ASIA TREATY ORGANIZATION (SEATO); THIRD WORLD; UNITED NATIONS; WARSAW PACT.

FORESTER, C. S. (1899–1966). Cecil Scott Forester was born in Cairo, Egypt, to English parents. Although an avid reader as a child, even reading encyclopedias, he had no interest in a formal **education**. Instead, after wanting to pursue a career in medicine, he decided to devote his life to writing. During World War II, he went to Hollywood, where he wrote and produced propaganda films, including in 1942 the feature-length film *Eagle Squadron*. He had an incredible knowledge of ships and the sea, which he made use of in his popular *Horatio Hornblower* series. Forester also wrote *The African Queen*, which became an Academy Award–winning movie. Forester battled arteriosclerosis in his later years. *See also* CINEMA; LITERATURE.

FORMOSA RESOLUTION, 1955. The U.S. Congress passed the Formosa Resolution in late January 1955, which gave President **Dwight D. Eisenhower** the right to use American troops against the Chinese Communists, and to defend Taiwan, the Pescadores, and other areas that were in the hands of America's friends. *See also* CHINA, RELATIONS WITH; QUEMOY AND MATSU CRISES.

FORMOSA STRAITS CRISES. *See* QUEMOY AND MATSU CRISES.

FRANCE, RELATIONS WITH. When President **Dwight D. Eisenhower** was inaugurated in 1953, he immediately faced a crisis involving France. The French army was fighting a losing war in **Vietnam**. The fear of communism in this region led to a pledge from the newly elected president to provide aid to the French military. But Eisenhower kept the U.S. military out of Vietnam.

In 1956, France, builder of the Suez Canal with the Egyptians, joined with **Great Britain** and **Israel** to attack Egypt in an effort to seize control of the canal. Eisenhower was critical of the attack. The **Suez Crisis** was finally turned over to the **United Nations**. In 1958, after becoming prime minister of France, **Charles de Gaulle** decided to establish a French nuclear defense program independent of the **North Atlantic Treaty Organization (NATO)**. In response, Eisenhower stated that such a change in NATO's structure could lead the United States to remove its troops from Western Europe.

Eisenhower had kept the U.S. military out of direct involvement in Vietnam. The defeat of the French at **Dien Bien Phu**, however, led to the deployment of U.S. troops during the administration of President **John F. Kennedy**. *See also* DILLON, DOUGLAS; DOMINO THEORY; DULLES, JOHN FOSTER; FOREIGN RELATIONS.

FRANCHISES, CHAINS, AND SHOPPING CENTERS. The 1950s witnessed the expansion of franchises and large shopping centers, in part as a result of the new **Interstate Highway System** and the growth of **suburbia**. Long journeys on the new highways meant people had to eat along the way or sleep overnight. Dunkin Donuts opened shops along the new roads and franchised them to others. By 1969, two of the biggest franchises were Kentucky Fried Chicken and McDonald's, with 1,800 outlets and 1,000 outlets, respectively. Suburban chains were a profitable arrangement; however, they led to the demise of many mom and pop businesses, as well as shopping in the heart of a town. As the suburbs grew, many shops in the downtown areas closed or moved to the suburbs. Some of the other companies franchising their business were Holiday Inn, AAMCO Transmissions, Manpower, Roto-rooter, Culligan water softeners, and H & R Bloch tax preparers. *See also* ECONOMY; KROC, RAY.

FRANKFURTER, FELIX (1882–1965). Associate justice of the **Supreme Court** 1939–62. Born in Austria and raised in New York City, Felix Frankfurter was educated at the College of the City of New York (B.A., 1902) and Harvard University Law School (1906), where he was the top student in his class. His work in the law office of Henry L. Stimson opened doors for Frankfurter. In 1910, he joined Stimson's campaign to become governor of New York. Although he lost, Stimson was appointed secretary of war by President William H. Taft. Again Frankfurter joined Stimson and became his confidant as well as the legal officer responsible for America's territorial possessions.

After World War I, he became one of the original members of the **American Civil Liberties Union (ACLU)**. He defended Nicola Sacco and Bartolomeo Vanzetti when they were arrested and accused of murder in a payroll robbery. Because they were immigrants and considered anarchists, prejudice and fears about the **Red Scare** worked against them. Frankfurter thought the case against them was unfair. He published an article and a book about the trial. Both defendants were convicted and executed.

Before his appointment to the Supreme Court, Frankfurter became close friends with Justice Oliver Wendell Holmes and Louis Brandeis, who was also destined to become a Supreme Court justice. After World War I, Frankfurter and Brandeis, both Zionists, had hoped that the Paris Peace Conference would result in a mandate for Palestine to help European Jews who wanted to immigrate to the Middle East. During President Franklin D. Roosevelt's first term, Frankfurter served as a counsel to Roosevelt. In 1939, he became a Supreme Court justice, replacing Justice Benjamin Cardozo. Frankfurter and Chief Justice **Earl Warren** worked to ensure a unanimous decision in *Brown v. Board of Education* (1954). The force of Frankfurter's decisions make his opinions, even today, far more interesting than those by the majority of the justices. *See also BROWDER V. GAYLE*; CIVIL RIGHTS MOVEMENT; ISRAEL, RELATIONS WITH; RACIAL INTEGRATION.

FRIEDAN, BETTY (1921–2006). A 1942 graduate of Smith College, Illinois-born Elizabeth Naomi Friedan stayed at home to raise her family, like so many other American women with a college education. But she always believed there was more for a woman to do to fulfill her life. After World War II, many women left their jobs and returned to a life of domesticity while veterans of the war replaced them in the workforce.

While at her 15th reunion in 1957 at Smith College, Betty Friedan circulated a survey among her classmates asking how they felt about their lives. She found that many felt as unfulfilled as she did, since they were unable to use their education as members of the workforce. Friedan compiled her findings into an article. When she was unable to find a **magazine** that would publish her findings, she turned the article into a book, *The Feminine Mystique* (1963). The book, a best seller, made women question what their lives were and what they could be. Friedan almost single-handedly changed the role of women in American society by raising the consciousness of women. Friedan was also one of the founders of the National Organization for Women (NOW) and a leading figure in the **women's movement**.

FROST, ROBERT (1874–1963). Often referred to as the unofficial poet laureate of the United States, Frost was born in California but raised and educated in New England. Although he did not graduate, he attended Dartmouth College for a semester in 1892 and later Harvard University (1897–99). Winner of several Pulitzer Prizes for his published works, he also taught and lectured but eventually concentrated solely on his poetry. He read his poem "The Gift Outright" at the 1961 inauguration of President **John F. Kennedy**. His poem "Stopping by Woods on a Snowy Evening" is included in many anthologies. Some of his other well-known poems are "Mending Walls," "Birches," "Fire and Ice," and "The Road Not Taken." *See also* LITERATURE.

FULBRIGHT, J. WILLIAM (1905–1995). U.S. senator 1945–74. James William Fulbright was born in Sumner, Missouri. After graduating from the University of Arkansas in 1925, he went to Oxford University in 1928 as a Rhodes Scholar. In 1934, he received a law degree from George Washington University Law School and taught law in Washington, D.C., and Arkansas. He was elected in 1942 to the U.S. House of Representatives and, three years later, to the U.S. Senate. During the presidency of **Dwight D. Eisenhower**, Fulbright became chair of the Foreign Relations Committee. As a senator, he was responsible for the Fulbright Act of 1946, which established Fulbright Scholarships for students and teachers to study overseas. He was an outspoken critic of the federal government's intervention in the foreign affairs of other countries, and critical as well of Senator **Joseph McCarthy**, who nicknamed Fulbright "Halfbright."

As a southerner, Fulbright was opposed to **racial integration** in the public schools, a decision that would later haunt him. When Vice President **Lyndon B. Johnson** urged President **John F. Kennedy** to make Fulbright his secretary of state, Kennedy remembered Fulbright's opinion on **civil rights**. Fulbright would later criticize Kennedy for the **Bay of Pigs** failure and the **Vietnam War**. He was also a well-known critic of President **Richard M. Nixon**. *See also* EDUCATION; FOREIGN POLICY.

– G –

GAGARIN, YURI (1934–1968). A Soviet astronaut and the first man in **space**, Yuri Alekseyevich Gagarin was born in Russia. After World War II, he entered an apprenticeship in metalworking. His background in math and science led to his selection for more training in a technical high school, where he joined a club to learn to fly light planes. In 1955, he completed his technical school education and trained in the military to be a pilot. In 1957, he obtained his pilot's wings.

In 1961, Gagarin was one of 20 pilots selected to train for the **Soviet Union**'s first manned orbital flight. Only a little over five feet tall, Gagarin was small enough to fit into the cockpit of the *Vostok 1*, in which he circled Earth on 12 April 1961. Later that year, he orbited Earth for almost two hours. Gagarin continued to work as a test pilot. He died in 1968 when a new plane he was flying crashed. *See also* *SPUTNIK*; TECHNOLOGICAL INNOVATIONS.

GATES, THOMAS S. (1906–1988). Secretary of the navy 1957–59, secretary of defense 1959–61. Born in Germantown, Pennsylvania, Thomas Sovereign Gates Jr. graduated from the University of Pennsylvania in 1928 and joined his father's investment firm, Drexel and Company. In 1935, he joined the Naval Reserve. During World War II, Gates was placed on active duty and achieved the rank of commander. After the war, he became director of the Beaver Coal Corporation. In 1948, he was promoted to vice president of the corporation. In 1953, he entered government service when he was appointed undersecretary of the navy by President **Dwight D. Eisenhower**. In 1959, Eisenhower elevated him to secretary of defense.

During his service in the Eisenhower administration, Gates made the military one of the strongest fighting forces in the country's history. By the time he left office in 1961, long-range bombers, **intercontinental ballistic missiles (ICBMs)**, **intermediate-range ballistic missiles (IRBMs)**, nuclear submarines, and surface-to-air missiles had become part of the U.S. arsenal. Gates also created early defense warning systems used throughout the continental United States. He also proposed the use of spy planes over the **Soviet Union**. This led to one of the most contentious meetings between President Eisenhower and Soviet Premier **Nikita Khrushchev** in 1959 after one of the **U-2** spy planes was shot down over the Soviet Union and the pilot, Francis Gary Powers, was captured. *See also* COLD WAR; FOREIGN RELATIONS; USS *NAUTILUS*.

GENEVA CONFERENCE AND ACCORDS, 1954. The Geneva Conference was intended to restore peace after the fall in 1954 of **Dien Bien Phu**, a French stronghold in **Vietnam**. The two-day meeting (20–21 July) ended with an agreement called the Geneva Accords, which had several major provisions. Indochina, formerly a French colony, was divided into three independent countries: Cambodia, Laos, and Vietnam. Cambodia and Laos would be neutral, not tied to the **Soviet**-led communist bloc or the U.S.-led anticommunist bloc. Vietnam was divided along the 17th parallel, with the Viet Minh and its leader, **Ho Chi Minh**, retreating to the north of that line and the French regrouped to the south. The two Vietnams were to remain neutral. Neither was to join into an alliance with any other country. In July 1956, Vietnam would hold national elections under international supervision; the winner of those elections would then become the leader of a reunified Vietnam.

Though not a signatory to the accords, the United States agreed to abide by its provisions. But with the approval of **Dwight D. Eisenhower**'s administration, the South Vietnamese refused to meet with the North Vietnamese and hold elections. Instead, the United States gradually pushed the French out of South Vietnam and helped install Ngo Dinh Diem as the leader of that nation. The failure of the elections to take place led to hostilities between North and South

Vietnam and, eventually, to direct U.S. involvement in South Vietnam. *See also* FOREIGN POLICY; FRANCE, RELATIONS WITH; VIETNAM WAR.

GENEVA SUMMIT CONFERENCE, 1955. After the death of **Joseph Stalin**, the **Soviet Union** showed signs of moderating its attitude toward the noncommunist West. Most notably, in 1955, the Soviets, who had occupied the eastern part of Austria, signed a treaty with that country that gave it independence. Then the Kremlin announced it was ready to discuss proposals put forward by the White House on disarmament. Believing he had to respond to these moves, President **Dwight D. Eisenhower** agreed to meet with Soviet leader **Nikita Khrushchev** at Geneva in July 1955. Hoping to score a propaganda victory while simultaneously reducing the possibility of a superpower war, he proposed an "open skies" policy by which the United States and Soviet Union would open their airspace to one another, thereby allowing each to monitor their respective military strengths and verify compliance with any disarmament agreement. Moscow rejected the proposal, regarding it as an attempt by the United States to spy on it. While no major settlements were reached at Geneva, the meeting did generate what reporters called the "Spirit of Geneva": a hope that the **Cold War** was thawing. Unfortunately, relations between the superpowers during Eisenhower's term ended on a sour note as a result of the **U-2 incident**. *See also* AUSTRIAN STATE TREATY; FOREIGN POLICY; POWERS, FRANCIS GARY.

GERMANY, RELATIONS WITH. At the end of World War II, the United States, **Great Britain**, and the **Soviet Union** met at the Potsdam Conference (1945) to determine the future of Germany. The country was divided into four zones under the United States, Great Britain, **France**, and the Soviet Union, respectively. The first three sectors eventually united to form West Germany. The Soviet zone became East Germany. East Germany remained under Soviet control, while West Germany had strong ties with the Western nations and became a close ally of the United States. In 1949, **Konrad Adenauer** became the first chancellor of West Germany. The Soviet Union continued to veto decisions involving East Germany and was able to control its zone as it wished. While he was president, **Dwight D. Eisenhower** had repeated confrontations with the Soviet Union concerning Germany. The United States helped West Germany rebuild its manufacturing plants, which supplied Allied forces during the **Korean War**. *See also* BERLIN CRISIS; BRANDT, WILLY; FOREIGN POLICY; GENEVA SUMMIT CONFERENCE.

GERSHWIN, GEORGE. *See* GERSHWIN, IRA, AND GEORGE GERSHWIN.

GERSHWIN, IRA (1896–1983), AND GEORGE GERSHWIN (1898–1937). Lyricist Ira Gershwin and his brother George Gershwin, a composer, were born in New York. In the 1920s, the brothers began their collaboration. Their first Broadway hit was *Lady, Be Good!*, the first of 20 Broadway hit shows in the 1920s. In 1931, the Gershwins went to Hollywood, where they wrote the scores for several movies, including *Shall We Dance* and *Damsel in Distress*. They continued to write together until 1937, when George died of a brain tumor.

Ira and George Gershwin were considered one of the most important duos in American **music** history. Some of their songs were "Summertime," "The Man I Love," "They Can't Take That Away from Me," and "I Got Rhythm." *Porgy and Bess*, which opened on Broadway with a cast of only **African Americans**, is still considered one of the most beautiful musicals ever written. After George died, Ira did not write any music for almost three years. Then he teamed up with various composers, including Jerome Kern, Kurt Weill, and Harold Arlen. Ira Gershwin received three Oscars for his lyrics for "They Can't Take That Away from Me" (1938), "Long Ago and Far Away" (1945), and "The Man That Got Away" (1955). *See also* CINEMA; THEATER.

GIBSON, ALTHEA (1927–2003). Born in South Carolina but raised in Harlem, New York, Althea Gibson was active in athletics at school. She became a member of the Harlem Cosmopolitan Tennis Club, often winning tennis tournaments. Donations were raised to pay for her membership and lessons. In 1942 and again in 1944 and 1945, she won the New York Tournament of the American Tennis

Association (ATA), an **African American** organization. In 1950, with the help of a wealthy South Carolina sponsor, Gibson took private tennis lessons while studying at Florida A&M University. In 1953, after graduating, she became an athletic instructor at Lincoln University in Missouri.

Gibson was the first African American to win championships at major tennis tournaments. These included Wimbledon, the French Open, the U.S. Open, and the Australian Doubles. By the late 1950s, Gibson had won 11 major titles. In 1957, the Associated Press named her Athlete of the Year, an honor she also won the following year. For 10 years, beginning in 1975, she was the New Jersey state commissioner of athletics. She ended her career in 1992 as a member of the Governor's Council on Physical Fitness. *See also* SPORTS; WOMEN'S MOVEMENT.

GINSBERG, ALLEN (1926–1997). A **Beat Generation** poet and antiwar activist, Allen Ginsberg was born in New Jersey. Both his parents were political liberals. Growing up, Ginsberg got into trouble with the law several times because of his left-wing politics, including during his years at Columbia University (B.A., 1949). He was influenced by the writings of **William Carlos Williams**, Ken Kesey, Timothy Leary, **William S. Burroughs**, and **Jack Kerouac**.

Ginsberg became a member of the drug and antiwar cultures of the 1950s and 1960s. His most famous poem, *Howl!*, was written while he was living in San Francisco. When he read it at a poetry reading, it was an immediate success. But when the poem was published by a local press, the police stopped its publication on the grounds that it was obscene. *Howl!* was a long poem in free verse meant to be read aloud. It decried the 1950s, a decade of political conservatism, capitalism, and consumerism. Ginsberg's own life was characterized by nonconformity and an interest in Buddhism. During the 1950s and 1960s, he became a favorite with college students as a symbol of the Beat Generation and because of his activism against the **Vietnam War**.

In 1993, Ginsberg won the National Book Award for *The Fall of America*. Some of his other works are *Reality Sandwiches*, *Selected Gay Poems and Correspondence*, and *Plutonian Ode*. *See also* LITERATURE; MAILER, NORMAN.

GLEASON, JACKIE (1916–1987). The actor and comedian Jackie Gleason was born Herbert John Gleason in Brooklyn, New York. His alcoholic father abandoned the family when he was a child. Gleason left school while very young to fend for himself by working as a boxer, a pool hustler, and in a carnival. Beginning a career in vaudeville, he signed a contract with Warner Brothers in 1940, and in the 1950s continued his success on television. From 1955 to 1956, Gleason starred as Ralph Kramden, a bus driver, on *The Honeymooners*, which is still in syndication. *The Honeymooners* was followed the next year by *The Jackie Gleason Show*, which consisted of *Honeymooners* segments and variety acts. Gleason also played various comedic characters.

A heavy man, Gleason often made fun of his size, being referred to as "The Great One." He was as adept at playing dramatic roles as comedic roles. In 1961, he played a pool shark in the highly acclaimed film *The Hustler*. In 1977, he played a comic southern sheriff in *Smokey and the Bandit* and its two sequels, which introduced him to a new generation. Gleason died of cancer soon after appearing in the movie *Nothing in Common* (1986). *See also* CINEMA.

GLEN CANYON DAM. One of the most controversial decisions President **Dwight D. Eisenhower** made was the construction of the Glen Canyon Dam in 1956. Since it was built, environmentalists have realized the problems the dam created. When President Eisenhower approved the construction of the Glen Canyon Dam, Utah's government praised the idea because it would create new water and recreation areas, including Lake Powell, a large lake constructed in southern Utah. Conservationists, however, were worried about the long-range effects of damming the Colorado River near the Grand Canyon.

The dam produced problems for the growing West. Both Las Vegas and Los Angeles were growing in size and needed the water that went to Utah. The dam affected American Indian archeological sites and natural scenery by covering them with water. In other areas, the dam prevented the once natural flow of the Colorado River. When wildlife, forests, and towns no longer received the water they needed to survive, they died. Today water from the Colorado River is still a major bone of contention among the western cities, all thirsty for water. In 1965, Secretary of the Interior Morris Udall referred to the problems created by the Glen Canyon Dam as a reason to end the construction of dams in the Grand Canyon. *See also* MISSION 66.

GODFREY, ARTHUR (1903–1983). Radio and **television** personality. Arthur Godfrey was born in New York City. He received radio training in the 1920s when he served in the U.S. Navy and later in the Coast Guard. Godfrey obtained his first radio announcing job in Baltimore and then continued his radio career in Washington, D.C., as a staff announcer on NBC. In 1945, he joined CBS Radio. Godfrey's popularity led to a television program in 1948, *Arthur Godfrey's Talent Scouts*. He helped further the careers of **Pat Boone**, Tony Bennett, Connie Francis, Eddie Fisher, and many others. Prior to 1959, few other personalities on television did more for the medium than Godfrey, who was one of the highest-paid television celebrities of the decade. He was known for his unique voice and for the humorous manner in which he promoted the products of his advertisers. Godfrey's greatest talent was his ability to identify with his audiences. His program was live, and the end of live television in 1959 spelled the end of his program.

GOLDEN AGE OF TELEVISION. *See* TELEVISION.

GOLF. President **Dwight D. Eisenhower** popularized golf by his love of the game and by playing with the greatest athletes in the sport. Three golf greats in the 1950s were Ben Hogan, Arnold Palmer, and Sam Snead. During his career as a professional golfer, Hogan won the four top major golf tournaments in the world: PGA, Masters, U.S. Open, and British Open. Only three other golfers have done the same. Arnold Palmer began his career in 1955 when he won the Canadian Open. He has won three of the major golf tournaments. Nicknamed "Slammin' Sammy" for his swing, Snead won more PGA tour events than anyone, but he won only three of the major tournaments. While Arnold Palmer never won the PGA, Snead never won the U.S. Open.

In 1950, **Babe Zaharias** and 12 other women interested in golf founded the Ladies Professional Golf Association (LPGA). It is still in operation today, hosting golf tournaments in conjunction with other countries' women's golf associations. *See also* SPORTS.

GOODPASTER, ANDREW JACKSON (1915–2005). Born in Illinois and educated at West Point (1939) and Princeton University (1948), Andrew Jackson Goodpaster worked closely in the 1950s with the Joint Chiefs of Staff at the Pentagon. His next assignment was with General **Dwight D. Eisenhower**, who was the first commander of the **North Atlantic Treaty Organization (NATO)**. In 1954, President Eisenhower chose Goodpaster as his staff secretary. Working closely with **Sherman Adams**, Goodpaster served as a liaison with all departments involved in national security. His duties included attending daily briefings, attending both cabinet and National Security Council meetings, and seeing that all of the president's decisions were executed.

During the **Vietnam War**, President **Lyndon B. Johnson** turned to Goodpaster as his liaison with former President Eisenhower. He was also a military advisor to President **Richard M. Nixon**. In 1977, West Point was involved in a cheating scandal, and the retired general was appointed superintendent of the military academy in order to restore its reputation. He retired from West Point in 1981. *See also* FOREIGN POLICY.

GOODSON-TODMAN PRODUCTIONS. No other **television** game show producers were as successful as Mark Goodson (1915–92) and Bill Todman (1918–79). Working in radio in the 1940s in New York City, the two met and immediately realized their mutual love of game shows. They made their fame in television beginning in 1948 with their first game show, *Winner Takes All*, which aired on the Columbia Broadcasting System (CBS) in New York City. Some of the most successful and long-running television game shows of Goodson-Todman Productions were *I've Got a Secret* (1952–76), *What's My Line?* (1950–67), *To Tell the Truth* (1956–67), *The Price Is Right* (1956–72), and *Concentration* (1958–73). *See also* QUIZ SHOW SCANDALS.

GREAT BRITAIN, RELATIONS WITH. Throughout its history, the United States has worked more closely with Great Britain than with any other country. President **Dwight D. Eisenhower** dealt with three British prime ministers: **Winston Churchill**, **Anthony Eden**, and **Harold Macmillan**.

In 1951, Churchill proposed overthrowing **Iran**'s Prime Minister **Mohammed Mossadegh**, who had ousted the shah of Iran and seized the British-owned oil fields. In 1953, the British and the **Central Intelligence Agency (CIA)** devised a covert operation and arrested Mossadegh. The shah of Iran, an ally of the West who had been living in Italy, returned to head the Iranian government.

In 1956, **Gamal Abdel Nasser**, the newly elected president of Egypt, seized control of the Suez Canal. For decades, Britain and **France** had had military bases in the area, and Nasser wanted all foreign military forces to leave the region. British Prime Minister Anthony Eden joined with France and **Israel** to send forces into Egypt to take control of the canal, thereby creating the **Suez Crisis**. Eisenhower was strongly critical of the attack.

In 1958, when **Lebanon** was on the verge of a civil war, the president of Lebanon, **Camille Chamoun**, referring to the **Eisenhower Doctrine**, asked the United States for military help to restore peace in his country. British Prime Minister Harold Macmillan offered help, and together the United States and Great Britain helped resolve the crisis. *See also* FOREIGN POLICY; PAHLAVI, MOHAMMAD REZA.

GUATEMALA, RELATIONS WITH. In 1951, Jacobo Arbenz Guzman became president of Guatemala and sought to nationalize industry. The United States regarded his election as a threat to the **United Fruit Company**, one of several American companies in Guatemala that could be forced to relinquish its holdings to the Guatemalan government. The **Central Intelligence Agency (CIA)**, headed by **Allen Dulles**, devised a plan to overthrow Arbenz's government using the U.S. military. In 1954, fearing for his life, Arbenz fled the country, which allowed the United States to put a more friendly government in place. *See also* ECONOMY; FOREIGN POLICY.

– H –

HAGERTY, JAMES (1909–1981). White House press secretary 1953–61. Born in New York and educated at Columbia University (B.A., 1934), James Campbell Hagerty worked for the *New York*

Times (1934–42) before becoming New York Governor Thomas E. Dewey's press secretary (1943–52). In 1953, he was appointed President **Dwight D. Eisenhower**'s White House press secretary. Responsible for answering questions about the administration in a timely manner, he informed reporters of the president's daily schedule as well as his reaction to world events. Hagerty was one of the longest-serving press secretaries in history. In 1961–75, Hagerty headed the news bureau at the American Broadcasting System (ABC).

HAIRSTYLES. The most popular hairstyle of the 1950s for young women was the ponytail. Going to the beauty parlor was common, and hairstyles became more involved. As the decade progressed, women began to tease their hair and sculpt it into a beehive, which was piled on one's head.

Many young men followed the hairstyles of **Elvis Presley** and **James Dean**, long sideburns and hair combed in the back into ducktails. Brylcreem was a popular hair-dressing product that gave a "wet look" to men's hair and kept it in place. *See also* FADS; CLOTHING AND FASHION.

HALLECK, CHARLES A. (1900–1986). U.S. House majority leader 1947–48 and 1953–54, and minority leader 1959–60. Born in Indiana, Charles Abraham Halleck received his B.A. (1922) and law degree (1924) from the University of Indiana, Bloomington. He then practiced law in Rensselaer, Indiana. Elected to the House of Representatives (1935) to replace Frederick Landis, who died in office, Halleck, a **Republican**, became a close friend and ally of both President **Dwight D. Eisenhower** and Senator **Everett Dirksen** of Illinois. His voting record was very similar to Dirksen's. While conservative on most issues, both men were major supporters of **civil rights** legislation. He almost always supported Eisenhower's policies. Halleck was a delegate to every Republican National Convention from 1936 to 1968. *See also* CIVIL RIGHTS ACT OF 1957; CIVIL RIGHTS ACT OF 1960.

HAMMARSKJOLD, DAG (1905–1961). UN secretary-general 1953–61. Swedish-born Dag Hammarskjold received two degrees from Uppsala University (1925 and 1928), a law degree in 1930, and a doctoral degree in economics from the University of Stockholm in 1934. In 1930, he began a career in government service that spanned over 30 years. In 1951–53, he was Sweden's foreign minister. In 1953, he became the secretary-general of the **United Nations (UN)**. During the **Suez Crisis** (1956), he organized the UN forces sent to Sinai and Gaza. In 1957, Hammarskjold played a vital role in ending the standoff begun by **Abdel Gamal Nasser**. His life was cut short on 18 September 1961 when he died in a plane crash while trying to end the **Congo Crisis**. He was awarded the Nobel Peace Prize posthumously (1961). *See also* FOREIGN POLICY.

HAMMERSTEIN, OSCAR, II. *See* RODGERS AND HAMMER-STEIN.

HAMMOND, JOHN (1910–1987). Record producer and critic John Hammond was one of the most important people in the popular **music** industry during the 20th century. He is credited with discovering Benny Goodman, **Pete Seeger**, Billie Holiday, Count Basie, Aretha Franklin, and Bob Dylan, among many other singers and musicians. Hammond was a producer, critic, and writer. He also served on the board of the **National Association for the Advancement of Colored People (NAACP)**.

Born into a wealthy New York family, Hammond learned as a young child to play the piano and violin. He entered Yale University (1928) but dropped out to pursue a career in the music industry. At the age of 20, he was a record producer making thousands of dollars by selling copies of the recordings of pianist Garland Wilson. Racial inequities in the music industry made him intent on integrating it, a difficult feat in the 1930s, but one he accomplished in the world of **jazz**. He integrated Benny Goodman's orchestra and invested money in the Café Society, the first integrated nightclub.

Hammond worked for Columbia Records in the 1950s and 1960s, during which time he signed Pete Seeger and Bob Dylan to recording contracts. Retiring in 1975, Hammond scouted the country for new talent. *See also* AFRICAN AMERICANS; *AMERICAN BANDSTAND*; RACIAL INTEGRATION.

HANSBERRY, LORRAINE. *See RAISIN IN THE SUN, A.*

HARLAN, JOHN MARSHALL (1899–1971). Associate justice of the **Supreme Court** 1955–71. Born in Chicago, John Marshall Harlan attended Princeton University (B.A., 1920) and studied for three years as a Rhodes Scholar at Balliol College, Oxford, before completing his education at New York University School of Law (1925). For 25 years, he combined private law practice at a New York law firm with public service for New York State. During World War II, he served in the U.S. Air Force. After the war, he returned to his law practice. In 1951–53, he served as chief counsel to the New York State Crime Commission.

In 1954, President **Dwight D. Eisenhower** appointed Harlan to the U.S. Court of Appeals Second Circuit and later that year to the U.S. Supreme Court, following the death of Justice **Robert Jackson**. A conservative, Harlan often sided with Justice **Felix Frankfurter**. At the same time, he was an outspoken advocate of freedom of speech and the **civil rights movement**. In the 1958 case of *NAACP v. Alabama*, Harlan gave the Court's opinion, which was that the **National Association for the Advancement of Colored People (NAACP)** did not have to disclose its members' names, which invalidated an Alabama law. He agreed with the Court's opinion in *Cooper v. Aaron* (1958), that Arkansas had to desegregate its public schools, and concurred in *Gomillon v. Lightfoot* (1960), which prohibited states from gerrymandering to keep **African Americans** from voting. In 1967, in *Loving v. Virginia*, he agreed that interracial marriages could not be banned by state law.

In other important Supreme Court cases, Harlan's opinions made the suing of newspapers by public officials more difficult. In *New York Times Co. v. Sullivan* (1964), he stated that actual malice had to be proven before a libel suit could go forward. The Court's ruling in *Miranda v. Arizona* (1965) led to the Miranda warning: police must advise people of their rights when taking them into custody. However, he believed too many court rulings made the jobs of law enforcement agencies unnecessarily difficult. *See also* CIVIL RIGHTS ACT OF 1957; CIVIL RIGHTS ACT OF 1960; CIVIL RIGHTS MOVEMENT.

HAWAII. Strategically positioned in the Pacific Ocean, Hawaii became a territory of the United States in 1898. In 1908, Congress authorized construction of a naval base at Pearl Harbor, upsetting many Hawaiians who believed a shark god lived in the area of construction. In 1935, Hickham Field was built. In 1941, it became the home of America's Pacific Fleet. The United States entered World War II after the Japanese attacked Pearl Harbor on 7 December 1941.

In 1959, activists led the way to statehood. One obstacle was the Big Five, plantation owners who could import cheap labor, which by law would end with statehood. However, on 21 August 1959, Hawaii became the 50th state.

HELLMAN, LILLIAN (1905–1984). Born in New Orleans, Lillian Hellman briefly attended New York and Columbia Universities. She worked at a publishing house in New York before moving to California, where she read plays for Metro-Goldwyn-Mayer (MGM). While employed at MGM, she met author Dashiell Hammett, who encouraged her to write. In 1934, her successful play *The Children's Hour* opened, and it ran for over a year on Broadway. Her other popular plays include *Days to Come*, *The Little Foxes*, and *Watch on the Rhine*. Hellman's liberal views eventually led in the 1940s to her being **blacklisted** during the witch hunts of the **House Un-American Activities Committee (HUAC)** and Senator **Joseph McCarthy**. In the 1960s, her views were better received. She taught at several colleges during that period, including Yale and Harvard.

Hellman's life was the subject of three of her books: *An Unfinished Woman*, *Pentimento: A Book of Portraits*, and *Scoundrel Time*. All depicted a woman who was strong during a time of crisis in the country. Many believe these books gave strength to women at the beginning of the **women's movement** in the United States. *See also* CINEMA; LITERATURE; RED SCARE; THEATER.

HEMINGWAY, ERNEST (1899–1961). Journalist and novelist Ernest Hemingway was born in Illinois. He gained his love of hunting and other **sports** from his father, who took his own life when Hemingway was a young man. Hemingway began his writing career as a reporter for the *Kansas City Star* during World War I. His personal experiences during the war became themes in his novels.

Like many writers in the 1920s, Hemingway went to Paris, where he met some of the most notable authors of the period, including Ezra

Pound, Gertrude Stein, James Joyce, and F. Scott Fitzgerald. His first two novels, *In Our Time* and *The Sun Also Rises*, were critically acclaimed. After serving as a journalist in World War II, he lived in **Cuba** until **Fidel Castro**'s revolution.

Hemingway's books reflect his passions: *The Sun Also Rises* (life in Paris in the 1920s), *Death in the Afternoon* (bullfighting), *For Whom the Bell Tolls* (the Spanish Civil War), and *Green Hills of Africa* (big game hunting). One of his most popular works was *The Old Man and the Sea*. Some of Hemingway's novels were made into successful motion pictures.

Unfortunately, Hemingway was a heavy drinker and suffered from depression. In 1961, Hemingway, like his father, took his own life. *See also* CINEMA; LITERATURE.

HERTER, CHRISTIAN A. (1895–1966). Secretary of state 1959–61. Born in Paris and educated at private schools in New York, Christian Archibald Herter received his B.A. from Harvard University (1915). Interested in international relations, he joined the State Department in 1917. He resigned after two years to become an assistant to Herbert Hoover, who was director of the American Relief Administration. He worked with Hoover for four years.

In 1924, Herter resigned from government service to become a **magazine** publisher. In 1931–43, he served in the Massachusetts House of Representatives. This was followed by 10 years in Congress (1943–53). He was governor of Massachusetts from 1953 until 1957, when he was appointed undersecretary of state. Following the death of Secretary of State **John Foster Dulles** in 1959, President **Dwight D. Eisenhower** appointed Herter as Dulles's replacement. During the 1960s, Herter served Presidents **John F. Kennedy** and **Lyndon B. Johnson** on various councils and commissions and in trade negotiations. *See also* FOREIGN POLICY.

HIDDEN PERSUADERS, THE. Journalist **Vance Packard**'s book *The Hidden Persuaders* (1957) was published when advertisers were perfecting subliminal ads. Packard exposed them as manipulative. He also explained how advertisements could make political candidates more appealing. Although some critics disagreed with his book, he was on the cutting edge of consumerism. Whether it was **television**, radio, or **magazines**, advertisers quickly learned the importance of demographics to sell particular products. *See also* ADVERTISING.

HILL, JOSEPH LISTER (1894–1984). Member of the U.S. House of Representatives 1923–38, U.S. senator 1938–69. Born in Montgomery, Alabama, Joseph Lister Hill received his undergraduate and law degrees from the University of Alabama at Tuscaloosa (1914 and 1915). In 1916, he was admitted to the Alabama bar. In 1923, he was elected to Congress to fill a vacancy resulting from the death of John R. Tyson. He served in the House of Representatives (1923–38) before representing Alabama in the U.S. Senate, where he was responsible for more than 60 pieces of legislation related to health care. While in Congress, he was called "the statesman of health." In 1946, he was co-sponsor of the Hill-Burton Act, which provided health care in low-income areas. In Alabama alone, over 67 medical facilities were built as a result of the legislation he co-sponsored. Hill was also one of the most important people behind the creation of the National Institutes of Health and the National Library of Medicine. In addition to his work on health issues, Hill was author or co-author of such other important measures as the Rural Housing Act, the G.I. Bill of Rights for veterans of World War II and the **Korean War**, the **Library Services Act** (1956), and the **National Defense Education Act** (1958). He also supported creation of the **United Nations**.

HITCHCOCK, ALFRED (1899–1980). In **cinema** history, director Alfred Hitchcock is considered the master of suspense. His movie plots were unparalleled and his use of the camera was unequaled. Born in England, Alfred Joseph Hitchcock had a strict father who once sent him to the police station with a note asking that he be briefly jailed. His father wanted the young Hitchcock to know what happened to people who committed crimes or did bad things. This event would haunt him for years.

Hitchcock's interest in the cinema led to a job at a movie studio in London, where he learned the basic skills of filmmaking. *The Lodger* (1926), his breakthrough film, showed Hitchcock's classic plotline, the problems one faced when wrongly accused of a crime. *The Lodger* led to other suspense-filled films, including *Murder!* (1930), *The 39 Steps* (1935), and two 1936 films, *Sabotage* and *Secret Agent*.

In 1940, Hitchcock began his film career in Hollywood, where he mastered cinematic techniques, especially lighting, to create some of the most unforgettable movies, including *Rebecca* (1940), *Spellbound* (1945), *Rope* (1948), *Rear Window* (1954), *To Catch a Thief* (1955), *Psycho* (1960), and *The Birds* (1963). His marketing of *Psycho* was brilliant: he allowed no one to enter the movie theater after the film began. The film's star, Janet Leigh, was killed at the beginning of the movie, unheard of before that time. Hitchcock always had a cameo scene in his movies, often so quick that audiences did not notice his presence. His leading ladies usually were beautiful blondes.

In 1955, Hitchcock began hosting *Alfred Hitchcock Presents*, a half-hour **television** mystery series, which in 1962 became the *Alfred Hitchcock Hour*. Hitchcock introduced each episode with dry wit and closed with an explanation of the culprit's mistake. The television show continued until 1986. Although Hitchcock died in 1980, **computer** processing colorized past episodes, making it seem that Hitchcock was introducing a totally different story. He was the only person in television history to rise from the dead to host a new series. In 1980, Hitchcock was knighted by **Queen Elizabeth II** for his work in the entertainment industry. *See also* DAY, DORIS; KELLY, GRACE; STEWART, JIMMY.

HO CHI MINH (1890–1969). President of the Democratic Republic of **Vietnam** 1945–69. Born in Vietnam, a French colony, Ho Chi Minh watched the French mistreat the peasants in his country. Longing to see French politics for himself, Ho sailed in 1911 for Marseilles, where he worked as a photo retoucher; however, his reputation preceded him, since he had been involved in protests in Vietnam. While in **France**, he became interested in socialist politics and began to advocate Vietnamese independence. In 1920, he helped found the French Communist Party and met with other French Vietnamese with whom he developed his ideas for the liberation of his country.

In 1923, Ho met with Vladimir Lenin in Moscow and in 1925 with **Chiang Kai-shek** in **China**. In 1927, when Chiang denounced communism, Ho returned to Moscow, where he remained until 1940. Returning to Vietnam, he formed the Viet Minh to fight for Vietnam's independence. In 1945, he led a rebellion which seized control of northern Vietnam, occupied Hanoi with little resistance, and established the Democratic Republic of Vietnam. In 1954, the Viet Minh broadened its hold over Vietnam by defeating the French at **Dien Bien Phu**. President **Dwight D. Eisenhower** provided monetary support to the French in their fight against the Viet Minh, but he would not involve the United States militarily.

Following Dien Bien Phu, a conference was held in Geneva in July that divided Vietnam into North and South Vietnam, pending elections for reunification. When South Vietnam refused to hold elections, Ho lent his support to insurgents there. During the presidency of **John F. Kennedy**, the United States sent troops to fight the North Vietnamese. The United States was now at war in Vietnam. *See also* GENEVA CONFERENCE AND ACCORDS; JOHNSON, LYNDON B.; VIETNAM WAR.

HOBBY, OVETA CULP (1905–1995). Secretary of health, education, and welfare 1953–55. Born in Texas, Oveta Culp Hobby received a law degree from the University of Texas (1925). During World War II, she directed the Women's Auxiliary Army Corps (WAAC). After the war, she returned home to Houston, where her husband, former governor of Texas William P. Hobby, owned the *Houston Post*. During **Dwight D. Eisenhower's** presidential campaign, Hobby headed Democrats for Eisenhower. President Eisenhower rewarded her with his newest cabinet position, secretary of health, education, and welfare. In 1955, she resigned to care for her sick husband. *See also* DEPARTMENT OF HEALTH, EDUCATION, AND WELFARE.

HOLLYWOOD. *See* CINEMA.

HOOVER, J. EDGAR (1895–1972). Director of the **Federal Bureau of Investigation** 1924–72. John Edgar Hoover was born in Washington, D.C. He received a law degree from George Washington University in 1917 and began practicing law in Washington, but within two years he was employed by the Department of Justice when Attorney General A. Mitchell Palmer chose Hoover as his assistant. The two men began a campaign to rid the country of communist agitators and anarchists using any means to do so. Even though Hoover was part of the program to spy on Americans, it was Palmer who suffered the brunt of the country's anger.

In 1924, President Warren G. Harding chose Hoover to head the Bureau of Investigation, which was renamed the Federal Bureau of Investigation (FBI) in 1935. As director of the FBI, Hoover made the Bureau an efficient department, but he also dominated his employees. After World War II, Hoover, Senator **Joseph McCarthy**, and the **House Un-American Activities Committee (HUAC)** were involved in witch hunts for Americans who were, or had been, involved with the Communist Party. Even after the **Red Scare** of the 1950s ended, Hoover was still running the FBI with a firm hand. Three presidents, **Harry S. Truman**, **John F. Kennedy**, and **Lyndon B. Johnson**, considered firing Hoover for his obsession to look, often illegally, for subversives. The FBI had files on some of the most important people in politics and the **civil rights movement**, including **Martin Luther King Jr.** *See also* COHN, ROY.

HOPE, BOB (1903–2003). Born in London, Leslie Townes Hope moved with his family to the United States when he was five years old. As a young, man he boxed for a while, but he also sang and danced in vaudeville. In his first feature film, *The Big Broadcast of 1938*, he sang "Thanks for the Memories," which became his theme song. In 1940–52, Bob Hope appeared in a series of *Road to . . .* movies with **Bing Crosby** and Dorothy Lamour, all of which were box office hits. By the 1960s, his **cinema** career was virtually over, but he was a familiar face on **television**. During 1950–95, he starred in television specials and his annual Christmas special, which began in 1953. His quick wit, wisecracks, and impeccable timing delighted audiences. During World War II, the **Korean War**, and the **Vietnam War**, Hope did more for the morale of U.S. troops than any other entertainer. His travels with an entourage of other performers brought delight to U.S. forces in combat areas and hospitals.

Hope garnered two honors in the *Guinness Book of World Records* for holding the longest contract with one network (60 years on NBC), and with over 1,500 awards, the most honored entertainer in history. He received five special Academy Awards for his contributions to the U.S. armed forces.

HORNE, LENA (1917–). The first **African American** to sign a long-term contract with a major Hollywood studio, Lena Horne was born in Brooklyn, New York. She left school at the age of 14 and was soon singing and dancing in the Cotton Club. Her talent led to sell-out audiences. At age 21, she made her first feature film, *The Duke Is Tops* (1938). Racial discrimination limited her roles. During the 1950s, she became involved with the **civil rights movement**. Her friendship with **Paul Robeson** led to her being **blacklisted**.

In the 1940s, Horne appeared in 13 films. In the 1943 movie *Stormy Weather*, she performed the title song, which also became her signature song. Between 1950 and 1956, the period during which she was blacklisted, she did not appear in any films. Horne focused instead on her nightclub career, and she appeared on Broadway in several musicals. Her one-woman show, *Lena Horne: The Lady and Her Music*, still holds the record for the most performances. *See also* CINEMA; HOUSE UN-AMERICAN ACTIVITIES COMMITTEE (HUAC); MCCARTHY, JOSEPH.

HOUSE UN-AMERICAN ACTIVITIES COMMITTEE (HUAC). In 1938, the U.S. House of Representatives formed the House Un-American Activities Committee. The committee's focus was communist subversives within the United States. During the 1950s, the committee terrorized many Americans. Anyone publicly named by HUAC was **blacklisted**, resulting in the loss of employment and friends. Senator **Joseph McCarthy** used a similar committee in the Senate. In 1954, the once powerful HUAC lost much of its importance. Its name was changed to the Committee on Internal Security during **Richard M. Nixon**'s presidency. In 1975, the committee was abolished and its tasks were given to the House Judiciary Committee. *See also* ARMY-MCCATHY HEARINGS; BELAFONTE, HARRY; CINEMA; COHN, ROY; COLD WAR; HELLMAN, LILLIAN; HORNE, LENA; KAZAN, ELIA; MILLER, ARTHUR; MURROW, EDWARD R.; PARKER, DOROTHY; RED SCARE; ROBESON, PAUL; SEEGER, PETE; THEATER; WEAVERS, THE.

HOUSING ACTS. President **Dwight D. Eisenhower** signed five housing acts between 1954 and 1959. The Housing Act of 1954 provided for the building of 35,000 homes in one year for people who had lost their homes due to urban projects. The Housing Act of 1955 provided for the building of 45,000 homes over a two-year period. The Housing Act of 1957 provided more funds for urban renewal. The Housing Act of 1958 reduced minimum down payments and increased available funds for home mortgages. The Housing Act of 1959 cleared slums and provided funds for more urban renewal projects. *See also* ECONOMY; SUBURBIA.

HUGHES, EMMET (1920–1982). Speechwriter for **Dwight D. Eisenhower**. Emmet John Hughes was born in New Jersey and attended Princeton University (B.A., 1941). During World War II, he was stationed in Spain and served as press attaché with the U.S. Embassy, the Office of Strategic Services (OSS), and Office of War Information. In 1949, he moved to New York and worked for Time-Life, Inc., in 1949–56 and again in 1957–60. During Eisenhower's 1952 presidential campaign, Hughes served as his main speechwriter. He wrote Eisenhower's famous speech in which he promised, if elected, to go to Korea to end the **Korean War**.

In 1959, Hughes published the first of several books critical of Eisenhower's presidency. *America the Vincible* ended any relationship he had with Eisenhower. His best-selling 1963 book *The Ordeal of Power: A Political Memoir of the Eisenhower Years* was another attack on Eisenhower. In 1968, Hughes was a speechwriter for **Nelson Rockefeller** in his unsuccessful presidential bid. In 1970, Hughes became a professor of political science at Rutgers University. *See also* ELECTION, 1952; ELECTION, 1956.

HUGHES, LANGSTON (1902–1967). James Langston Hughes was born in Missouri. He began writing poetry while in high school in Ohio. In 1921, he entered Columbia University but left the following year to travel. Offered a scholarship to Lincoln University in Pennsylvania, Hughes returned to complete his college education (B.A., 1929). Hughes wrote poetry, radio and **television** scripts, books, short stories, musicals, and operas. He loved **jazz** and the blues, and the rhythm of this **music** became evident in his writing, particularly his poetry. Three of his many books of poetry are *The First Book of Jazz*, *Tambourines to Glory*, and *Selected Poems*. Hughes was a leading figure in the Harlem Renaissance, an outpouring of **literature**, music, and **art** by **African Americans** in the 1920s. In his attempt to popularize black authors, he edited several anthologies, including *An*

African Treasury and *New Negro Poets: USA*. His book *I Wonder As I Wander* was autobiographical.

HUMPHREY, GEORGE M. (1890–1970). Secretary of the treasury 1953–57. Born in Michigan, George Magoffin Humphrey received his law degree from the University of Michigan (1912) and then began working for his father's steelworks firm, M. A. Hanna and Company, becoming chairman of the board by 1952. In 1953, President **Dwight D. Eisenhower** appointed Humphrey secretary of the treasury. Considered one of the most influential people in Eisenhower's cabinet, he reduced government spending. In 1954, Congress reduced individual income taxes and eliminated excess-profit taxation. In 1956, the federal government had a budget surplus, the first since 1951. Humphrey resigned in 1957 to return to the Hanna Company as its president. *See also* BANKING; ECONOMY; SOCIAL SECURITY.

HUMPHREY, HUBERT H. (1911–1978). U.S. vice president 1964–65. Born in South Dakota, Hubert Horatio Humphrey received degrees from the University of Minnesota (B.A., 1939) and Louisiana State University (M.A., 1940). He taught at Louisiana State University and the University of Minnesota before deciding to enter politics. In 1945, he was elected mayor of Minneapolis after narrowly losing two years earlier. He quickly became one of the rising stars of the **Democratic Party**. In 1948, he was elected to the U.S. Senate, where he championed tax reforms, **civil rights**, and pro-labor legislation. He also formed a close relationship with **Lyndon B. Johnson**. Humphrey was reelected to the Senate in 1954. After trying unsuccessfully to gain the Democratic nomination for president in 1956, he ran for president in 1960 but lost after a bitter primary struggle to **John F. Kennedy**.

In the 1964, presidential campaign, Lyndon B. Johnson chose Humphrey as his running mate in his successful bid for a full term as president. As vice president, Humphrey served mainly as the country's goodwill ambassador. He was also a member of several presidential commissions. Using his former Senate position, he tried to defend the president's policies on the **Vietnam War**.

Johnson decided not to seek reelection in 1968, and Humphrey won the Democratic presidential nomination. He narrowly lost the election to **Republican** candidate **Richard M. Nixon**. Humphrey's support of President Johnson's war policies was his downfall. Humphrey remained in the Senate until his death in 1978.

HUNGARIAN REVOLUTION, 1956. In 1956, students in Budapest held protest marches against control of Hungary by the **Soviet Union**. They were soon joined by other citizens angered because of poor housing and working conditions. When the Soviet secret police fired on the protestors, Hungarians tried to fight back. Premier **Nikita Khrushchev** sent in Soviet troops to end the protests. A new pro-Soviet government was established, headed by Janos Kadar. During Kadar's years in office, many Hungarians were executed or held in prison. Nine years after the 1956 Hungarian Revolution, Kadar freed all political prisoners.

When the Hungarians were fighting for their freedom, the United States was involved in the **Suez Crisis**. After leaving the presidency, **Dwight D. Eisenhower** stated his regret at his inability to help the Hungarian people. *See also* REFUGEE RELIEF ACT.

HYDROGEN BOMB. After the **Soviet Union** detonated its first **atomic** bomb in 1949, President **Harry S. Truman** approved the development of the more powerful hydrogen bomb (H-bomb). In 1952, the United States tested its first hydrogen bomb. The following year, the Soviets dropped an even more powerful H-bomb. The development of the hydrogen bomb has been severely criticized by many scientists opposed to the proliferation of nuclear weapons. *See also* TECHNOLOGICAL INNOVATIONS.

– I –

IMMIGRATION AND NATIONALITY ACT, 1952. In response to the **Cold War** and the threat of communism, Senator Pat McCarran and Representative Francis Walter, both **Democrats**, won approval for the Immigration and Nationality Act, also known as the McCarran-Walter Act, which allowed the federal government to deport anyone who was involved in sabotage against the United States. It also barred suspected subversives from entering the United States, including former Communist Party members, even if they had not been a member of the party for many years. *See also* COHN, ROY; HOUSE UN-AMERICAN ACTIVITIES COMMITTEE (HUAC); MCCARTHY, JOSEPH.

IN GOD WE TRUST. In 1953, the phrase "In God We Trust" was added to U.S. coins. In 1955, President **Dwight D. Eisenhower** signed legislation that added the phrase to all currency. The phrase was added as part of a widespread reaction against communism, which advocated atheism. *See also* COLD WAR; HOUSE UN-AMERICAN ACTIVITIES COMMITTEE (HUAC); MCCARTHY, JOSEPH; RED SCARE; RELIGION.

INDIA, RELATIONS WITH. Even before gaining independence from **Great Britain** in 1947, India had established in 1925 a department to keep in contact with the outside world. **Jawaharlal Nehru**, who had always been interested in world affairs, kept other nations informed about India's struggle for independence. When independence was finally attained, Nehru became prime minister. He criticized America's **foreign policy** during the administrations of **Harry S. Truman** and **Dwight D. Eisenhower**, especially during the **Korean War** and the **Cold War**. India believed in nonalignment, but it was an active participant in the **United Nations (UN)** and an important power in world affairs.

India's belief in not aligning with either the Western or Soviet power blocs kept the country neutral during the Korean War. Its location, however, made it vulnerable during conflicts in South Asia. During the Korean War, India approved the UN Security Council's resolution calling for military sanctions against North Korea. India also wanted **China** admitted to the UN. India and China were on good terms at this time, and since China had intervened in the Korean War, Nehru believed China's admittance into the UN might help end the war. Nehru's idea was rejected. He repeatedly sent the United States and the **Soviet Union** messages in his attempt to restore peace to the region. It took Eisenhower's election to the U.S. presidency and his promise to go to Korea to end the war.

During the Cold War, Secretary of State **John Foster Dulles** was particularly angered by India's policy of nonalignment. He viewed nonalignment as the inability to choose freedom over communism. To strengthen relations, the United States gave India economic aid. However, Nehru was angry when the United States signed a military alliance with Pakistan, one of India's border enemies.

In accordance with his belief in **Atoms for Peace**, Eisenhower offered nuclear **technology** to India. By 1974, India detonated its first nuclear weapon. *See also* ATOMIC AND NUCLEAR ENERGY; FOREIGN POLICY.

INGE, WILLIAM (1913–1973). William Motter Inge, who was born in Kansas, graduated from the University of Kansas (B.A., 1935) and continued his education at the George Peabody College for Teachers (M.A., 1938). He began his career as a drama teacher at Stephens College in Missouri (1938–43). He loved the **theater**, and while working as a drama and music critic on a St. Louis newspaper, he met **Tennessee Williams**, who encouraged him to write plays. While teaching at Washington University in St. Louis (1946–49), Inge wrote *Come Back Little Sheba*. The critically acclaimed Broadway play was turned into a film in 1952, winning a number of academy awards. Other **cinema** successes adapted from his plays include *Picnic* (1953), based on his Pulitzer Prize play; *Bus Stop* (1956), which starred **Marilyn Monroe**; and *The Dark at the Top of the Stairs* (1960). His script for the 1961 movie *Splendor in the Grass* won an Academy Award. Except for *Splendor in the Grass*, none of his subsequent works met with much box office success. Believing he had lost his ability to write, Inge fell into a deep depression. In 1973, he committed suicide.

INTEGRATED CIRCUIT. *See* KILBY, JACK; TECHNOLOGICAL INNOVATIONS.

INTER-AMERICAN DEVELOPMENT BANK (IADB). After his election in 1956, President Juscelino Kubitschek of Brazil sought to raise living standards throughout Latin America. As a result of his influence and that of President **Dwight D. Eisenhower**, the **Organization of American States (OAS)** created the Inter-American Development Bank in 1959 to promote social and economic development in Latin America and the Caribbean. Initially the financial institution was funded at $1 billion. As a result of the threat of communism following **Fidel Castro**'s revolution in **Cuba**, another $500 million were added to the bank's funding. Located in Washington, D.C., the IADB continues to finance social and economic projects for the 47 countries that are its members. *See also* FOREIGN POLICY.

INTERCONTINENTAL BALLISTIC MISSILE (ICBM). President **Dwight D. Eisenhower** realized that nuclear weapons had changed the way future wars would be conducted. He wanted to focus on missiles with nuclear warheads that could travel long distances and quickly end hostile activities. Three military advances during the **Cold War** allowed for the creation of intercontinental ballistic missiles (ICBMs): more powerful **atomic** and **hydrogen** bombs were developed; guidance systems for missiles were improved; and boosters became more powerful, allowing missiles to travel farther and faster. Since ICBMs are large, they cannot be fired from ships at sea, as can their smaller counterparts, the **intermediate-range ballistic missiles (IRBMs)**. When detonated, an ICBM can travel 5,000–6,000 miles in about half an hour to its designated target.

INTERMEDIATE-RANGE BALLISTIC MISSILE (IRBM). Developed during the **Cold War**, ballistic missiles are categorized by the distance they can travel. Intermediate-range ballistic missiles (IRBMs) can travel between 200 and 1,500 miles. Although traveling shorter distances than **intercontinental ballistic missiles (ICBMs)**, IRBMs are more versatile and smaller than ICBMs. They have the capability of being launched from ships or submarines as well as from land.

INTERNATIONAL ATOMIC ENERGY AGENCY (IAEA). In 1946, **Harry S. Truman** sent **Bernard Baruch** to the first meeting at the **United Nations** of the **Atomic Energy Commission (AEC)**. Since only the United States had the **atomic** bomb, Baruch proposed that the United States head the commission, a plan the **Soviet Union** rejected. After the Soviet Union developed nuclear weapons, President **Dwight D. Eisenhower** proposed an **Atoms for Peace** plan at the United Nations in 1953. He proposed allowing only the peaceful use of atomic energy. His speech led to the creation of the

International Atomic Energy Agency, which today has 130 member nations. The IAEA headquarters is in Vienna, Austria.

INTERNATIONAL GEOPHYSICAL YEAR, 1957–1958. For 18 months, scientists from 67 countries participated in a study of the earth, the oceans, the atmosphere, and the sun. Similar research had been done in the 1930s, but the enormous advances in **technology** since that time provided for more advanced scientific study. Scientists gave Antarctica particularly close scrutiny. **Space** satellites were used by scientists from the **Soviet Union** and America to probe the atmosphere, a technology not available in the 1930s. Major discoveries were made concerning the climate, the ocean floor, and the earth's atmosphere. Antarctica was designated as a nonmilitary area to be used only for scientific research. To this day, Antarctica is still used for gathering scientific information, including the effects of moisture and carbon dioxide on the atmosphere.

INTERSTATE HIGHWAY SYSTEM. Because of the increased number of **automobiles** and the development after World War II of **suburbia**, American automakers lobbied the federal government for an interstate highway system. The **Cold War** and the possibility of nuclear war also underscored the need for roads to evacuate large cities. Recalling the difficulty he had encountered on dirt roads in 1918 when he drove across the country, President **Dwight D. Eisenhower** signed into law the 1956 Federal-Aid Highway Act. It authorized an interstate highway system to crisscross the United States from north to south and east to west. The Interstate Highway System was later renamed the Dwight David Eisenhower National System of Interstate and Defense Highways, and these roads are part of the National Highway System.

The system is funded by the federal government but is maintained by the individual states. Even-numbered highways cross the United States from east to west while odd-numbered highways go from north to south. The highway system has proved invaluable during evacuations prior to hurricanes and other natural disasters. The speed limit on these highways varies. In the more populated areas of the eastern United States, the speed limit is lower than in the more sparsely populated western states.

Eisenhower's Atoms for Peace address before the United Nations Assembly, 8 December 1953.

Eisenhower giving one of his many radio and television broadcasts from the Oval Office and the White House Broadcast Room.

Eisenhower and Mamie during the 1956 campaign for reelection, Washington, D.C., November 1956.

Eisenhower signing legislation for Alaska Statehood, 3 January 1959, in the White House. Some in attendance were Richard M. Nixon, E. L. Bartlett, Fred Seaton, Waine Hendrickson, David W. Kendall, Sam Rayburn, Michael Stepovich, and Robert Atwood.

Dwight D. Eisenhower and Richard M. Nixon with Anne and David Eisenhower and Julie and Tricia Nixon at the 1957 inauguration.

President Eisenhower discussing the Middle East situation in a radio and television broadcast from the Oval Office and the White House Broadcast Room.

President Eisenhower signing the 1954 Federal-Aid Highway Act, the White House, 6 May 1954.

Senate luncheon on 4 March 1953; those in attendance were John F. Kennedy, Hubert Humphrey, Mike Mansfield, A. S. Mike Moroney, Harley M. Kilgore, Albert Gore, Henry M. Jackson, Price Daniel, Earle Clements, Wilton Pearsons, Stuart Symington, Paul Douglas, Herbert Lehman, Thomas Hennings, and Sherman Adams.

November 1953, Eisenhower with members of the Supreme Court.

The first time an entire official family attended church services with an incoming president was on 20 January 1953, when President-elect Eisenhower and his staff attended a preinaugural service at the National Presbyterian Church on Connecticut Avenue, Washington, D.C. The Rev. Edward L. R. Elson, pastor of the church, conducted the service.

Second inauguration. The first president to be sworn in on 20 January was Franklin D Roosevelt when he was sworn in for his second of four terms in 1937. Eisenhower tool the oath for his second term on Sunday, 20 January 1957, and was formally inaugurated in public on Monday, 21 January. Ronald Reagan followed the same scenario in 198! after winning reelection. Every 28 years, 20 January falls on a Sunday.

Eisenhower and Nixon during the 1952 presidential campaign.

General Eisenhower and Winston Churchill, northern France, June 1944.

John Foster Dulles, Winston Churchill, Eisenhower, Anthony Eden, 25 June 1954, the White House.

Denver, Colorado: Dwight and Mamie's wedding portrait, 1 July 1916.

Roy Rogers, Mamie, Barbara, John, Mamie's mother Elivera Doud, Eisenhower, and Dale Evans, at David Eisenhower's birthday party, March 1956.

British Queen Elizabeth II at the St. Lawrence Seaway dedication, 26 June 1959.

IRAN, RELATIONS WITH. American oil interests in Iran were compromised when **Mohammed Mossadegh** became Iran's prime minister and nationalized the Iranian oil fields. Mossadegh threatened to turn to the **Soviet Union** for help should the United States attempt to intervene. In response, President **Dwight D. Eisenhower** and the **Central Intelligence Agency (CIA)**, under the direction of **Allen Dulles**, devised a plan known as "Operation Ajax" to overthrow Mossadegh and reinstate the pro-Western shah, **Mohammad Reza Pahlavi**. Operation Ajax was a covert operation, spearheaded by the United States and **Great Britain**, that used a CIA-financed coup to topple Mossadegh in 1953. Mossadegh was imprisoned and the shah was reinstated as Iran's leader. *See also* COLD WAR; FOREIGN POLICY.

ISRAEL, RELATIONS WITH. From the establishment of the state of Israel in 1948 to the present, the location of the Jewish state among Arab countries has led to conflicts. During the 1950s, for example, Egyptian Intelligence trained fighters and stationed them on bases in Egypt, Jordan, and **Lebanon** to carry out attacks within Israel. These attacks, in 1951–56, violated a **United Nations** Armistice Agreement made in 1949 prohibiting the use of paramilitary forces. In 1955, Egypt purchased arms from the **Soviet Union** and seized control of the Suez Canal. In response, Israel sought military aid from the United States. President **Dwight D. Eisenhower** refused to get involved, telling the Israelis instead to seek help from **France**. Eisenhower believed in Israel's right to exist, but some historians contend he minimized relations with Israel during his presidency. During his second term, Israel was accused of making nuclear weapons, but Eisenhower did not pursue this matter. *See also* ATOMIC AND NUCLEAR ENERGY; FOREIGN POLICY; NASSER, GAMAL ABDEL; SUEZ CRISIS.

– J –

JACKSON, CHARLES D. (1902–1964). Special assistant to President **Dwight D. Eisenhower**. Born in New York City and educated at Princeton University (B.A., 1924), Charles Douglas Jackson developed a background in psychological warfare. During World War II, he worked in the Office of Strategic Services (OSS). In 1945–49, he was Time-Life International's managing director and publisher of *Fortune*. Jackson's expertise in psychology was invaluable when dealing with the **Soviet Union** during the **Cold War**. One of those responsible for Eisenhower's famous 1953 **Atoms for Peace** speech, he served as the president's special assistant for international affairs in 1952–53. After **Sherman Adams** resigned as Eisenhower's chief of staff in 1958, Jackson returned to assist Eisenhower. In 1960, however, he resigned to become publisher of *Life*.

JACKSON, ROBERT H. (1892–1954). Associate justice of the **Supreme Court** 1941–54. An eloquent speaker and lifelong **Democrat**, Robert Houghwout Jackson was born in Pennsylvania. After only a year at Albany Law School (1911), he passed the bar. He practiced law for a year before entering politics, but finding political life demanding, he returned to his law practice. During Franklin D. Roosevelt's administration, Jackson was appointed to various legal positions culminating in his appointment as attorney general of the United States in 1940. In 1941, Roosevelt appointed Jackson to the Supreme Court. At the Nuremberg trials of war criminals at the end of World War II, he served as the chief prosecutor for the United States. In the Supreme Court's decision in *West Virginia State Board of Education v. Barnette* (1943), Jackson stated schoolchildren did not have to salute the American flag. He predicated this decision on his strong belief in freedom of speech. His belief in freedom of **religion** influenced many of his decisions.

JAPANESE PEACE TREATY, 1951. Before becoming President **Dwight D. Eisenhower**'s secretary of state, diplomat **John Foster Dulles** negotiated and signed the 1951 Japanese Peace Treaty. Its purpose was twofold, to end the formal state of war with Japan, and to make Japan an ally of the United States. A major provision of the treaty allowed U.S. troops to remain in Japan. It was officially signed by 49 nations on 8 September 1951 in San Francisco, California, and is therefore also known as the San Francisco Treaty.

JAZZ. In the 1950s, jazz was a popular form of **music**. Many Americans listened to jazz performances in nightclubs, on the radio, and on

television. But a new sound was becoming popular, **rock and roll**, a combination of gospel, jazz, and rhythm and blues. Jazz musicians responded with their own sound, free jazz.

In 1954, Elaine and Louis L. Lorillard of Newport, Rhode Island, heirs to a tobacco fortune, announced the first Newport Jazz Festival. From 1954 until 1971, the event was held in Newport. In 1972, the festival moved to New York City, but since 1981, it has been held in both New York City and Newport. In 1986, the name was changed to the JVC Jazz Festival.

During the 1950s, the Newport Jazz Festival featured some of the greatest jazz composers and musicians. Two of the most memorable performances in the history of the festival were Miles Davis's rendition of jazz artist Thelonious Monk's "Round Midnight" (1955) and the Duke Ellington Orchestra's performance of Ellington's composition "Diminuendo and Crescendo" (1956). Ray Charles, **John Coltrane**, Count Basie, and Herbie Mann have performed at the festival.

American jazz guitarist **Les Paul** introduced the solid-body electric guitar. The guitar and Paul's other innovations, including overdubbing and delay effects, gave jazz a whole new sound. Improvisation was also part of free jazz. Ella Fitzgerald and Frank Sinatra were two of the 1950s best jazz singers.

JOHN BIRCH SOCIETY. In response to the growing fear of communism in the 1950s, Robert Welch Jr., a retired candy manufacturer, formed a right-wing group that he named after John Birch, who had been killed in 1945 by the Chinese Communists. In Welch's opinion, Birch was "the first American victim of the Cold War." Thousands of Americans joined Welch in his support of Senator **Joseph McCarthy**'s hunt for alleged communists. Welch accused Presidents **Harry S. Truman** and **Dwight D. Eisenhower** of being **Soviet Union** agents as well as communist sympathizers. Welch also accused Eisenhower's brother, **Milton Eisenhower**, of communist beliefs that influenced the president. President Eisenhower never responded to Welch's accusations. *See also* COLD WAR; HOUSE UN-AMERICAN ACTIVITIES COMMITTEE (HUAC); RED SCARE.

JOHNSON, LYNDON B. (1908–1973). U.S. president 1963–68. A lifelong **Democrat**, Lyndon B. Johnson was born and raised in Texas.

He received his college education at Southwest Texas State Teachers College (B.A., 1929) and became involved in Texas politics when he was in his 20s. In 1937, he was elected to the U.S. House of Representatives and was reelected five times, running unopposed in some elections. In 1949–61, Johnson served in the U.S. Senate. Through most of the 1950s, Johnson voted with other southern Democrats against **civil rights** legislation. Johnson believed in civil rights, but he was caught between his southern roots and his position in Congress. He opposed the **Supreme Court**'s decision in *Brown v. Board of Education* because he thought it would cause riots in the South. He was, however, one of Eisenhower's main supporters in the passage of the **Civil Rights Act of 1960**, which helped protect **African Americans'** right to vote. In 1960, **John F. Kennedy** chose Johnson as his running mate on the Democratic ticket. Johnson became president in November 1963 after Kennedy's assassination. In 1964, he won a landslide victory for president against his **Republican** opponent, Barry Goldwater. The **Vietnam War**, however, destroyed Johnson's presidency, and he chose not to run for a second term. *See also* CIVIL RIGHTS ACT OF 1957; CIVIL RIGHTS MOVEMENT; RACIAL INTEGRATION.

JONES, JAMES (1921–1977). Author James Jones was born and educated in Robinson, Illinois. After serving in World War II he returned to Robinson, where he began to write about his experiences during the war. In 1951, he published the critically acclaimed novel *From Here to Eternity*, which in 1953 became a major motion picture. In 1949, Jones helped to establish the Handy Writers' Colony in Marshall, Illinois, where fledgling authors studied with established writers. In the mid-1960s, Jones joined other American expatriates in Paris, where he continued to write. His novels include *Some Came Running* (1957) and *The Thin Red Line* (1962), both of which became feature films. During the **Vietnam War**, which he bitterly opposed, the *New York Times Magazine* employed Jones as a war correspondent. *See also* CINEMA; LITERATURE.

– K –

KAYE, DANNY (1913–1987). Born David Daniel Kaminski in Brooklyn, New York, Danny Kaye began performing at the age of

13 in Catskill Mountain resorts. His ability to do tongue twisters quicker than anyone else delighted audiences. He also performed on Broadway and later signed a contract with Metro-Goldwyn-Mayer. His movies often included his tongue twisters. During the 1950s, he starred in some of MGM's most popular musical comedies, including *The Court Jester*, which some critics considered his best performance. He also performed for four years (1963–67) in his own **television** show and appeared as a guest conductor with some of the finest orchestras in the world. From 1954 until his death in 1987, he worked as a goodwill ambassador for the **United Nations** Children's Fund (UNICEF). In 1965, when UNICEF received the Nobel Peace Prize, Danny Kaye was asked to represent the organization at the ceremony. *See also* CINEMA.

KAZAN, ELIA (1909–2003). Director Elia Kazan was born in Turkey but raised in New York. Educated at Williams College (A.B., 1930), Yale University (1930–32), and Wesleyan University (M.F.A., 1955), he began his directing career on Broadway. He later founded the Actors Studio with Lee Strasberg. In addition to his work in **theater**, Kazan directed some of Hollywood's best actors in **cinema**, including Gregory Peck in *Gentleman's Agreement* (1947), **Marlon Brando** in *Viva Zapata* (1952) and *On the Waterfront* (1954), and Lee J. Cobb in *America, America* (1963).

When Kazan was called to testify before the **House Un-American Activities Committee (HUAC),** he refused at first to provide names of suspected communists in Hollywood. When he was informed that if he did not do so, he would be **blacklisted**, he testified giving the names of several communist sympathizers or Communist Party members. As a result, he was blacklisted in his own way by many colleagues in the entertainment industry. In 1999, the Academy Awards honored Kazan with an Oscar for his lifetime achievement. Many in the entertainment industry did not believe Kazan deserved to receive the honor, while others understood his predicament in the 1950s. Kazan wrote in his biography that he had to think of himself and his family first when he finally named people before HUAC. During the 1950s, when Senator **Joseph McCarthy** was promoting fears about communists in America, no other director was as controversial as Kazan. *See also* COLD WAR; RED SCARE.

KEFAUVER, ESTES (1903–1963). U.S. representative 1939–49, U.S. senator 1949–63. Born and raised in Tennessee, Carey Estes Kefauver received his B.A. from the University of Tennessee (1924) and his law degree from Yale University Law School (1927). A member of the **Democratic Party**, he was elected to the U.S. House of Representatives in 1939. After his election to the Senate in 1948, he became chair of the Senate Committee on Organized Crime, better known as the Kefauver Committee. Its two-year investigation resulted in Kefauver's book *Crime in America* (1951), and it made him a nationally known political figure. Although Kefauver was unsuccessful in his bid for the Democratic presidential nomination in the **1952** and **1956 elections**, **Adlai Stevenson** chose him as his running mate in 1956.

KELLER, HELEN (1880–1968). Stricken with an illness as a child, Helen Keller was left blind and deaf. With the help of her teacher Anne M. Sullivan, Keller learned to speak and write. As the first deaf and blind graduate of Radcliffe College (1904), Keller became an activist for those with disabilities. A pacifist, socialist, and advocate of **birth control**, Keller traveled around the world promoting her causes. She met with President **Dwight D. Eisenhower** in 1954 and President **John F. Kennedy** in 1961. In 1964, President **Lyndon B. Johnson** honored her with the Medal of Freedom for her work helping others who are handicapped.

KELLY, GRACE (1929–1982). Actress Grace Kelly was born in Pennsylvania. After graduating from high school in 1947, she left for New York, where she worked as a model until 1949, when she debuted on Broadway. In 1951, she went to Hollywood to begin her career in **cinema**. In 1952, she starred opposite Gary Cooper in the highly acclaimed western *High Noon*. In 1953, she starred in *Mogambo*. Director **Alfred Hitchcock**, notorious for starring beautiful blondes in his movies, chose Kelly for several of his films, including *Dial M for Murder* and *Rear Window*. She also appeared opposite **Bing Crosby** in the 1954 film *The Country Girl*, for which she won an Academy Award for Best Actress.

On a trip to the Cannes Film Festival in 1955, Kelly met Prince Rainier, the ruler of Monaco. Within six months, the prince and Kelly were engaged. Their wedding was a worldwide **television** event. After her marriage, Kelly did not continue her acting career. She died in an automobile accident in 1982.

KENNAN, GEORGE F. (1904–2005). George Frost Kennan was born in Wisconsin. After graduation from Princeton University (1925), he served in minor diplomatic posts in Geneva and Hamburg. From 1929 to 1931, he studied the Russian language and culture while living in Berlin. At the beginning of World War II, Kennan was interned by the Germans. Freed in 1942, he spent the following two war years in Lisbon and London. In 1944–46, he served as minister-counselor in Moscow.

Kennan returned to the United States in 1946. Having lived in the **Soviet Union** he had developed theories about postwar Soviet **foreign policy**. In 1947–49, while the director of the Policy Planning Staff of the State Department, he wrote an article in *Foreign Affairs* calling for the **containment** of the **Soviet Union**. That article, famous as "Article X," became the blueprint for much of American foreign policy during the **Cold War**.

In 1952, President **Dwight D. Eisenhower** appointed Kennan ambassador to Russia. His appointment was short-lived. While on a trip in Berlin, Kennan made comments about the poor treatment that Western diplomats received in the Soviet Union, which led to his recall as ambassador. Soon thereafter he left the foreign service. For the remainder of the 1950s he was a professor of history at Princeton University.

In 1961, President **John F. Kennedy** appointed Kennan ambassador to Yugoslavia. After two years, he returned to Princeton University, angered by the Cold War attitude of the Kennedy administration. Kennan wrote several books, including *American Diplomacy, 1900–1950* (1951), *Russia, the Atom, and the West* (1958), and *A Cloud of Danger* (1977). *See also* FOREIGN POLICY.

KENNEDY, JOHN F. (1917–1963). U.S. president 1961–63. John Fitzgerald Kennedy was born into a wealthy Massachusetts family. Educated at Harvard University (B.A., 1940), he served in the U.S. Navy during World War II. He entered politics in 1946, winning three terms in the U.S. House of Representatives. In 1952, he was elected to the U.S. Senate. While ill for a time from an old back injury and unable to be in Washington, he wrote his Pulitzer Prize–winning *Profiles in Courage* (1956).

In 1956, Kennedy almost won the **Democratic Party**'s nomination for vice president. The Democratic national convention proved to be a launching pad for his successful bid for the presidency in 1960. His 1960 campaign was well-organized; money was no object. A series of **television** debates between Kennedy and his **Republican** opponent Vice President **Richard M. Nixon** proved decisive in Kennedy's narrow victory in November. Kennedy was knowledgeable, extremely photogenic, and promised progressive ideas concerning **civil rights**, housing, health, and defense.

In 1962, Kennedy learned the **Soviet Union** had positioned missiles in **Cuba** aimed at the United States. This was one of the most trying times in the nation's history; however, the president's cool handling of the crisis helped to avoid a nuclear war. On 22 November 1963, Kennedy was assassinated in Dallas, Texas. *See also* BAY OF PIGS; CASTRO, FIDEL; FOREIGN POLICY.

KEROUAC, JACK (1922–1969). Massachusetts-born Jack Kerouac always knew he wanted to be a writer. He carried a notebook with him in which he wrote down his thoughts. He was also an athlete who won a scholarship to Columbia University in 1940, but in 1942 he dropped out before graduating. In 1948–49, he attended the New School for Social Research. A wanderer, in 1957 he published *On the Road* about his travels. Some of the characters in his books were patterned after his friends, who included **Allen Ginsberg** and **William S. Burroughs**. Kerouac was a leading figure of the **Beat Generation**. His drinking led to his death at the age of 47. *See also* LITERATURE.

KHRUSHCHEV, NIKITA (1894–1971). Premier of the **Soviet Union** 1957–64. Nikita Sergeyevich Khrushchev was a shepherd and a locksmith before he joined the Communist Party. He rose quickly to become a top member of the Soviet leadership by 1939. During World War II, he was instrumental in thwarting the German invasion into the Ukraine. After the war, he headed the reconstruction of that area. After **Joseph Stalin**'s death in 1953, Khrushchev became first secretary of the party. In 1957, he became the premier of the Soviet Union.

Khrushchev ended riots in Poland and East Germany and crushed the **Hungarian Revolution** in 1956. In 1957, the Soviet Union launched the first satellite, *Sputnik*. The **space** race had officially begun. But in 1959, there was a brief thaw when Khrushchev visited President **Dwight D. Eisenhower** and traveled on to California.

But the rivalry continued. In 1962, he attempted to place missiles in **Cuba** aimed at the United States. Khrushchev is often remembered for pounding his shoe on a desk at the **United Nations**. The event was in response to the downing of an American **U-2** spy plane over the Soviet Union in 1959. His actions at the UN were embarrassing to the Soviet Union. In 1964, Khrushchev was replaced as Soviet leader by Leonid Brezhnev and Aleksei Kosygin. *See also* COLD WAR; FOREIGN POLICY.

KILBY, JACK (1923–2005). A scientist and inventor, Jack St. Clair Kilby was born in Missouri but grew up in Kansas. He attended the University of Illinois at Champaign-Urbana (B.S., 1947), where he majored in electrical engineering, and the University of Wisconsin (M.S., 1950). He was employed at Texas Instruments, where he worked with **computer** circuits. The materials used in these circuits were not only slow but also expensive. Kilby tried putting the transistors in germanium and then into a crystal chip that was no bigger than a paper clip. In this way, the integrated circuit was born in 1958 and patented in 1959. Months later, Robert Noyce, co-founder of Intel, used silicon in place of germanium. Kilby was also the co-inventor of the pocket calculator. He taught at Texas A&M for several years while still employed at Texas Instruments. Recipient of over 60 patents, he is considered one of the world's greatest electrical engineers. His invention of the integrated circuit, or microchip, has made computing and communications affordable, convenient, and extremely efficient. Kilby won a Nobel Prize in 2000. *See also* TECHNOLOGICAL INNOVATIONS.

KIM IL SUNG (1912–1994). Premier of North Korea 1948–72, president of North Korea 1972–94. Kim Il Sung was born in Pyongyang, Korea. In 1920, his family, opposed to the Japanese occupation of their country, fled to Manchuria, where Kim became fluent in Chinese. In the 1930s, he joined the Chinese Communist Party. He was able to return to Korea in 1945 and founded the Workers' Party. By 1947, the **Soviet Union** controlled North Korea and made Kim Il Sung leader of the country. In 1948, Kim proclaimed North Korea a republic. He was a shrewd politician who knew how to challenge other communist leaders. When Kim decided to invade South Korea, some American politicians, including Secretary of State **Dean Acheson**, concluded Kim did not believe the United States would retaliate. Fearing the spread of communism, the United States took military action against North Korea's invasion of South Korea, which led to the **Korean War** (1950–53).

While Kim kept North Korea closely allied to the Soviet Union, he also pursued a more generally isolationist policy. He groomed his son to be his heir, and upon his death in 1994, Kim Jong Il became North Korea's president. *See also* FOREIGN POLICY.

KING, CORETTA SCOTT (1927–2006). Civil rights activist Coretta Scott King was born in Alabama. When she was admitted to Antioch College (A.B., 1951), she was the first female **African American** accepted to the Ohio school. She later trained at the New England Conservatory of Music in Boston with the intention of being a singer. While living in Boston, she met **Martin Luther King Jr.**, whom she subsequently married. She joined him in the civil rights movement. After her husband was assassinated, she continued the work he had begun. In 1968, she founded the King Center, whose mission is to continue Martin Luther King Jr.'s legacy of solving problems nonviolently. In addition to her work in behalf of African Americans, she was an advocate of rights for women, gays, and lesbians. She also sought to prevent the spread of AIDS. During her life, she received many awards and honorary degrees. *See also* CIVIL RIGHTS ACT OF 1957; CIVIL RIGHTS ACT OF 1960; EDUCATION; FAUBUS, ORVAL; MONTGOMERY BUS BOYCOTT; PARKS, ROSA; RACIAL INTEGRATION; SIT-IN; SOUTHERN CHRISTIAN LEADERSHIP CONFERENCE (SCLC); SUPREME COURT.

KING, MARTIN LUTHER, JR. (1929–1968). Minister and **civil rights** activist Martin Luther King Jr. was born in Atlanta, where his father was the minister of the Ebenezer Baptist Church. After receiving his Ph.D. from Boston University (1955), King followed in his father's footsteps. Graduating from the Chicago Theological Seminary (D.D., 1957), he became a minister of a Baptist church in Montgomery, Alabama. The arrest of **Rosa Parks**, after her refusal to give up her seat on a bus, led to the **Montgomery Bus Boycott** (1955–56). King was instrumental in organizing the boycott that made him a national figure in the civil rights movement. His nonviolent approach to ending discrimination and his eloquence as a speaker were his greatest strengths.

In 1960, King left Montgomery to become co-pastor at his father's Atlanta church. When students began **sit-ins** in North Carolina at a lunch counter, he asked the **Southern Christian Leadership Conference (SCLC)** to finance a meeting with the students. With both King's and the SCLC's help, the Student Non-violent Coordinating Committee (SNCC) was formed. As he traveled back to Atlanta, he was arrested for violating a one-year probation stemming from a past protest demonstration. His imprisonment at a rural penal camp led to a national outcry. **John F. Kennedy**, the **Democratic** presidential candidate in the **1960 election**, with help from his brother Robert F. Kennedy, won the release of King, which virtually guaranteed the **African American** vote for Kennedy in the election.

In 1961, a group of Americans, who came to be known as Freedom Riders, went to Montgomery to protest segregation at bus terminals in the South. When violence against the protesters began, King immediately sought to quell it. He also led peaceful demonstrations in Albany, Georgia.

The protests proved unsuccessful. To regain momentum, he ordered demonstrations in 1963 in Birmingham, Alabama, that included children. The protestors marched on city hall but were repelled by water cannons and nightsticks. President Kennedy sent his assistant attorney general to end the violence. In response to the violence and federal intervention, city leaders decided to integrate city businesses, upgrade black workers, and establish a biracial committee. Reaction to these changes led to the bombings of the home of King's brother and the headquarters of the SCLC. In response, Kennedy spoke to the country, labeling discrimination a moral issue. He also sent Congress a civil rights bill, which eventually became the Civil Rights Act of 1964, signed by President **Lyndon B. Johnson**.

Birmingham was followed by other protests throughout the South. In 1963, King led a march on Washington, D.C., during which he delivered his famous "I Have a Dream" speech. Throughout the 1960s, King was able to bridge the gap between black activists and civil rights advocates. His nonviolent message was followed by the majority of African Americans.

In 1968, King traveled to Memphis, Tennessee, to support striking garbage workers. While standing on the balcony of his motel room, he was assassinated. His murder caused major outbreaks of violence throughout the country. In 1986, President Ronald Reagan signed a bill making the third Monday in January a national holiday in honor of the birthday of Martin Luther King Jr. (15 January). Some states balked at the idea of a holiday honoring King; however, by 2000, all 50 states recognized the national holiday. *See also BROWDER V. GAYLE; BROWN V. BOARD OF EDUCATION;* CIVIL RIGHTS ACT OF 1957; CIVIL RIGHTS ACT OF 1960; EDUCATION; FAUBUS, ORVAL; RACIAL INTEGRATION; SUPREME COURT.

KINSEY, ALFRED (1894–1956). Alfred Kinsey was born and raised in New Jersey. His parents were strict, and the topic of sex, which later brought Kinsey fame, was never discussed in his home. A graduate of Bowdoin College (1916) and Harvard University (Sc.D., 1920), Kinsey joined the faculty of Indiana University, where he conducted research on human sexual practices. In 1948, he published *Sexual Behavior in the Human Male.* He followed this in 1953 with *Sexual Behavior in the Human Female.* His observations and comments, including a belief that sexual experiences should not be delayed, caused a major national sensation. Critics question some of Kinsey's findings, but his work contributed to the sexual revolution of the 1960s. *See also* LITERATURE.

KNOWLAND, BILL (1908–1974). U.S. Senate majority leader 1953–55, U.S. Senate minority leader 1955–59. At the age of 12, William Fife Knowland was campaigning for **Republican** presidential candidate Warren G. Harding. A graduate of the University of California, Berkeley (A.B., 1929), he was elected in 1933 to the California State Assembly when he was only 25. After serving in World War II, he returned to California. When U.S. Senator Hiram Johnson died in 1945, Governor **Earl Warren** appointed Knowland to complete Johnson's term.

Elected on his own in 1946, Knowland represented California in the Senate for the next 14 years. During this time he was a vocal opponent of President **Harry S. Truman**. He also developed a lifelong dislike for Senator **Richard M. Nixon**. After President **Dwight D. Eisenhower** suffered a heart attack and his political future was uncertain, Knowland considered running for president as Eisenhower's successor. He left the Senate to run for governor of California in 1960 but was unsuccessful. After leaving politics, he became the editor of his father's *Oakland Press*. His death in 1974 was ruled a suicide.

KOREAN WAR. After World War II, the United States and the **Soviet Union** divided Korea into two sections at the 38th parallel. Their purpose was to end Japan's 30-year occupation of Korea. The northern part was under communist rule; the southern part would be watched, but not occupied, by the United States. In 1950, fighting developed along the 38th parallel.

The **United Nations (UN)** Security Council tried to intervene, ordering the North Koreans back behind the 38th parallel. Instead, the North Koreans continued their invasion. The Soviet member of the UN Security Council never attended the meetings. At the end of June, President **Harry S. Truman** ordered American troops to South Korea. The Security Council also sent troops. With UN approval, General **Douglas McArthur** commanded all fighting forces.

By July 1950, the communist forces were deep inside South Korea. In September, McArthur landed troops at the port of Inchon, which was about 200 miles behind the North Koreans' front. His plan worked and the North Korean troops were forced back to the border with China along the Yalu River. The United States had been warned by the Chinese Communists that if troops ventured too close to their border, China would enter the conflict. MacArthur had thought the Chinese would not enter the war, but they did. Hundreds of thousands of Chinese soldiers, supported by the Soviet Union, pushed the Americans back. American casualties were heavy.

MacArthur asked President Truman to let his troops invade Manchuria. When the president refused, MacArthur made public statements that infuriated Truman. In April 1951, Truman fired MacArthur. Given MacArthur's popularity among Americans, it was a controversial action.

In July 1951, peace talks began. As talks proceeded, it was obvious that a unified Korea was impossible. Meanwhile, troops continued fighting and casualties mounted on both sides. Throughout 1952, the peace talks continued, as well as the fighting.

Campaigning for the U.S. presidency in 1952, **Dwight D. Eisenhower** promised that if elected, he would go to Korea to end the war. In December, Eisenhower kept his promise. He traveled to Korea and threatened the Chinese with the possible use of **atomic** weapons to end the conflict. In March 1953, **Joseph Stalin**, leader of the Soviet Union died. Stalin's death ended much of the Soviet Union's support for the Chinese army. Finally, in July 1953, a cease-fire was signed.

In 1954, the **Geneva Conference** was held, but it was impossible to agree on how to reunite the two Koreas. After three years of fighting, the troops returned to roughly their original positions, split along the 38th parallel, which became the demarcation line between North and South Korea. *See also* FOREIGN POLICY; RHEE, SYNGMAN.

KROC, RAY (1902–1984). The trend toward "fast food" began in the 1950s when an entrepreneur named Ray Kroc purchased a restaurant from the McDonald brothers in California. Born in Illinois, Kroc was a high school dropout who had tried many jobs, including one as a milkshake mixer salesman. While holding that job, Kroc had noticed the McDonald brothers' mass-production skills as they made six milkshakes at one time. Kroc asked if he could copy their production methods. He opened his first successful restaurant in his hometown. In time, he purchased the McDonald brothers' restaurant and name. Shortly thereafter, he began selling McDonald's **franchises**. By 1963, he had become a millionaire many times over. Using consistent ingredients and shapes, his assembly-line methods could mass produce popular foods and drinks in minutes. At the time of his death in 1984, Kroc owned restaurants worldwide as well as the San Diego Padres baseball team.

– L –

LABOR MANAGEMENT REPORTING AND DISCLOSURE ACT, 1959. The Labor Management Reporting and Disclosure Act was passed in 1959 in order to prevent gangsters, blackmailers, and racketeers from infiltrating labor unions. The measure prohibited union members from participating in any form of criminal activities. It also provided for carefully supervised elections and prohibited unfair labor practices. The bill was sponsored by three senators, including **John F. Kennedy** of Massachusetts. *See also* AMERICAN FEDERATION OF LABOR AND CONGRESS OF INDUSTRIAL ORGANIZATIONS (AFL-CIO); RANDOLPH, A. PHILIP.

LALANNE, JACK (1914–). Fitness expert and bodybuilder Jack LaLanne was born in California. He was not concerned about diet and nutrition until he heard a lecture on the subject. He entered a chiropractic college but left to open a health spa. He emphasized improving health through weightlifting and proper diet. He later promoted the idea when he hosted his own **television** program (1951–84). LaLanne realized television and women at home were a perfect combination for promoting women's health by encouraging them to lift weights. In addition to his television program, he wrote books, made videos to promote fitness and nutrition, and designed bodybuilding machines, many of which are still in use today. By the 1980s, about 200 health clubs used his name although he no longer was associated with any of them.

LANDRUM-GRIFFIN ACT. *See* LABOR MANAGEMENT REPORTING AND DISCLOSURE ACT.

LAPIDUS, MORRIS (1902–2001). Architect Morris Lapidus was born in Russia and raised in New York City. After graduating in 1927 from Columbia University, he created unique stores with large windows through which shoppers could view much of the store.

Miami, Florida, in the postwar years, was experiencing a building boom. It became a glamorous place for Hollywood entertainers. The combination of glitz and prosperity produced an elegance in **architecture**. Lapidus was commissioned to build a hotel there suitable to the high economic status of its guests. In 1954, the Fountainbleau Hotel opened. The quarter-circle curved hotel was strongly criticized by fellow architects; however, Lapidus was commissioned to build the Eden Roc Hotel next door. He believed travelers wanted a fantasy place to stay in, and this concept was evident in his designs: curves, lots of color, unusual lighting effects, and luxury.

In 1985, tired of the criticism from his colleagues, Lapidus closed his office and retired. By the 1990s his designs, always enjoyed by the public, finally received the accolades of younger architects. In 1998, Lapidus's innovative architecture had become known as "MiMo" or Miami Modern. The term was coined to promote preservation of the structures built during the 1950s and 1960s in Miami.

LEBANON CRISIS. In 1956, **Camille Chamoun**, the pro-Western president of Lebanon, failed to side with Egypt during the **Suez Crisis**, which angered Egyptian President **Gamal Abdel Nasser**. Complicating matters was the fact that Muslims in Lebanon wanted to join Egypt and Syria in the newly created United Arab Republic (UAR) while the minority Christians wanted to remain aligned with Western powers. A Muslim rebellion ensued. Its purpose was to topple Chamoun's government. President Chamoun called on President **Dwight D. Eisenhower** for help during the rebellion. Eisenhower responded by sending U.S. marines into Lebanon in July 1958. By the end of October 1958, order had been restored. Eisenhower also sent diplomat Robert D. Murphy to persuade Chamoun to resign. General Faud Chehab, a Christian, was Chamoun's replacement. *See also* EISENHOWER DOCTRINE; FOREIGN POLICY.

LEMAY, CURTIS (1906–1990). Born in Ohio and educated at Ohio State University (1932), Curtis Emerson LeMay joined the Air Corps in 1928. During World War II, he was responsible for the effective night bombing of Japan and oversaw the dropping of the **atomic** bombs on Japan in 1945. After the war, he headed the Berlin Airlift, which was followed by his appointment as head of the newly created **Strategic Air Command (SAC)**. He turned SAC into a highly efficient military force, ready to strike at a moment's notice.

During **Dwight D. Eisenhower**'s presidency, LeMay proposed attacking the **Soviet Union**. Eisenhower rejected his recommendation. LeMay continued to argue for the strong use of military force during the administrations of Presidents **John F. Kennedy** and **Lyndon B. Johnson**, especially regarding the Cuban Missile Crisis and the **Vietnam War**. In the 1968 presidential race, after retiring from the

Air Force, he was Alabama Governor George Wallace's running mate. After Wallace, running as a third-party candidate, lost the election, LeMay retired from public life. In the movie *Dr. Strangelove*, General Jack D. Ripper was patterned after LeMay. *See also* CUBA, RELATIONS WITH; FOREIGN POLICY; MARSHALL PLAN.

LEVITTOWN. *See* SUBURBIA.

LEWIS, JERRY. *See* MATIN, DEAN, AND JERRY LEWIS.

LIBERATION. A **foreign policy** term coined by **John Foster Dulles**, liberation was the opposite of the policy of **containment**. **Dwight D. Eisenhower** hoped European and Asian countries dominated by communism could be liberated or freed from communist rule. Unfortunately, during the **Hungarian Revolution** in 1956, Eisenhower's focus was on the **Suez Crisis**, leaving the Hungarians under the communist yoke.

LIBERIA. *See* TUBMAN, WILLIAM V.S.

LIBRARY SERVICES ACT, 1956. For over 10 years, the American Library Association had been trying to win support for rural Americans who did not have access to public libraries. In 1956, President **Dwight D. Eisenhower** signed legislation providing books to rural communities on topics specifically requested by the citizens in the area. The books were delivered by bookmobiles. The Library Services Act has been updated twice. In 1964, the measure became the Library Services and Construction Act. In 1996, the Library Services and Technology Act reflected the inclusion of **technology**.

LIPPMANN, WALTER (1889–1974). Pulitzer Prize–winning journalist and author Walter Lippmann was born in New York, entered Harvard University at the age of 17, and graduated in three years. He was employed by journalist and social critic Lincoln Steffens as his secretary. Lippmann's experiences with Steffens during the 1912 presidential election led to his first book, *A Preface to Politics*. Following this success, he co-founded the *New Republic* **magazine**. Lippmann had been a socialist but moved to the **Democratic Party**

when Woodrow Wilson was the party's presidential candidate. He worked with Wilson on his famous Fourteen Points Peace Program and was a delegate to the 1919 Paris Peace Conference, where the League of Nations was created.

In 1920, he left the *New Republic* to become the editor of the *New York World*. In 1931, he became a columnist for the *New York Herald Tribune*, where for 30 years he wrote his column "Today and Tomorrow." He wrote two books in the 1920s which questioned whether a true democracy could be possible. *Public Opinion* and *The Phantom Public* were both controversial, and by the 1950s, he was one of the most outspoken and respected political columnists in the country.

LITERATURE. The end of World War II brought changes in science, **technology**, and lifestyles. The fear of communism was rampant, forcing many to turn to patriotism and **religion**. The allure of **space** became paramount in people's minds, especially after the **Soviet Union** launched ***Sputnik***. These factors were reflected in many of the popular books published during the 1950s.

Science fiction authors such as **Isaac Asimov**, Arthur C. Clarke, and Robert Heinlein became immensely popular. These prolific writers tackled topics such as robots, other planets, atoms, new technology, space travel, medicine, and politics. Their novels opened new worlds to the reader. Heinlein's *Starship Troopers* (1959) had an anticommunist message. Asimov's *Fantastic Voyage* (1966) placed the reader in a microscopic submarine injected into a person's bloodstream. The reader was tossed and turned as the body tried to reject the foreign object. Clarke's *2001: A Space Odyssey* (1968) pitted humans against a **computer**.

A number of books with religious themes became best sellers, including *The Cardinal* (1950), *Moses* (1951), *The Silver Chalice* (1952) , *The Robe* (1953), and *Exodus* (1959). *The Cardinal* and *The Silver Chalice* were best sellers two years in a row.

Because **teenagers** were more affluent in the 1950s, they had more freedom as well as time to experience life. They identified with the characters in **J. D. Salinger**'s *Catcher in the Rye* (1951), which was banned by many groups, as was William Golding's *Lord of the Flies* (1954). *Lolita* (1955) involved an older man who was sexually obsessed with a 12-year-old girl. The book, first published in France, was extremely controversial when it was sold in the United States.

Antimaterialism was reflected in books by **Beat Generation** authors **Jack Kerouac, William S. Burroughs**, and **Allen Ginsberg**. Their groundbreaking writing reached its peak in the 1950s. **Norman Mailer** wrote of his World War II experiences in his novel *The Naked and the Dead* (1948), and he tackled politics and social issues in other books and articles. **James Jones** wrote *From Here to Eternity* (1951) based on his wartime experiences. **Ernest Hemingway** wrote *The Old Man and the Sea* (1952) while he lived in **Cuba**. In *The Man in the Gray Flannel Suit* (1955), Sloan Wilson tackled the problems confronting men as a result of the demands made on them at work and at home in **suburbia**. The aftermath of **atomic** war was the theme of Nevil Shute's *On the Beach* (1957). *The Ugly American* (1959), by Eugene L. Burdick, was an indictment of U.S. **foreign policy**. In *The Ugly American*, diplomats were sent to countries where they were unaware of the customs and could not speak the language.

Perhaps the most explosive novel of the 1950s was *Peyton Place* (1956), by **Grace Metalious**. Based on real people in a New Hampshire town near where she lived, the novel involved sex, incest, abortion, adultery, and murder. The book sold 60,000 copies in 10 days. *See also* AGEE, JAMES; BALDWIN, JAMES; BUCKLEY, WILLIAM F., JR.; CAPOTE, TRUMAN; CARSON, RACHEL; COMIC BOOKS; CUMMINGS, E. E.; DOS PASSOS, JOHN; DRURY, ALLEN; ELIOT, T. S.; FAULKNER, WILLIAM; FORESTER, C. S.; FREIDAN, BETTY; FROST, ROBERT; HANSBERRY, LORRAINE; HELLMAN, LILLIAN; HUGHES, LANGSTON; KINSEY, ALFRED; LUCE, CLARE BOOTH; MAGAZINES; MILLER, ARTHUR; MUMFORD, LEWIS; O'CONNOR, FLANNERY; PACKARD, VANCE; PARKER, DOROTHY; *RAISIN IN THE SUN, A*; RAND, AYN; ROBBINS, HAROLD; SANDBURG, CARL; WARREN, ROBERT PENN; WILDER, THORNTON; WILLIAMS, TENNESSEE; WILLIAMS, WILLIAM CARLOS; WOUK, HERMAN; WRIGHT, RICHARD.

LODGE, HENRY CABOT, JR. (1902–1985). U.S. senator 1937–44 and 1947–52. Educated at Harvard University (1924), Henry Cabot

Lodge Jr. represented Massachusetts in the U.S. Senate in 1937–44, resigned to serve in the U.S. Army during World War II, and returned to the Senate again in 1947–53. When **Dwight D. Eisenhower** ran as the **Republican Party**'s candidate for president in the **1952 election**, Lodge served as his campaign manager. Eisenhower was successful, but Lodge lost his Senate seat to his **Democratic** opponent in Massachusetts, **John F. Kennedy**. In 1953–60, Lodge served as ambassador to the **United Nations**. In the **1960 election**, he ran for vice president on the Republican ticket. In 1963 and again in 1965–67, he served as ambassador to South **Vietnam**. During both **Richard M. Nixon**'s presidency and Gerald Ford's term, Lodge served as special envoy to the Vatican. *See also* FOREIGN POLICY.

LUCE, CLARE BOOTH (1903–1987). Member of the U.S. House of Representatives 1943–47. Clare Booth Luce was born in New York City. Although she had hoped to be an actress, she became a journalist with *Vogue* (1930) and later associate editor of *Vanity Fair* (1931). She resigned from *Vanity Fair* (1934) in order to write. Married to Henry Luce, her second husband, who was the founder of *Time*, *Fortune*, *Sports Illustrated*, and *Life*, she began a new phase in her life, traveling and writing. Her three plays in the 1930s—*The Women*, *Kiss the Boys Goodbye*, and *Margin of Error*—were well received and made her one of the country's best-known playwrights.

In 1942, Luce entered politics as a **Republican**, winning a Connecticut race for the U.S. House of Representatives. She served two terms in the House (1943–47). In 1944, her only child, a daughter, was killed in an automobile accident. Luce suffered a nervous breakdown but was helped by psychotherapy and her religion. After serving her two terms in the House of Representatives, she returned to writing. Her screenplay for the movie *Come to the Stable* won an Academy Award (1949).

In the **1952 election**, Luce campaigned for Republican presidential candidate **Dwight D. Eisenhower**. President Eisenhower rewarded her by appointing her ambassador to Italy in 1954. This was the first time in the country's history that a woman held a diplomatic position. She campaigned for Barry Goldwater in the 1964 presidential election and ran for a U.S. Senate seat from New York the same year but, like Goldwater, was not elected.

In 1967, after her husband died, Luce retired to their home in Hawaii. In 1981, she returned to Washington, D.C., when President Ronald Reagan appointed her to the President's Foreign Intelligence Advisory Board. She died of a brain tumor in her Watergate Hotel apartment. *See also* CINEMA; LITERATURE; THEATER.

– M –

MACARTHUR, DOUGLAS (1880–1964). U.S. general and military hero Douglas MacArthur was born into a military family. His father was a lieutenant general in the army stationed in Arkansas when MacArthur was born. The family moved to San Antonio, Texas, where MacArthur was educated in military schools. In 1903, he graduated at the top of his West Point class.

MacArthur displayed his bravery during the 1916–17 raids on Pancho Villa in Mexico and in **France** during World War I, for which he received a number of medals and honors. By 1930, he had become the U.S. Army's chief of staff, but his far-right politics affected his career. President Franklin D. Roosevelt thought MacArthur was a dangerous man who would do anything to get what he wanted. One columnist saw him as a potential dictator if given the opportunity.

During World War II, MacArthur was the triumphant commander of the Pacific theater of operations. He was best known for liberating the Philippine Islands. In the **Korean War**, he headed the **United Nations** forces. MacArthur wanted to use **atomic** weapons in Korea, which stunned Truman. When MacArthur openly criticized Truman, the president fired him. Many Americans responded by calling for Truman's impeachment.

In 1951, when MacArthur spoke to a joint session of Congress, he stated, "Old soldiers never die, they just fade away." His speech was well received. After **Dwight D. Eisenhower** was elected president, he turned to MacArthur for advice concerning Korea. MacArthur again suggested using atomic weapons. His advice was ignored. *See also* FOREIGN POLICY.

MACMILLAN, HAROLD (1894–1986). Prime minister of **Great Britain** 1957–63. The grandson of the founder of Macmillan

Publishers, Maurice Harold Macmillan was born in London and educated at Balliol College, Oxford. In 1924, he entered politics as a member of Parliament. He met General **Dwight D. Eisenhower** during World War II, and they became friends. After the failed **Suez Crisis** led to Prime Minister **Anthony Eden's** forced resignation, Macmillan was appointed the new prime minister. The Suez Crisis had affected the friendship between the United States and Great Britain; however, Macmillan restored relations between the two countries. In 1963, he resigned from his position as prime minister to head his family's publishing company. *See also* FOREIGN POLICY.

MAGAZINES. A host of magazines made their debut during the 1950s. *Mad* first appeared in 1952 as a satirical publication. It poked fun at everything from **television** programs to everyday life. As the magazine gained popularity, it also became more brazen. The witch hunts of Senator **Joseph McCarthy** as well as the **Vietnam War** were satirized. In 1956, a *Mad* icon was introduced, Alfred E. Neumann. His face came from a postcard and his name from an old radio program. He had a big grin with a gap in his front teeth and a look quickly associated with the *Mad* question, "What, me worry?" When one needed to show stupidity, Alfred E. Neumann was pictured. *Mad* is still published in many countries today.

In 1953, with the growth in the number of television programs, *TV Guide* was introduced. **Lucille Ball** and her first child graced the first cover. The weekly publication included news and reviews of new programs, gossip, and a crossword puzzle.

Hugh Hefner introduced *Playboy* in 1953, gambling on his belief that the time was right for a magazine for men. The war was over, leisure time had increased, economic prosperity had spread, and movies had tested the censors. The first issue featured a pullout centerfold of sex symbol **Marilyn Monroe**. *Playboy* was an immediate success. The second issue introduced the famous *Playboy* bunny logo, designed to look like a tuxedo-dressed rabbit. *Playboy* became increasingly explicit, and full nudity in the centerfold became the norm. The magazine's articles covered **sports**, men's fashions, and interviews with people in the news. Today, *Playboy* still has the largest circulation of all magazines aimed at men. Hugh Hefner's empire includes Playboy clubs, mansions, and adult television stations.

Sports Illustrated appeared in 1954, a magazine for men covering sports events. Photos were in color and articles were timely, appearing the week after an event. The magazine annually named a "Sportsman of the Year," and many little-known athletes were introduced.

William F. Buckley Jr., who believed conservatism had lost its voice in a more liberal world, sought a way to revive those ideas and ideals. In 1955, with the help of an ex-communist editor, he sought the financial backing to begin the *National Review*, a biweekly magazine. In 1957, it appeared on the newsstands for the first time. Contributors with the same values as Buckley became reporters and writers. Libertarians were welcome to express their ideas. The magazine is still influential among conservatives today. *See also* COMIC BOOKS; LITERATURE.

MAILER, NORMAN (1923–2007). Author Norman Mailer was born in New Jersey but raised in Brooklyn. He graduated from Harvard University (1943) with a degree in engineering science. The following year, he was drafted into the army and served in the Philippines. His wartime experiences were the basis of *The Naked and the Dead* (1948), his first book, which was an immediate best seller and later a movie. Enjoying instant success, Mailer embraced the counterculture of the 1950s that was reflected in **Beat Generation** authors **Jack Kerouac** and **Allen Ginsberg**. During this period, Mailer co-founded the *Village Voice*, for which he wrote political and social commentary. For a short time during the 1950s, Mailer also wrote screenplays.

His books often covered timely subjects. *Barbary Shore* (1951) was set during the **Cold War**. *The Armies of the Night* (1968) was a nonfiction narrative written during the **Vietnam War**. Apollo 11 was the subject of *A Fire on the Moon* (1971). *The Prisoner of Sex* (1971) expressed his disapproval of the **women's movement**, which he openly opposed. His books won many of the notable prizes for **literature**. He published articles in at least 75 different journals and **magazines**. Mailer also reported on presidential elections, gave advice to several presidents, and was frequently interviewed on radio and **television**. *See also* BURROUGHS, WILLIAM S.; CINEMA.

MALCOLM X (1925–1965). The outspoken black nationalist Malcolm X was born Malcolm Little in Nebraska and grew up in Michigan.

His father was a radical Baptist minister. Malcolm was a troubled **teenager** with a history of drugs, violence, and petty crimes. In 1952, he was released from a prison term for burglary and joined the Black Muslims, a group he had learned about while incarcerated. He became more outspoken and stressed the importance of Black Power. When this led to a disagreement with the Black Muslims, he formed his own group of activists, the Organization of Afro-American Unity. He continued making inflammatory statements that scared whites and angered moderate **civil rights** activists. In 1965, while in Harlem, he was assassinated by Black Muslims who viewed him as a traitor to their group. *See also* AFRICAN AMERICANS.

MANILA PACT. *See* SOUTHEAST ASIA TREATY ORGANIZA-TION (SEATO).

MAO ZEDONG (1893–1976). Born in Hunan Province, **China**, in 1893, Mao Zedong grew up in poverty. He became an avowed follower of communism and one of the delegates to the First Congress of the Chinese Communist Party (CCP), held in 1921. A few years later, he joined with the Chinese Kuomintang, or Nationalists, who were fighting to unite China under their leadership.

In 1925, **Chiang Kai-shek** became the leader of the Nationalists. Two years later, when the alliance broke down, communists under Mao withdrew into the countryside, where they began a 20-year revolution against Chiang. In 1949, they succeeded in ousting Chiang from power; the Nationalist leader fled to Taiwan (Formosa).

As Chiang was a U.S. ally, Mao believed that the United States would attempt to put his old foe back into power. He therefore signed an alliance with the **Soviet Union** in 1950, ordered Chinese troops to intervene in the **Korean War**, and offered assistance to **Ho Chi Minh** and the Viet Minh, who were fighting the French in **Vietnam**. Mao also ordered the bombardment of the Nationalist-controlled islands of **Quemoy and Matsu** in 1954–55 and 1958.

In 1958, Mao instituted the Great Leap Forward, his plan to expand China's industrial base. Crop production fell as people left the land to make steel, and a drought made matters worse. Internal criticism of his leadership grew. Relations with the Soviet Union worsened as Soviet officials concluded that the goal of the Great Leap Forward was to make China, and not the Soviets, the leader of the communist world. Although Mao would successfully overcome the internal dissent, ties between his country and the Soviet Union would remain sour throughout the remainder of his life. *See also* DULLES, JOHN FOSTER; EISENHOWER, DWIGHT D.; FOREIGN POLICY; JOHNSON, LYNDON B.; KENNEDY, JOHN F.; KHRUSHCHEV, NIKITA.

MARSHALL, GEORGE C. (1880–1959). U.S. general and diplomat George Catlett Marshall was born in Pennsylvania. His father owned a coal business; however, Marshall wanted a military career. After graduating from the Virginia Military Institute (1901), he served in the Philippines and the United States. He continued his military education at Fort Leavenworth's Infantry-Calvary School and then the Army Staff School. During World War I, he had a distinguished career. After the war, his reputation as an officer led to his assignment as the aide-de-camp to General John J. Pershing. He continued to serve in various military positions, being promoted frequently. By the mid-1930s, he was a brigadier general. In 1938, Marshall was part of the General Staff in Washington, D.C., and the next year was chief of staff. In 1944, he became a five star general, a new rank Congress implemented that year.

As chief of staff during World War II, Marshall oversaw the activities of 8 million soldiers. He also served on the policy committee that supervised scientists engaged in **atomic** research. After the war, Marshall served the country in diplomatic positions, finally becoming President **Harry S. Truman**'s secretary of state in 1947. During his two years in Truman's cabinet, Marshall promoted his European economic plan, later referred to as the **Marshall Plan**. During the **Korean War**, he served as secretary of defense for one year. In 1951, Senator **Joseph McCarthy** accused Marshall of being soft on communism. During the **1952 election**, **Republican** presidential candidate **Dwight D. Eisenhower** wanted to defend Marshall against McCarthy's attacks, but for political reasons did not do so, something Eisenhower later regretted. In 1951, Marshall resigned from public life. He won the Nobel Peace Prize in 1953. *See also* FOREIGN POLICY.

MARSHALL PLAN. The Marshall Plan was an economic aid program extended to 16 European nations in 1947–51. After World War II, much of Europe was devastated; food was in short supply, and the spread of communism was a major concern. Secretary of State **George C. Marshall**'s impression of the **Soviet Union**'s postwar ambitions in Europe became the basis of the plan. Although the Soviet Union was included in the original plan, it opted out, not wanting to expose its citizens to America's charity or disclose its economic problems after the war.

In June 1947, speaking at Harvard University, Marshall unveiled his plan to aid Europe. It had two major parts: to keep communism from spreading and to make the international economy embrace capitalism. Each European nation submitted a recovery plan. President **Harry S. Truman** asked Congress for $17 billion to be spent over four years. Congress allocated between $13 and $14 billion. Most of the money went to **Great Britain**, **France**, and West **Germany**. Overall, the plan was an economic success. The Marshall Plan also helped to bring the Western nations together through peaceful means. *See also* FOREIGN POLICY; KENNAN, GEORGE F.

MARSHALL SPACE FLIGHT CENTER, 1960. After World War II, a number of German scientists were employed by the U.S. Army. One was **Wernher von Braun**, who with his colleagues had developed the V-2 rockets used by **Germany** during the war. Von Braun's real interest was **space** travel, and after the **Soviet Union** launched the satellite *Sputnik*, the space race was on.

In the 1950s, von Braun and his team were moved to Huntsville, Alabama, to develop rockets at the Redstone Arsenal. On 31 January 1958, the first successful Redstone rocket was sent into space. In 1960, President **Dwight D. Eisenhower** officially opened the Marshall Space Flight Center in Huntsville, named for **George C. Marshall**. Wernher von Braun was the first director. Still in operation today, the center provides support to the Kennedy Space Center in Florida. Research in jet propulsion, lunar robotics, and space exploration are a few of the center's projects. The Marshall Space Flight Center is part of the **National Aeronautics and Space Agency (NASA)**.

MARSHALL, THURGOOD (1908–1993). Associate justice of the **Supreme Court** 1967–91. Thurgood Marshall was born in Baltimore and educated at Howard University Law School, where he graduated at the top of his class (1933). His first position was as legal counsel to the **National Association for the Advancement of Colored People (NAACP)**. Then he became the director of the NAACP Legal Defense and Education Fund. In this position, he won a series of **civil rights** cases before the U.S. Supreme Court, including *Murray v. Pearson* (1936), his first case. He argued 32 cases in front of the Supreme Court and won 27. His greatest success was the decision in *Brown v. Board of Education*, leading to the end of segregation in public schools.

In 1961, President **John F. Kennedy** nominated Marshall for a judgeship on the Second Circuit Court of Appeals. The Senate Judicial Committee, under the leadership of Mississippi Senator James Eastland, held up the nomination until 1962. With his appointment to the Supreme Court in 1967, by President **Lyndon B. Johnson**, Thurgood Marshall became the first **African American** to sit on the Court.

MARTIN, DEAN, AND JERRY LEWIS. Singer Dean Martin (born Dino Crocetti, 1917–1995) and comedian Jerry Lewis (born Jerome Levitch, 1926–) met in the mid-1940s when both were performing separately in Atlantic City at the 500 Club. Lewis did not garner many laughs during his first few nights on stage and suggested to Martin that they appear together. Martin would sing and Lewis would interrupt with silly comments or antics. Their personalities and their timing were perfect together, and audiences loved their shows. In 1947, they became a duo. Almost immediately, they became a hit, moving from radio to **television** guest appearances and finally to movies. During the 1950s, they were the most popular duo in **cinema**; however, by the mid-1950s the two began to go their separate ways. Martin became successful with his records and television program. Lewis had success with a series of films and became one of the most popular movie stars in **France**, where his movies were always major money-makers. Since 1966, Lewis has hosted a televised Labor Day marathon to raise money for muscular dystrophy research. *See also* MUSIC.

MARTIN, JOSEPH W., JR. (1884–1968). Speaker of the House of Representatives 1947–48 and 1953–54. Joseph William Martin Jr. was born in Massachusetts. He started working as a journalist at age 18. By 24, he was editor and publisher of the *North Attleboro Chronicle*. In 1911, he was elected to the state legislature. In 1924, he was elected to the U.S. House of Representatives and remained there for 40 years. In 1966, he was defeated in the **Republican** primary election. One of President **Dwight D. Eisenhower**'s major allies in Congress, he supported Eisenhower's foreign aid policies as well as federal funding for **education**. No one, to date, has chaired as many Republican National Conventions as Martin, from 1940 to 1956.

MARTIN, MARY (1913–1990). One of the **theater**'s superstars in the 1950s, Mary Martin was born in Weatherford, Texas. She began dancing and singing as a teenager in the local theater. In 1935, she opened a dance school in Weatherford and then began singing on a Dallas radio station. Later she appeared in Los Angeles nightclubs, where she was discovered by a major talent agent. In 1938, she sang "My Heart Belongs to Daddy" in the Cole Porter musical *Leave It to Me* on Broadway. Her rendition made her a star. In 1943, she starred in the Broadway play *One Touch of Venus*. In the 1940s, she had small parts in several Paramount movies. In 1950, she returned to the Broadway stage to star in *South Pacific*. She received Tony Awards for *South Pacific*, *Peter Pan* (1955), and *The Sound of Music* (1960). She appeared in the **television** production of *Peter Pan*, the role for which she is most remembered. *See also* CINEMA.

MASSIVE RETALIATION. First adopted by President **Dwight D. Eisenhower**'s secretary of state, **John Foster Dulles**, the policy of massive retaliation was closely related to **brinksmanship**. Massive retaliation meant the use of **atomic** weapons in response to military aggression by an enemy power. To threaten massive retaliation meant going to the brink of a nuclear war. When **John F. Kennedy** became president, he believed massive retaliation was too radical. He wanted a more flexible military posture, one that relied more on special ground forces and less on the air force. *See also* COLD WAR; CONTAINMENT; FOREIGN POLICY.

MATHIS, JOHNNY (1935–). Born in Texas but raised in San Francisco, Johnny Mathis began singing when he was eight years old. His father played the piano while giving singing instructions to his son. At age 13, Mathis received professional singing lessons. Mathis also starred on the track team in high school as a hurdler and high jumper. At San Francisco State College, he studied to be a teacher. He also continued to excel in the high jump, coming within two inches of the **Olympic** record at that time. On weekends, he sang in clubs. The owner of one of these clubs contacted Columbia Records to send someone to hear Mathis sing. The performance led to a record contract but also to a dilemma for the young singer. He was scheduled to try out for the 1956 Olympic team, but his father persuaded him to pursue a musical career. He recorded his first album in 1956. Although the album was not a hit, he continued to sing in various New York clubs.

In 1955, Mathis was under the supervision of Mitch Miller, a band leader and producer. Miller had Mathis record "It's Not for Me to Say" and "Wonderful, Wonderful." These two hits were followed by "Chances Are" as well as an appearance on **Ed Sullivan**'s popular **television** show, which introduced the singer to a wider audience. Mathis is one of only five singers to have a hit record for four decades in a row (1950s–80s). He also enjoyed the distinction of being the first recording star ever to have an album of "Greatest Hits." *See also* MUSIC.

MCCARRAN-WALTER ACT. *See* IMMIGRATION AND NATIONALITY ACT.

MCCARTHY, JOSEPH (1908–1957). U.S. senator 1946–57. Born and educated in Wisconsin, Joseph Raymond McCarthy received a law degree from Marquette University (1935). After graduation, he worked at a law firm and later served in World War II. In 1946, he was elected to the U.S. Senate. His first four years in the Senate were unimpressive. In 1950, he made a speech in West Virginia that became the template for a series of speeches in which he claimed to have the names of communists employed in the federal government.

In 1952, when **Dwight D. Eisenhower** was elected president, McCarthy was reelected to the Senate. With **Republicans** in the majority in Congress, McCarthy became chair of the Senate Permanent Subcommittee on Investigations. From this position, he began his search for communists in the government and the military. Slowly his importance grew. As in the hearings of the **House Un-American Activities Committee (HUAC)**, individuals called before McCarthy's subcommittee were grilled about alleged connections with communism and were expected to name communists with whom they worked. People refusing to testify or to name names were **blacklisted**, which could mean an end to their careers.

In 1954, reporter and **television** news host **Edward R. Murrow** began to question McCarthy's tactics on his program *See It Now*. McCarthy's downfall resulted from his accusation that army personnel, including ones working closely with the president, were communists. Up to that time, Eisenhower had hoped McCarthy's power would dwindle on its own, but accusing people he knew to be innocent was intolerable. McCarthy was relieved of his position in the Senate and called to testify on his own behalf in televised hearings. His testimony led to his censure in the Senate. McCarthy became an alcoholic and died of cirrhosis of the liver. Joseph McCarthy's tactics led to the term **McCarthyism**. *See also* ARMY-MCCARTHY HEARINGS; BELAFONTE, HARRY; CINEMA; COHN, ROY; COLD WAR; HELLMAN, LILLIAN; HORNE, LENA; KAZAN, ELIA; MCCARTHY, JOSEPH; MILLER, ARTHUR; PARKER, DOROTHY; RED SCARE; ROBESON, PAUL; SEEGER, PETE; SCHINE, G. DAVID; THEATER; WEAVERS, THE.

MCCARTHYISM. Derived from Senator **Joseph McCarthy**'s name, the term McCarthyism refers to a form of demagoguery. McCarthy's tactics in the 1950s as he pursued suspected communists became notorious. Unsubstantiated attacks in order to defame someone's character were part of McCarthy's strategy. *See also* BLACKLIST; COHN, ROY; HOUSE UN-AMERICAN ACTIVITIES COMMITTEE (HUAC).

MCCONE, JOHN A. (1902–1991). CIA director 1961–65. Born in California, John Alexander McCone received a degree from the University of California, Berkeley (B.S., 1922). McCone worked his way through the ranks to become executive vice president of the

Llewelyn Ironworks. In 1937, he began his own extremely successful engineering company, building refineries for oil companies. In 1947, McCone, a fanatical anticommunist, was introduced to **Allen Dulles**. He also met and became friends with **Dwight D. Eisenhower**.

In 1948, President **Harry S. Truman** named McCone deputy to the secretary of defense. In 1950, he became undersecretary of the U.S. Air Force. In 1956, he attacked **Adlai Stevenson** for suggesting a nuclear test ban. McCone was named chair of the **Atomic Energy Commission** in 1958, after **Lewis Strauss** resigned to become secretary of commerce. In 1961, McCone became director of the **Central Intelligence Agency (CIA)**. An opponent of the **Vietnam War**, he resigned from the CIA in 1965. *See also* ATOMIC AND NUCLEAR ENERGY.

MCDONALD'S CORPORATION. *See* KROC, RAY.

MCELROY, NEIL H. (1904–1972). Secretary of defense 1957–59. Born and raised in Ohio, Neil Hosler McElroy returned to his home state after graduating from Harvard University in 1925. He began his career at Procter & Gamble in Cincinnati, becoming its president in 1948. In 1957, President **Dwight D. Eisenhower** appointed McElroy secretary of defense after **Charles E. Wilson** resigned. At the time of his appointment, the United States was behind in the field of missiles and rocket research. The **Soviet Union** had already launched its satellite, *Sputnik*. Eisenhower knew defense preparedness was vital; however, neither he nor McElroy chose to increase the defense budget. Although he ordered production of **intercontinental ballistic missiles (ICBMs)**, he wanted them placed overseas before they were completely tested. McElroy had agreed at the time of his appointment as defense secretary to serve for only two years, but he was criticized for leaving when he resigned in 1959. He was succeeded by **Thomas S. Gates Jr**.

MCKAY, DOUGLAS (1893–1959). Secretary of the interior 1953–56. Born in Oregon, James Douglas McKay worked his way through Oregon State College (B.S., 1917). Injured during World War I, he was unable to return to the strenuous work of his family's farm. Instead, he sold automobiles and eventually owned his own dealerships. Elected mayor of Salem, Oregon, in 1932, he helped the city remain afloat during the Great Depression. In 1934, he was elected to the Oregon state senate. In 1948, he successfully ran for governor. A staunch **Republican** in the **1952 election**, McKay threw his support behind **Dwight D. Eisenhower**. His appointment as secretary of the interior by President Eisenhower was well received. McKay was from the West, where the environment and natural resources were carefully guarded. He remained secretary of the interior until 1956, when he ran unsuccessfully against Wayne Morse for a seat in the U.S. Senate.

MEAD, MARGARET (1901–1978). Anthropologist and author Margaret Mead was born in Philadelphia, Pennsylvania. Her father was a university professor and her mother was a social activist. After receiving her Ph.D. from Columbia University (1929), Mead traveled to Samoa and New Guinea to study primitive cultures. Mead believed culture was more important than heredity in shaping one's personality. She wrote a number of books on anthropology, including *Coming of Age in Samoa*, *Growing Up in New Guinea*, *Male and Female*, and *Growth and Culture*. *Coming of Age in Samoa* (1928) has been criticized for some inaccuracies, but her books were popular and opened the world of anthropology to readers worldwide. Mead was employed by the American Museum of Natural History in New York (1926–69) and also taught at Columbia University. Her book *Blackberry Winter* is autobiographical.

MEDICAL ADVANCES. The 1950s were a time of medical breakthroughs. Tranquilizers were first produced in 1950, and by 1955 many doctors were prescribing them. The **birth control pill** (1952) allowed women to decide when they were ready to have children. Streptomycin, discovered in 1952, was used to cure tuberculosis. In 1952, the first successful open-heart surgery was performed on a five-year-old girl.

In 1953, lung cancer was attributed to smoking. Steroids were introduced to help improve muscular strength. And the first accurate model of DNA structure was illustrated in the magazine *Nature*. In 1958, ultrasound allowed doctors to view an embryo in the womb.

A vaccine against polio was one of the most important break-throughs in medicine. In 1954, **Jonas Salk** began inoculating school-children with the new polio vaccine. In 1956, Albert Sabin developed an oral vaccine for polio. *See also* POLIOMYELITIS VACCINA-TION ACT.

MERMAN, ETHEL (1908–1984). Stage and film star Ethel Merman was born Ethel Agnes Zimmerman in Queens, New York. Early in her career, she worked as a stenographer during the day and sang at various clubs at night. In order to fit her name on **theater** marquees, she shortened her last name. In 1930, she appeared on Broadway for the first time, belting out "I've Got Rhythm." An overnight sensa-tion, she appeared on Broadway and in the **cinema** for the next five decades. In 1934, she appeared in movies with **Bing Crosby** and Eddie Cantor. Returning to the stage, she won accolades for her performance in *Girl Crazy* (1934). Broadway successes continued with *Panama Hattie* (1940–42), *Something for the Boys* (1943–44), *Annie Get Your Gun* (1946–49), *Happy Hunting* (1956–57), *Call Me Madam* (1950–52), and *Gypsy* (1959–61). In 1964–70, she starred in *Hello Dolly!* One of her most memorable cinema performances was in *It's a Mad, Mad, Mad, Mad World* (1963). Merman will always be remembered for her renditions of "Everything's Coming Up Roses" and "There's No Business like Show Business." *See also* MUSIC.

METALIOUS, GRACE (1924–1964). Best-selling author Grace DeRepentigny Metalious was born in New Hampshire into a work-ing-class family. Her father abandoned the family when she was 11. By the time she was 17, she was married to a teacher, and they soon had four children. She wanted to write and often heard stories about people living in another New Hampshire town. One story involved a girl who had murdered her father for molesting her. Using this real-life situation as well as other sordid stories about various townspeo-ple, she wrote the novel ***Peyton Place***. When the book was published, it was a blockbuster. The book sold out within the first 10 days.

People who believed they were the basis for the characters in the book felt betrayed. Her husband, a school principal, was fired. The family was ostracized. Other children were not allowed to play with

Metalious's children. She wrote three more novels, but none met with the success of *Peyton Place*. In the end, the novel proved the bane of her existence. She became an alcoholic who spent her wealth frivolously. Divorced and alone, she died at the age of 39. Even today, an event or place that is shockingly immoral might be called "a regular Peyton Place." *See also* LITERATURE.

MIDDLE EAST TREATY ORGANIZATION. In 1955, Iraq, Iran, Turkey, Pakistan, and **Great Britain** signed a security agreement known as the Baghdad Pact, forming the Middle East Treaty Organization (MENTO). The treaty was encouraged by the United States and patterned after the **North Atlantic Treaty Organization (NATO)**. It was part of the **containment** strategy against the **Soviet Union**. In 1959, when Iraq withdrew from the pact, the alliance was renamed the Central Treaty Organization (CENTO). In 1965, Pakistan, in a war with **India**, tried but was unable to obtain aid from the alliance. In 1979, the withdrawal of Iran and Pakistan spelled the end of the organization. *See also* COLD WAR; FOREIGN POLICY.

MILITARY-INDUSTRIAL COMPLEX. First used in President **Dwight D. Eisenhower's Farewell Address**, the term military-industrial complex referred to an alliance between government and military arms manufacturers to build huge weapons arsenals. Eisenhower worried that this relationship was dangerous to world peace. While arms manufacturers became wealthy from their sales, countries built up weapons arsenals. Misuse of these arsenals jeopardized world peace. *See also* MILLS, C. WRIGHT.

MILLER, ARTHUR (1915–2005). Playwright Arthur Miller was born in New York City. Educated at the University of Michigan (A.B., 1938, L.H.D., 1956), Miller began writing plays in the 1940s. His first success was *All My Sons* (1947), which dealt with the wartime morality of an arms manufacturer. In 1949, he wrote the internationally acclaimed *Death of a Salesman*. The play won a Pulitzer Prize. During the 1950s, Miller was called to testify before the **House Un-American Activities Committee (HUAC)**. His experience before the committee, coupled with the anticommunist witch hunts of Senator **Joseph McCarthy**, led to *The Crucible* (1953), about the

Salem witch trials of the 1600s. Miller's many plays have appeared on Broadway as well as on **television**. *Death of a Salesman* and *The Crucible* are the most popular and most performed.

In 1956–61, Miller was married to actress **Marilyn Monroe**, for whom he wrote the screenplay for *The Misfits* (1961). The film was the last movie in which Hollywood legends Marilyn Monroe and Clark Gable starred. *See also* CINEMA; LITERATURE; THEATER.

MILLS, C. WRIGHT (1916–1962). Social scientist Charles Wright Mills was born in Texas and graduated from the University of Texas (M.A., 1939) and the University of Wisconsin (Ph.D., 1942). From 1946 until his death in 1962, he taught at Columbia University. Mills expressed his controversial beliefs about society in the 1950s in two of his most famous works, *White Collar* and *The Power Elite*. Written during the postwar growing economy, *White Collar* tells the story of the new middle class. *The Power Elite* explains Mills's premise that society is controlled by three groups: corporations, the military, and politicians. Like President **Dwight D. Eisenhower**, Mills was critical of the **military-industrial complex**, an opinion that influenced the political thinking of the New Left of the 1960s. Mills believed too much political power in the hands of a few people was dangerous. He also thought that intellectuals could provide the best political decisions. He believed notoriety gained in **sports** or entertainment did not qualify one to hold political office.

MINTON, SHERMAN (1890–1965). Associate justice of the **Supreme Court** 1949–56. Born in Indiana, Sherman Minton graduated from the University of Indiana (L.L.B., 1915) and finished at the top of his Yale University law class (1915). A firm believer in serving the public, he was elected to the U.S. Senate in 1934. During his time in Washington, Minton was one of the most fervent backers of President Franklin D. Roosevelt's New Deal, and he served as **Democratic** whip (1939–41). Minton was later appointed to the Seventh Circuit Court of Appeals, which included his home state of Indiana. In 1949, after the death of Justice Wiley B. Rutledge, **Harry S. Truman** appointed Minton to the Supreme Court. During Senator **Joseph McCarthy**'s anticommunist hearings in the 1950s, Minton supported the conviction of people involved in subversive activities. He was a staunch supporter of **civil rights**, and he agreed with the Court's decision in ***Brown v. Board of Education*** that ended segregation in public schools. His health was a constant problem and forced his resignation from the Supreme Court in 1956. During his service on the Court, Minton often feuded with Justices **Felix Frankfurter** and **William O. Douglas**.

MISSION 66. With the new **Interstate Highway System**, tourism increased throughout the United States. The national parks saw a growing number of visitors but lacked the facilities to accommodate them. In 1956, Congress approved Mission 66, a 10-year project in honor of the Park Service's 50th anniversary. Congress allocated $1 billion for new or improved park roads, campsites, visitors centers, homes for park employees, and various buildings housing park services. In 1951, an estimated 37 million visitors had visited the national parks. In 1956, the estimate was 60 million visitors, and in 1966, 80 million. During President **Dwight D. Eisenhower**'s administration, the Park Service acquired approximately 30 new parks, including the Glen Canyon National Recreation Area, which surrounded the **Glen Canyon Dam**, the most controversial part of Mission 66.

MITCHELL, JAMES P. (1900–1964). Secretary of labor 1953–61. James Paul Mitchell, who was born in New Jersey, was unable to afford a college education after graduating from high school in 1917. His first job was in a grocery store. He tried unsuccessfully to run his own store. After his business failed, he was employed at Western Electric. During the Depression, he was the director of the Emergency Relief Administration in Union County, New Jersey. When he was 38, he was employed in New York City by the Works Progress Administration (WPA). His expertise in labor relations during World War II led to a position at Macy's in New York. By 1947, he was in charge of personnel at Bloomingdale's. New York Governor Thomas Dewey brought Mitchell to the attention of President **Dwight D. Eisenhower**, who appointed him secretary of labor in 1953. Mitchell worked to increase the minimum wage and provided programs to improve workers' skills.

Mitchell was nicknamed "the social conscience of the **Republican Party**." He was considered for **Richard M. Nixon**'s running mate in the **1960 election** but was not chosen. In 1961, he ran for governor of New Jersey. Even though Eisenhower campaigned for Mitchell, he lost the election.

MONROE, MARILYN (1926–1962). Born Norma Jean Mortenson in Los Angeles and raised in foster homes, Marilyn Monroe married at age 16. The marriage lasted only a few years. After working as a model and acting in small roles in movies, Monroe had starring roles in the 1953 films *Gentlemen Prefer Blondes* and *How to Marry a Millionaire*. In both movies, she played a dumb, sexy blonde. In 1953, she was also the centerfold in the first issue of the **magazine** *Playboy*. Her status as a Hollywood sex symbol and cultural icon continues to this day. Monroe married **baseball** player Joe DiMaggio in 1954, but the marriage lasted less than a year. She was later married to playwright **Arthur Miller** (1956–61).

Monroe starred in some of the **cinema**'s most acclaimed comedies, including *The Seven Year Itch* (1956) and *Some Like It Hot* (1959). She was rumored to have had affairs with both Robert F. Kennedy and President **John F. Kennedy**. In 1961, she sang "Happy Birthday" to President Kennedy in her soft, sexy voice. In 1962, when Monroe was found dead in her home of an apparent overdose, rumors spread that she had been murdered. Although she most likely committed suicide, the cause of her death remains something of a mystery.

MONTGOMERY BUS BOYCOTT. After the 1954 **Supreme Court** decision in *Brown v. Board of Education* made segregation in public schools unlawful, **civil rights** activists were ready to fight other unfair practices. In Montgomery, Alabama, on 1 December 1955, **Rosa Parks**, tired from a day's work, refused to give up her seat on a bus to a white man and was arrested. In response, E. D. Nixon, president of the local and state chapters of the **National Association for the Advancement of Colored People (NAACP)**, spoke with several other activists about how to proceed with a boycott of the bus system. Nixon bailed Parks out of jail and made a flier calling for the boycott. Since three-fourths of the Montgomery bus riders were **African American**, the action would have an impact on the city's economy. Nixon called on **Martin Luther King Jr.** to lead the boycott.

Beginning on 5 December 1955, African Americans opted to walk to work rather than ride the bus. Many whites gave their black employees rides. As the boycott progressed, buses that went into black areas stopped their routes. Whites, who had been providing rides for their black employees, were pressured to stop. In February 1956, 89 boycott leaders were arrested, including King, Parks, and Ralph Abernathy. The homes of both King and Nixon were bombed. This intimidation only made African Americans more determined to continue the boycott. City officials were pressured by the **White Citizens Council** not to give in. After 381 days, however, the enormous loss of revenue to the city's economy led officials to end segregation on buses, bringing an end to the boycott. *See also BROWDER V. GAYLE*; CIVIL RIGHTS ACT OF 1957; CIVIL RIGHTS ACT OF 1960; RACIAL INTEGRATION.

MOSSADEGH, MOHAMMED (1882–1967). Mohammed Mossadegh was born in **Iran** and educated as a lawyer. He was elected to the Iranian parliament at the age of 21 but was too young to serve. His most striking attribute was his desire to nationalize Iranian resources and businesses. The shah of Iran, a political ally of the West, repeatedly imprisoned Mossadegh for his views. In 1951, Mossadegh was elected prime minister, but the shah prevented his control of the army. In August 1953, citizens rioted against the shah, who fled to Italy.

Mossadegh nationalized the Iranian oil fields, which led to covert operations by the **Central Intelligence Agency (CIA)**. In 1953, with the aid of Iranians paid by the CIA, Mossadegh was overthrown and arrested. The shah of Iran was returned to power. *See also* COLD WAR; CONTAINMENT; FOREIGN POLICY.

MOTOWN RECORDS. Detroit songwriter Berry Gordy Jr. had his first hit in the 1950s when he co-wrote "Lonely Teardrops" for singer Jackie Wilson. In 1959, Gordy, his sisters, and a friend formed Motown Records in Detroit. Between 1961 and 1971, the company had over 100 hit records. Some of the recording stars were the Supremes, the Jackson Five, the Miracles, Stevie Wonder, Gladys Knight and the Pips, and the Temptations. In the 1970s, Gordy moved his business to California, where his company produced several successful motion pictures, including *Lady Sings the Blues* (1972) and *The Wiz*

(1978). By 1964, Motown Records was the most influential independent record company in the country. *See also* AFRICAN AMERICANS; CINEMA; MUSIC.

MUELLER, FREDERICK H. (1893–1976). Secretary of commerce 1959–61. Michigan-born Frederick Henry Mueller was the son of a furniture manufacturer. After graduating from Michigan State University (B.S., 1914), he joined his father's business and worked his way to president of the company. In 1959, President **Dwight D. Eisenhower** appointed Mueller secretary of commerce when his first nominee for the position, **Lewis L. Strauss**, was not confirmed by the Senate to replace **Sinclair Weeks**.

MUMFORD, LEWIS (1895–1990). Born in New York, Lewis Mumford attended the City College of New York but did not complete a degree program. Living in New York City, Mumford traveled around the streets, observing its citizens, and he always had a pad of paper and a pen with which to write down his thoughts. His career began as a writer for various **magazines**, including the *New Yorker*. Mumford worried that as the population of a city grew and technology became more prominent, people failed to care for each other. History showed that the Roman Empire collapsed from within as it grew and lost its moral values. He often used the Pentagon as an example of society's problems. Officials within the Pentagon's walls were deciding the fate of those on the outside. The Pentagon was a walled city unto itself. Some of Mumford's most notable works are *The Pentagon of Power*, *The Cultures of Cities*, *The City in History*, and *The Myth of the Machine*. Lewis Mumford is still viewed as one of the most unique and original thinkers of the 20th century. His works continue to be studied by architects, urban planners, historians, and environmentalists. *See also* ARCHITECTURE.

MURROW, EDWARD R. (1908–1965). Born in North Carolina to Quaker parents, Edward Roscoe Murrow grew up in Washington State. He majored in speech at Washington State University (B.A., 1930), and in 1935 he joined CBS radio. That year, CBS sent him to Europe as director of European operations. Murrow was in Poland when he received word that Adolf Hitler had annexed Austria.

Murrow chartered a plane to Vienna. From there, he did his first eyewitness report of what had happened to Austria. Murrow's reporting was exceptional. Soon he was reporting on World War II from London. After the war, Murrow worked for CBS in New York, where he produced and narrated the **television** program "See It Now." In 1954, at the height of Senator **Joseph McCarthy**'s anticommunist witch hunts, Murrow questioned McCarthy's tactics on his national television program. His employers at CBS feared reprisals from McCarthy; however, Murrow's reporting helped to bring the downfall of the senator. *See also* COLD WAR; HOUSE UN-AMERICAN ACTIVITIES COMMITTEE (HUAC); RED SCARE.

MUSIC. With his swiveling hips and long sideburns, **Elvis Presley** started a revolution among **teenagers** in the 1950s that made record companies and recording stars millions of dollars. He was the poster boy for recording studios who sought a new sound. Presley's music was partly rooted in the music of **African Americans**. His recording of "I'm All Right, Mama," written by a black songwriter, became a hit with teenagers. Influential disc jockey Alan Freed and the **television** show *American Bandstand* introduced Presley's songs to the country. The popular program and **Motown Records** also introduced black singers to a larger white audience. Color barriers were broken. Teenagers enjoyed these new sounds and new singers, both white and black. A song could often spawn a dance **fad**, as did "Hand Jive," "Mashed Potato," and "The Stroll."

Harry Belafonte introduced calypso music, native to the Caribbean Islands. His hit records included "Day-O" and the "Banana Boat Song." The rhythm of Cuban music made the cha-cha a popular dance.

Throughout the 1950s, the Metropolitan Opera in New York City continued its radio broadcasts of the Saturday afternoon opera performances. Some of the great artists to debut at the Met at this time were Giorgio Tozzi (1953), Renata Tebaldi (1955), Maria Callas (1956), Birgit Nilsson (1959), Jon Vickers (1960), and Franco Corelli (1961). Rudolf Bing, manager of the Metropolitan Opera from 1950 to 1972, integrated the opera company when, in 1955, he debuted **Marian Anderson**. Following Anderson's historic performance, other **African Americans** performed with the Metropolitan Opera, including George Shirley and Leontyne Price.

In the 1950s, American composer Charles Ives's "Symphony No. 2" premiered at Carnegie Hall in New York City, which also premiered compositions by many other American composers. **Leonard Bernstein** was an important American composer and conductor in the 1950s and 1960s. Other great composers during the 1950s were Dmitri Shostakovich, Gian Carlo Menotti, and John Cage. Shostakovich composed 15 symphonies. Menotti composed the popular Christmas opera *Amahl and the Night Visitors*, as well as two dozen other operas, two of which won Pulitzer Prizes. Cage is renowned for his postwar avant-garde compositions and was influential in the development of modern dance.

Violinists Jascha Heifetz and Isaac Stern recorded many classical works in the 1950s, and they appeared on television and around the world. Stern has made over 100 recordings. *See also* ARMSTRONG, LOUIS; BERRY, CHUCK; BOONE, PAT; COPLAND, AARON; CROSBY, BING; DAY, DORIS; GERSHWIN, IRA, AND GEORGE GERSHWIN; HAMMON, JOHN; HORNE, LENA; JAZZ; MARTIN, DEAN, AND JERRY LEWIS; MARTIN, MARY; MATHIS, JOHNNY; MERMAN, ETHEL; PAUL, LES; ROBESON, PAUL; ROCK AND ROLL; SEEGER, PETE; VOCAL GROUPS AND VOCALISTS; WEAVERS, THE.

MUTUAL DEFENSE ASSISTANCE AGREEMENT. In response to the **Korean War** and the **Cold War**, the governments of Japan and the United States signed the Mutual Defense Assistance Agreement in 1954, which allowed the United States to continue its military presence in Japan while the country recovered from World War II. Japan built up its defensive systems, but it was not allowed to rearm for offensive action. Japan's strategic location near **China**, Korea, and the **Soviet Union** was very important to the safety of the United States. *See also* FOREIGN POLICY; JAPANESE PEACE TREATY.

– N –

NASSER, GAMAL ABDEL (1918–1970). President of Egypt 1956–70. One of the most influential leaders in Arab history, Gamal Abdel Nasser was born in Alexandria, Egypt. Rebellious as a young man, he joined the military during the 1948 war with **Israel**. The loss to Israel reinforced Nasser's desire to overthrow the government of King Farouk. In 1952, Nasser and General Muhammed Naguib led a coup forcing Farouk to abdicate. In 1954, Naguib became Egypt's president and Nasser became premier. In the 1956, presidential election, Nasser ran unopposed. As the new president of Egypt, he began to purchase military weapons from the **Soviet Union**.

As the relationship between Nasser and the Soviet Union grew stronger, President **Dwight D. Eisenhower** became more concerned. The United States had promised funds to Nasser to build the Aswan Dam but withdrew the offer. Furious, Nasser responded by seizing control of the Suez Canal. British Prime Minister **Anthony Eden** feared Nasser would cut off oil to **Great Britain**. He met secretly with **France** and Israel to plan an invasion to take control of the canal. In October–November 1956, the three countries sent forces into Egyptian territory, creating the **Suez Crisis**. President Eisenhower, with the help of the **United Nations** and the Soviet Union, used diplomatic pressure to end the invasion. With the withdrawal of the three armies, the UN sent its troops to the area to maintain peace.

Nasser was a hero in the eyes of the Middle East. In 1958, Syria and Egypt formed the United Arab Republic (UAR). Nasser was its president until it dissolved in 1961. In 1967, Nasser provoked a war with Israel. The swift defeat by the Israeli military humiliated him. When he announced his resignation as president, however, the country rallied to his support and he remained in power until 1970, when he died of a heart attack. Vice president Anwar Sadat became the new president. *See also* COLD WAR; CONTAINMENT; FOREIGN POLICY.

NATIONAL AERONAUTICS AND SPACE ADMINISTRATION (NASA). After the **Soviet Union** sent a small satellite, *Sputnik*, into orbit in 1957, President **Dwight D. Eisenhower** and the U.S. Congress responded by creating the National Aeronautics and Space Administration (NASA) in July 1958. Earlier in 1958, the first American satellite, *Explorer I*, had been successfully launched. NASA would continue America's **space** program through aeronautic research and exploration. President **John F. Kennedy** set a goal for the United States to be the first country to land a man on the moon. In 1962,

John Glenn was the first American to orbit the earth. In July 1969, a **televised** transmission from the moon showed American astronaut Neil Armstrong setting foot on the moon. *See also* COLD WAR; TECHNOLOGICAL INNOVATION.

NATIONAL ASSOCIATION FOR THE ADVANCEMENT OF COLORED PEOPLE (NAACP). In 1905, a small group of prominent **African Americans** gathered near Niagara Falls in a Canadian hotel, which unlike U.S. hotels was not segregated, and discussed problems faced by people of color. This meeting led to the Niagara movement, in which black and white Americans organized to advance civil rights in the United States. This movement led to the formation in 1909–10 of the National Association for the Advancement of Colored People (NAACP). The multiracial group's main objective was to stop social injustice against people of color. The first director of the NAACP was **W. E. B. Du Bois**.

During President **Dwight D. Eisenhower**'s administration, the NAACP played a major role in the landmark **Supreme Court** decision in *Brown v. Board of Education* (1954). In 1955, it also came to the aid of **Rosa Parks** when she was arrested for refusing to give up her seat on a bus to a white passenger, leading to the **Montgomery Bus Boycott**. The 1960 **sit-ins** held in Greensboro, North Carolina, were started by members of the NAACP Youth Council. *See also* BELAFONTE, HARRY; *BROWDER V. GAYLE*, BUNCHE, RALPH; CIVIL RIGHTS ACT OF 1957; CIVIL RIGHTS ACT OF 1960; CIVIL RIGHTS MOVEMENT; EDUCATION; FAUBUS, ORVAL; HAMMOND, JOHN; HARLAN, JOHN MARSHALL; KING, MARTIN LUTHER, JR; MARSHALL, THURGOOD; PARKER, DOROTHY; POWELL, ADAM CLAYTON, JR.; RACIAL INTEGRATION; RANDOLPH, A. PHILIP; SOUTHERN CHRISTIAN LEADERSHIP CONFERENCE (SCLC).

NATIONAL DEFENSE EDUCATION ACT, 1958. The **space** race between the United States and the **Soviet Union** forced changes in **education** in the United States. More federal funds were funneled into education. The curriculum, at all levels, began to focus more on **science**, math, and foreign languages at the expense of the **arts**. Low-interest loans were made available to college students.

NATIONAL FRONT FOR THE LIBERATION OF SOUTH VIETNAM (NFL). After the splitting of Vietnam into North and South Vietnam in 1954, the National Front for the Liberation of South Vietnam (NFL), composed of citizens of both Vietnams, was formed to reunite the two parts into one country. In 1960, the Viet Cong became the military arm of the NFL in South Vietnam. The Viet Cong eventually became the guerrilla fighters against whom the United States fought the **Vietnam War**. *See also* GENEVA CONFERENCE AND ACCORDS; HO CHI MINH.

NEHRU, JAWAHARLAL (1889–1964). Prime minister of **India** 1947–64. Born in Allahabad, Jawaharlal Nehru was educated in the best schools in India and **Great Britain**. His years in Great Britain allowed him to study the Russian revolution as well as Ireland's fight for freedom from British rule. Upon his return to India, he worked for its independence from Britain. A follower of Mohandas Gandhi, he was imprisoned more than once in the struggle for India's freedom. In 1947, Nehru became independent India's first prime minister.

During the **Cold War** and the **Korean War**, Nehru attempted to follow a policy of nonalignment. His policy of not aligning his country with either the Western or Soviet power blocs angered U.S. Secretary of State **John Foster Dulles**, who claimed Nehru was unable to choose freedom over communism. President **Dwight D. Eisenhower** offered India economic aid as well as nuclear **technology**, as outlined in his **Atoms for Peace** speech. Eisenhower, however, angered Nehru when the United States signed a military alliance with Pakistan, one of India's enemies.

Nehru became a major participant in the **United Nations (UN)**. During the Korean War, he agreed with the UN resolution calling for military sanctions against North Korea, but Nehru never sent Indian troops to fight in the Korean War. When he argued that **China** should be admitted to the UN, his proposal was rejected.

India and China were on good terms during the 1950s; however, in 1962 a border dispute erupted between the two nations. It took 30 rounds of talks and a number of stalemates to reach an agreement that finally brought better relations between India and China. Nehru, however, never attained a lasting peace with Pakistan.

Like Gandhi, Nehru was a man of peace who sometimes acted as a go-between when countries were in conflict. He served as prime minister until he died in 1964. His daughter, Indira Gandhi, was prime minister of India in 1966–77 and 1980–84. *See also* ATOMIC AND NUCLEAR ENERGY; FOREIGN POLICY; SOVIET UNION, RELATIONS WITH.

"NEW LOOK." Soon after **Dwight D. Eisenhower** became president he announced changes in the military budget. He reduced the size of the military and focused on the production of **atomic** weapons. He believed **massive retaliation** coupled with the possible use of atomic weapons were deterrents to war. These changes were soon referred to as the "new look."

NIELSEN, A. C. (1897–1980). Born in Chicago and educated at the University of Wisconsin (B.S., 1918), Arthur Charles Nielsen began his career as an engineer in Chicago. During the Great Depression, he worked for the packaged goods industry. The importance of his reports on the volume and price of goods around the country led his company to expand into other forms of market research.

In 1942, Nielsen began to survey radio audiences, employing the audiometer, an instrument able to record audience ratings of programs. When **television** became an important medium, it was only natural for Nielsen to survey television audiences. The audiometer connected television sets in selected homes around the country to Nielsen's **computers** through phone lines, so the company could determine which programs were most popular.

Advertisers in television's earliest years did not focus on any particular audience group. With a limited number of television sets in the early 1950s, tracking audiences and their preferences was not a priority. The A. C. Nielsen Company changed that perception. Nielsen's company began to categorize the audiences of various programs using demographics. This information was a boon to advertisers. Now they knew which products to advertise during a particular program. After his death, Nielsen's company became part of Dun and Bradstreet, one of the leading providers of business information. *See also* ADVERTISING; TECHNOLOGICAL INNOVATIONS.

NIXON, RICHARD M. (1913–1994). U.S. president 1969–74. Richard Milhous Nixon was born in California. He received his law degree from Duke University (1937) and returned to California to practice law. He was a member of the U.S. House of Representatives in 1947–51 and a senator in 1951–53, during the communist witch hunts carried out by the **House Un-American Activities Committee (HUAC)** and by Senator **Joseph McCarthy**. One of the most notable cases during the HUAC hearings involved a former State Department official named Alger Hiss. After Hiss was accused by the editor of *Time* of having been a member of the Communist Party, Nixon probed into Hiss's background and established that he had been a communist in the 1930s. His findings led to Hiss's conviction on perjury charges and made Nixon a nationally known figure. In the **1952 election**, Nixon was chosen as the running mate of **Republican** presidential candidate **Dwight D. Eisenhower**. He was also Eisenhower's running mate in the **1956 election**.

During the 1952 campaign, Nixon was accused of having a personal business fund. He defended himself in a nationally televised speech in which he explained that the only gift he had received was a cocker spaniel, which he named Checkers. He would not return the dog, he said, since his daughters loved Checkers. The **Checkers Speech**, kept him on the ticket.

As vice president, Nixon had to take Eisenhower's place while the president was in the hospital in 1955, 1956, and again in 1957. Nixon showed his ability to take charge, all the time hoping to become the president after Eisenhower left office. In 1959, at Moscow's American National Exhibition, he displayed his ability to stand up to **Nikita Khrushchev** during their "kitchen debate" on communism versus capitalism.

But Nixon lost the **1960 election** to the **Democratic Party** candidate, **John F. Kennedy**. Afterward, he announced he would not enter the political arena again. In 1968, however, he was the Republican presidential candidate and narrowly defeated his Democratic opponent, **Hubert H. Humphrey**. During the campaign, Nixon stated that if elected, he would end the **Vietnam War**, which had become very unpopular with the American public.

As president, Nixon kept up a heavy bombing campaign in Vietnam and sent forces into Cambodia. But he also pursued peace negotiations and eventually secured an end to the war. He was the first U.S. president to travel to **China** (1972), reopening a relationship between the two countries. Nixon also traveled to the **Soviet Union** (1972), where he achieved a limited strategic arms treaty.

Prior to the 1972 presidential election, a break-in occurred at the Democratic Party's headquarters in the Watergate Hotel in Washington, D.C. Those arrested for the crime were soon revealed to have connections with high-level officials in the White House. Although Nixon said he had no knowledge of such actions, the truth surfaced during U.S. Senate hearings about the Watergate break-in. The president had participated in attempts to cover up his involvement. The testimony of those close to Nixon brought the president's downfall. Nixon resigned in August 1974 rather than face impeachment.

NORTH ATLANTIC TREATY ORGANIZATION (NATO). In 1949, 11 nations, including the United States, signed an agreement to aid each other should any one of them be attacked. President **Harry S. Truman** chose **Dwight D. Eisenhower** to head the new organization. NATO's primary purpose was to combat communism. During Eisenhower's second term as U.S. president, a crisis erupted with the **Soviet Union** over the status of Berlin. Soviet leader **Nikita Khrushchev** announced that the Western powers, which had occupied Berlin since the end of World War II, must leave the city. The member nations of NATO worried that the **Berlin crisis** might lead to a nuclear war with the Soviet Union. But Eisenhower knew the United States' reputation was at stake. When Khrushchev came to the United States to meet with Eisenhower, the two attempted to resolve the Berlin question. Although they could not come to an agreement, the threat of war was averted. In 1961, Khrushchev solved the Berlin question on his own by building a wall between East Berlin and West Berlin. *See also* ATOMIC AND NUCLEAR ENERGY; CONTAINMENT; FOREIGN POLICY; KENNAN, GEORGE F.; MASSIVE RETALIATION; SOUTHEAST ASIA TREATY ORGANIZATION (SEATO).

NUCLEAR ENERGY. *See* ATOMIC AND NUCLEAR ENERGY.

– O –

O'CONNOR, FLANNERY (1925–1964). Novelist and short story writer Mary Flannery O'Connor was born in Georgia and lived in the town of Milledgeville most of her life. She completed her undergraduate degree at Georgia State College for Women (1945) and her graduate degree at the University of Iowa (M.F.A., 1947). She soon became highly acclaimed for her novels and short stories, which were set in the South. Her books include *Wise Blood*, *The Violent Bear It Away*, *A Good Man Is Hard to Find*, and *Everything That Rises Must Converge*. A deeply religious woman, questions of faith played a major role in her stories. O'Connor's characters were often physically deformed, violent, or immoral, and her work showed a dark humor. Diagnosed with lupus, O'Connor returned home to Milledgeville in 1951 and was not expected to live many more years. But much of her mature work was completed in the intervening years before her death in 1964 at age 39. *See also* LITERATURE; RELIGION.

O'KEEFFE, GEORGIA (1887–1986). One of the finest women artists of the 20th century, Georgia O'Keeffe was born in Wisconsin. She studied at both the Art Institute of Chicago and in 1907 at New York's Art Students' League, where one of her paintings received a top prize. O'Keeffe was an early abstract painter. She turned to strong colors, especially in her paintings of flowers. After the death of her husband, photographer Alfred Stieglitz, she moved to New Mexico. The Southwest provided the setting for the paintings of flowers and desert scapes for which she became most famous. *See also* ART.

OLYMPICS. The **Soviet Union** did not participate in the 1952 Winter Olympics. A revolution and two world wars had led to their extended absence from the Olympics. Ironically, they did participate in the 1952 Summer Olympics in Helsinki, Finland, a country it invaded twice during World War II. The United States won 76 medals that year, the Soviet Union 71. During the 1952 Winter Olympics in Oslo, Norway, the United States won 11 medals.

World events affected the number of participants at the 1956 Summer Olympics, held in Melbourne, Australia. The **Suez Crisis** led Egypt, **Lebanon**, and Iraq to boycott the games. The failed **Hungarian Revolution** prompted Spain, the Netherlands, and Switzerland also to withdraw in protest against the Soviet Union's suppression of the revolution. Both the Soviet Union and Hungary participated in the summer games. The People's Republic of **China** boycotted the 1956 Summer Olympics because the Republic of China (Taiwan), their political rival, participated. The Soviet Union excelled in both the 1956 Summer Olympics in Melbourne and in the Winter Olympics in Cortina d'Ampezzo, Italy.

In the 1960 Winter Olympics in Squaw Valley, the Soviet Union dominated, winning 21medals; the Americans won 10. American **television** covered the Olympics for the first time. In the 1960 Summer Olympics in Rome, Italy, the Soviet Union led the participating 84 nations with 103 medals, followed by 71 for the United States. *See also* RUDOLPH, WILMA; SPORTS.

OPEN SKIES. *See* GENEVA SUMMIT CONFERENCE.

OPERATION AJAX. *See* IRAN, RELATIONS WITH.

OPPENHEIMER, J. ROBERT (1904–1967). Born in New York and educated at both Harvard University (A.B., 1925) and Gottingen University, Germany (Ph.D., 1927), Julius Robert Oppenheimer was the physicist who headed the secret Manhattan Project during World War II to develop an **atomic** weapon. After the war, Oppenheimer chaired the **Atomic Energy Commission** (1947–52) and opposed the further development of nuclear weapons. In contrast, his colleague **Edward Teller** wanted to continue research on the more powerful **hydrogen bomb**. Teller raised questions about Oppenheimer, who began to be regarded as a security risk. In 1953, after appearing before the **House Un-American Activities Committee (HUAC)**, Oppenheimer lost his security clearance. In the years that followed, Oppenheimer gave lectures, wrote, and continued to work in physics. *See also* COLD WAR; MCCARTHY, JOSEPH; RED SCARE.

ORGANISATION FOR EUROPEAN ECONOMIC COOPERATION (OEEC). After World War II, the **Marshall Plan** was developed to aid the devastated countries of Europe through economic aid. In April 1948, the Organisation for European Economic Cooperation was created to continue the work begun by the Marshall Plan. It originally consisted of 18 participants and was helpful in making better use of American assistance and increasing economic cooperation in Europe. In 1961, it was superceded by the Organisation for Economic Cooperation and Development (OCED), a worldwide body. The OECD continues to provide help to countries trying to develop a sustainable economy. It also promotes world trade. *See also* TRUMAN, HARRY S.

ORGANIZATION OF AMERICAN STATES (OAS). In April 1948, the Organization of American States was formed in Bogota, Colombia. The purpose of this organization was for the nations of the western hemisphere to deal with matters of importance to the region, including terrorism, illegal drugs, human rights, and corruption. **Cuba** was an initial member but was suspended in 1962, leaving 34 member nations. Four official languages are used by the OAS: English, Spanish, French, and Portuguese. Although international concerns are discussed throughout the year, the General Assembly meets once a year to set major goals and policies. *See also* COLD WAR; FOREIGN POLICY; INTER-AMERICAN DEVELOPMENT BANK (IADB).

ORGANIZATION OF PETROLEUM EXPORTING COUNTRIES (OPEC). The Organization of Petroleum Exporting Countries (OPEC) was organized in Baghdad, Iraq, in September 1960 in response to declining prices for Mideast oil. The original members—Saudi Arabia, **Iran**, Iraq, Kuwait, and Venezuela—resolved that they could "no longer remain indifferent to the attitude heretofore adopted by the oil companies in effecting price modifications." Over the next 10 years, OPEC was able to establish a revenue floor for Mideast oil that rose from $0.80 a barrel at the beginning of the 1960s to slightly below $1.00 a barrel by the end of the decade. By taking advantage of the world's hunger for oil (which by the beginning of the 1970s was already leading to spot shortages) and opening new fields to independent producers in Libya, OPEC was able to break the control over Mideast oil that the major oil companies had enjoyed since the 1920s.

– P –

PACKARD, VANCE (1914–1996). Author and marketing expert Vance Oakley Packard was born in Pennsylvania and earned degrees at Pennsylvania State University (B.A., 1936) and Columbia

University's School of Journalism (M.S., 1937). He gained national fame with the publication of his first book, *The Hidden Persuaders*, which exposed the manipulation methods used by the **advertising** industry to influence consumers. Candidates in elections used these same tricks to influence voters. *The Hidden Persuaders* was followed by other books of interest to consumers. *The Waste Makers* explained that businesses engaged in "planned obsolescence," making products that were not intended to last. As products changed or improved, consumers threw away the older products and replaced them with the newest models. *The Waste Makers* was another best seller. Packard's other books include *The Naked Society*, *The Sexual Wilderness*, *The People Shapers*, *Our Endangered Children*, and *Ultra Rich: How Much Is Too Much?*

PAHLAVI, MOHAMMAD REZA (1919–1980). Shah of Iran 1941–79. In 1941, Mohammad Reza Pahlavi succeeded his father as the shah of **Iran**. Pro-Western, he instituted many modernizing social reforms, and he worked closely with U.S. oil companies to increase Iran's oil production.

In 1951, Prime Minister **Mohammed Mossadegh**, leader of the National Front Movement, supported by the Iranian Communist Party, nationalized the British-owned Anglo-Iranian Oil Company, the country's main source of income. In 1953, the shah was forced to flee the country, taking refuge in Italy. Later that year, a covert operation by the **Central Intelligence Agency (CIA)** called Operation Ajax forced Mossadegh from office. The shah returned to head the Iranian government until 1979, when he was overthrown in a revolution. He died in Panama of cancer in 1980. *See also* COLD WAR; CONTAINMENT; FOREIGN POLICY.

PARIS CONFERENCE, 1954. In 22–23 October 1954, a nine-nation conference met in response to **France**'s concern about the future of postwar **Germany**. The conference agreed that the occupation of Germany should end soon and that Germany should be admitted to the **North Atlantic Treaty Organization (NATO)**. Fearful of a rearmed Germany, however, France opposed these plans. Prime Minister **Anthony Eden** of **Great Britain** assured France that Germany was not a threat. The conference adopted the proposals for Germany's future, and Germany entered NATO. *See also* FOREIGN POLICY.

PARKER, DOROTHY (1893–1967). Poet, critic, and screenwriter, Dorothy Parker was born into a well-to-do family in New Jersey. When she was five years old, her mother died. Later her father married a woman Parker despised. When she was in her teens, she left school and began writing poetry. Parker sent some of her poems to the editor of *Vogue*. In 1916, *Vogue* offered her a position at the **magazine**. In 1917, she left *Vogue* to work for *Vanity Fair* (1917–20), and in 1927–33 she wrote book reviews for the *New Yorker*. In the 1930s, she was a Hollywood screenwriter.

Although she was never a member of the Communist Party, Parker considered herself a communist and was called before the **House Un-American Activities Committee (HUAC)** during the **Red Scare** of the early 1950s. She was **blacklisted** by the committee for her leftist views and opinions.

Parker was married twice, had a number of affairs, attempted suicide more than once, and was a heavy drinker. Known for her biting criticism and quick wit, she spoke out freely on topics about which she was passionate. In her will, she left her estate to **Martin Luther King Jr**. After King's death, the estate went to the **National Association for the Advancement of Colored People (NAACP)**. *See also* CINEMA; LITERATURE.

PARKS, GORDON (1912–2006). Photographer Gordon Parks was born in Kansas. His mother's death forced 15-year-old Parks to move to Minnesota, where his married sister lived. Parks and his brother-in-law did not get along, and he was forced to move out. On his own, he did what he could to survive. When he was 26, he noticed photographs of migrant workers in a **magazine**.

In 1938, he purchased his first camera and began photographing the common lives of **African Americans**. When his photographs were displayed in an Eastman Kodak store in Minneapolis, they were noticed by the wife of boxer Joe Louis. She suggested Parks move to Chicago, where more opportunities would be available to him as an African American artist.

In 1948, his photo essay on Harlem led to a job at *Life*, where he worked until 1972. He photographed racism, poverty, black urban life, celebrities, Paris fashions, and politicians. In 1962, a co-worker suggested Parks write his life story. The result was *The Learning Tree*, which in 1969 was made into a movie with Parks as director. The success of *The Learning Tree* led to more **cinema** successes. In 1971, Parks wrote the screenplay and directed the box office hit *Shaft*.

Parks was a co-founder of *Essence*, a magazine whose focus and audience is the African American community. He was also a **civil rights** activist and marched in 1963 with **Martin Luther King Jr**. In 1990, he published his memoir *Voices in the Mirror*. *See also* LITERATURE.

PARKS, ROSA (1913–2005). Rights activist Rosa Parks was born and raised in segregated Alabama. As a child, she heard that Ku Klux Klan members lynched **African Americans**. Her biggest fear was that her home would one day be burned down. When she was 11 years old, she was sent to a school in Montgomery, Alabama, run by white women who believed in giving young black women an **education** in skills such as sewing. She became a seamstress and in 1924 married Raymond Parks, a barber who was active in the Montgomery chapter of the **National Association for the Advancement of Colored People (NAACP)**.

On 1 December 1955, Rosa Parks gained fame when she refused to give up her seat on a bus to a white person, as required by law. Once before, the driver had forced her off his bus when she would not move. In the past, he had also interfered when she had attempted to register to vote. This time, the driver stopped his bus and had Parks arrested.

Parks's arrest was the spark that began the **Montgomery Bus Boycott**, which was spearheaded by **Martin Luther King Jr.**, then a new minister in Montgomery. The largest number of bus riders in Montgomery were African American. For months they walked, leaving the buses virtually empty. Throughout the boycott, King brought national attention to Rosa Parks's arrest as well as the living and working conditions in the South for African Americans.

Parks's role in the boycott led to threats on her life and unemployment for her husband. In 1957, they moved to Detroit, where she worked as a receptionist for a young lawyer and future congressman, John Conyers. She returned to Montgomery to help King's marches and protests. For her work in the **civil rights movement**, Rosa Parks received many awards and honors, including the Medal of Freedom in 1996, presented to her by President Bill Clinton. She died in Detroit at the age of 92. Her body lay in the Rotunda of the U.S. Capitol, an honor normally granted only to high-ranking dignitaries. She was buried in Detroit. *See also BROWDER V. GAYLE*; CIVIL RIGHTS ACT OF 1957; CIVIL RIGHTS ACT OF 1960; RACIAL INTEGRATION.

PAUL, LES (1915–). Born Lester William Polsfuss in Wisconsin, Les Paul began playing the guitar at the age of 14. In 1936, he formed a **jazz** trio. Unhappy with the sound of his guitar, Paul worked to improve its quality. In 1941, he invented the solid-body electric guitar. In 1951, his Gibson Les Paul guitar was introduced to the public. For the **rock and roll** musicians of the 1950s, Paul's creation was extremely important.

Throughout his career, Paul continued to create new recording techniques. In the 1950s, Paul and his wife Mary Ford recorded several hit records using his system of overdubbing numerous tracks. Some of their songs were "Tennessee Waltz," "How High the Moon," and "Vaya Con Dios." The eight-track tape recorder was also Paul's invention.

Paul is one of the most influential people in modern string popular **music**. The solid-body electric guitar is still used by guitarists worldwide. In 1988, Les Paul was inducted into the Rock and Roll Hall of Fame.

PAYOLA. Although the practice of paying a disc jockey to play a song on the radio was a criminal offense in most states, record companies had traditionally engaged in such practices. The major difference when **rock and roll** became popular in the 1950s, however, was the influence disc jockeys had with their listeners. They could make or break a budding singer.

Alan Freed was one of the most influential disc jockeys of the 1950s to engage in payola. He introduced many of the **African Americans** in the recording industry to white audiences. Many of the singers in the 1950s credited Freed with their success. In 1958, he was singled out for engaging in payola and lost his job. In the 1960s, federal laws were passed prohibiting anyone at a radio station from taking money in return for playing certain records. *See also* MUSIC.

PEANUTS. For over 55 years, the comic strip *Peanuts* created by Charles M. Schulz has appeared in Sunday newspapers and in books, and it has been adapted for **television** and Broadway. Schulz's first cartoons appeared nationally in the *Saturday Evening Post* during the 1940s, and a series of his cartoons that were an early version of *Peanuts* were published in a St. Paul newspaper. In 1950, the United Feature Syndicate began to publish *Peanuts*. By the 1960s, *Peanuts* was so popular that Hallmark Cards used the characters in their greeting cards. In 1965, *A Charlie Brown Christmas* debuted on television. The show *You're A Good Man, Charlie Brown* began off Broadway in 1967. In 1973, *A Charlie Brown Thanksgiving* aired on television. By 1984, *Peanuts* appeared in 2,000 newspapers. By 1999, over 20,000 products based on *Peanuts* characters had been produced.

PEYTON PLACE. The first book to be called a blockbuster, *Peyton Place*, by novelist **Grace Metalious**, was published in 1956. Within the first 10 days, every copy sold out; soon after, the rights to the book were bought by Hollywood. Metalious had used fictional characters based on real people and a real-life event involving a young woman who killed her father for molesting her. The setting was an outwardly prudish small town in New England where illicit relationships were common. The book included wife-beating, rapes, and women striving to be independent. Three women in the book finally gain independence and self-respect, and they learn to put aside their past. These were some of the very ideals of the **women's movement**; thus, some critics saw the book as exploring women's struggles and drew parallels with **Betty Friedan**'s 1953 nonfiction book *The Feminine Mystique*. At a time when **television** shows commonly showed happy families and problems being easily solved,

Metalious wrote about a totally different side of life, taboos not so blatantly exposed before.

Although *Peyton Place* was a huge commercial success, a number of countries banned the book. Some libraries refused to purchase it. Critics called the book trash. Metalious, nevertheless, opened the door for women who wanted to write novels filled with lust and desire. The title of the book became synonymous with immorality. Even today, an event or place that is shockingly immoral might be called "a regular Peyton Place." *See also* CINEMA; LITERATURE.

PLEDGE OF ALLEGIANCE. In 1951, the national board of directors of the Knights of Columbus made the decision to insert the words "under God" into the Pledge of Allegiance anytime the organization's members recited the pledge. In 1954, Congress voted to add the phrase to the pledge, and President **Dwight D. Eisenhower** signed the legislation into law. America wanted to show the world, especially the atheistic **Soviet Union**, that **religion** and faith were part of the American way of life. *See also* COLD WAR; IN GOD WE TRUST; RED SCARE.

POITIER, SIDNEY (1927–). Actor Sidney Poitier was born in Miami. His parents were on a trip from their home in the Bahamas. When he was 16, he moved to New York and worked as a janitor at the American Negro Theater, where he was given acting lessons. As **Harry Belafonte**'s understudy, Poitier was able to appear in *Days of Our Youth* when Belafonte was unable to perform, and he made an impression on audiences. Throughout the 1940s, he continued to appear in plays. In 1950, he made his **cinema** debut in *No Way Out*. In films during the 1950s and 1960s, he portrayed characters of strength and confidence, making him a role model for **African Americans**. He appeared in important and controversial movies, including *Cry, the Beloved Country*, *Blackboard Jungle*, *A Raisin in the Sun*, *The Defiant Ones*, *Guess Who's Coming to Dinner*, and *To Sir, with Love*. For his role in *Lilies of the Field* (1963), he became the first African American to win an Academy Award for Best Actor. In addition to his acting career, Poitier directed several films, including *Buck and the Preacher*, *Uptown Saturday Night*, *Stir Crazy*, and *Ghost Dad*.

POLIO. *See* SALK, JONAS.

POLIOMYELITIS VACCINATION ACT, 1955. After **Jonas Salk** discovered a vaccine to prevent polio, the U.S. government allocated $30 million for states to purchase the vaccine. Twenty percent of the funds were to be used for vaccinations for those unable to pay for them. In 1952, prior to the polio vaccine, there were 60,000 cases of polio, the highest number ever recorded in the country. By 1960, the number had been reduced to 3,277, the lowest since 1938. *See also* MEDICAL ADVANCES.

POWELL, ADAM CLAYTON, JR. (1908–1972). Member of the House of Representatives 1945–67. Adam Clayton Powell Jr. was born in New Haven, Connecticut, but raised in Harlem, New York, where his father was pastor of the largest **African American** church. In 1930, he received his B.A. from Colgate University. He planned to study medicine but then decided to follow in his father's footsteps. After he received a master's degree in religious education from Columbia University Teachers' College (1932), he joined his father as an assistant pastor. In 1937, he replaced his father as pastor of the church. He quickly became known as an outspoken black leader.

In 1941, Powell became New York City's first African American councilman. A **Democrat**, in 1945 he was elected to the U.S. House of Representatives. In 1946, the House was considering a bill that proposed using federal funds to provide free school lunches to children. Powell succeeded in amending the bill so that it prohibited states from excluding African American children from the program.

In 1952, the Internal Revenue Service and the Justice Department investigated Powell for tax evasion. Although he was acquitted of all charges in 1960, he was investigated in 1966 for using House funds for personal use. In 1967, he lost his congressional seat over the scandal. Although he won his seat back in a special election that same year, he lost his seat in the 1970 election. *See also* CIVIL RIGHTS ACT OF 1957; CIVIL RIGHTS ACT OF 1960; CIVIL RIGHTS MOVEMENT.

POWERS, FRANCIS GARY (1929–1977). Born in Kentucky but raised in Virginia, Francis Gary Powers graduated from Milligan

College in Tennessee (1950). He was commissioned that same year in the U.S. Air Force and trained as a fighter pilot. During the **Korean War**, he was recruited by the **Central Intelligence Agency (CIA)**. In 1956, he left the air force and joined a CIA program involving observation flights over the **Soviet Union**. In 1960, at the height of the **Cold War**, his U-2 plane was shot down over Soviet air space and he was held as a spy for two years. The **U-2 Incident** was an embarrassment for President **Dwight D. Eisenhower**, who at first denied that such a flight had taken place.

When Powers was freed from Soviet prison and returned to the United States in 1962, his CIA colleagues were still angry at him for not destroying the plane or committing suicide when captured. Powers left his government position and continued his career as a test pilot. He was killed in a helicopter crash in 1977. Forty years after the U-2 Incident, his family received various military and government awards to honor his memory. *See also* GATES, THOMAS S.; KHRUSHCHEV, NIKITA.

PRESIDENTIAL DEBATES, 1960. For the first time in history, viewers in 1960 watched the two presidential candidates, **John F. Kennedy** and Vice President **Richard M. Nixon**, debate each other before **television** cameras. Nixon did not use makeup, and he looked tired. His gray suit was a poor choice against the drab background. Kennedy looked fit, was well prepared for the questions, and used the cameras to his advantage. He looked directly at the television audience. Viewers felt he was talking directly to them, not the journalists asking the questions.

When Nixon ran for president in 1968, he remembered the mistakes made in the 1960 debates. The lessons he learned helped him in his televised debates against **Hubert H. Humphrey**. *See also* ELECTION, 1960.

PRESIDENT'S COUNCIL ON PHYSICAL FITNESS AND SPORTS. When President **Dwight D. Eisenhower** learned that American children were less fit than European children, he established a council in 1958 to develop programs to improve their health and fitness. In one physical fitness study, 90 percent of European children passed a test of minimum muscular fitness; only half of American children passed the same test. Vice President **Richard M. Nixon** chaired the first meeting of the President's Council on Physical Fitness and Sports. The council worked with both public and private groups to encourage sports and other outdoor activities. President **John F. Kennedy** changed the council's name to the President's Council on Physical Fitness. Whereas Eisenhower had focused on children, Kennedy included all age groups.

PRESLEY, ELVIS AARON (1935–1977). Born in Mississippi, Elvis Aaron Presley began singing in his church choir. He learned to play the guitar and sing songs that combined **music** styles of white and black performers. In 1953, he made his first hit record, "That's All Right, Mama," for Sun Records. In 1956, "Heartbreak Hotel" topped the record charts. Presley's singing, combined with his hip movements, were unprecedented and shocking to many parents. When Presley appeared on **Ed Sullivan**'s highly-rated **television** program, censors prohibited him from being shown below the waist.

The popularity of Presley's music opened the door for a number of black singers. **Teenagers**, for the most part, did not care who sang a song. Many **African American** singers acknowledge that had it not been for Presley, they would never have been as successful. Presley has been credited with bringing about some of the most important cultural changes in the United States in the 20th century. His songs made **rock and roll** popular, and his movements opened the door to more provocative **dances**.

Presley starred in many movies but never believed he was given the chance to show his dramatic acting ability, for he was always expected to sing. Many of his films shared their titles with his popular songs, including *Love Me Tender* (1956), *Jailhouse Rock* (1957), *Blue Hawaii* (1961), and *Viva Las Vegas* (1964). *See also* CINEMA; FADS.

PROXMIRE, WILLIAM (1915–2005). U.S. senator 1957–89. Born in Illinois, William Proxmire was educated at Yale University (B.A., 1938) and Harvard University (M.B.A., 1940). After serving in World War II, he returned to Harvard and received a second graduate degree, from the Harvard Graduate School of Arts and Sciences

(1948). He then moved to Madison, Wisconsin, to work as a reporter for the *Capitol Times*.

In 1951, Proxmire was elected to the Wisconsin State Assembly. The following year he made an unsuccessful bid for governor. In 1957, he was elected to fill the seat of the late Senator **Joseph McCarthy**. In the Senate, Proxmire, a **Democrat**, was an outspoken critic of the **Vietnam War** and often criticized Presidents **Lyndon B. Johnson** and **Richard M. Nixon**. A member of the Armed Services Committee, he uncovered wasteful military spending. From the mid-1970s until 1988, his Golden Fleece Award was given yearly to government departments that funded unnecessary projects. He was chair of the Committee on Banking, Housing, and Urban Affairs, which saved New York City from bankruptcy in 1976–77. He was against the production of the supersonic transport and an early advocate of changing the rules on campaign financing. For almost 40 years, he worked to convince the United States to ratify a **United Nations** document banning genocide. In 1988, the United States finally signed the Convention on the Prevention and Punishment of the Crime of Genocide.

After leaving the Senate, Proxmire had an office in the Library of Congress. In 2005, he died from the effects of Alzheimer's disease.

PUERTO RICO. After the United States defeated Spain in the 1898 Spanish-American War, the island of Puerto Rico became a U.S. territory with considerable self-government. In time, rival political groups sought either independence or statehood. Some engaged in violence. In 1950, members of the Puerto Rican Nationalist Party attacked Blair House, the official residence of vice presidents. Oscar Collazo, the leader of the group, and one White House police officer were killed.

During the presidency of **Dwight D. Eisenhower**, violence in the name of Puerto Rican independence continued. In 1954, members of the Puerto Rican Nationalist Party, led by Lolita Lebron, entered the U.S. House of Representatives and opened fire, wounding five people. Lebron and her cohorts were caught and imprisoned. In response to these attacks, the government of Puerto Rico cracked down on such groups. In 1979, after 25 years in prison, Lebron was pardoned by President Jimmy Carter. She returned to Puerto Rico, where she was welcomed as a hero.

– Q –

QUEEN ELIZABETH II (1926–). When British King George VI died in 1952, he was succeeded by his eldest daughter, Elizabeth, who was in Kenya when she learned of her father's death from cancer. In 1953, the first major international **television** event was her coronation as Queen Elizabeth II.

Elizabeth II visited the United States twice during **Dwight D. Eisenhower**'s presidency. In 1957, she addressed the **United Nations** General Assembly. In 1959, she hosted a dinner for the president at the Canadian Embassy in Washington, D.C. *See also*, GREAT BRITAIN, RELATIONS WITH.

QUEMOY AND MATSU CRISES. Quemoy and Matsu are islands in the Taiwan Strait between **China** and Taiwan (Formosa). In 1949, losing the fight against **Mao Zedong** and his communist forces, the noncommunist Nationalist Chinese government led by **Chiang Kai-shek** fled to Taiwan. Retaining control over Quemoy and Matsu, Chiang used these islands as staging grounds to launch raids on the Chinese mainland. In August–September 1954, the Chinese Communists began to shell these islands, starting with Quemoy.

Fearful that the bombardment was part of a communist plan to take these islands and then Taiwan, President **Dwight D. Eisenhower** and Secretary of State **John Foster Dulles** made clear that they would support the Chinese Nationalist government. However, to keep the communists guessing, they did not make clear whether that commitment would include Quemoy and Matsu. As a further attempt to bring pressure to bear on the Chinese Communists, the Eisenhower administration brought the matter before the **United Nations** and signed a defense treaty with Taiwan. Then, the U.S. Congress in January 1955 passed the **Formosa Resolution**, which gave the president the right to use the U.S. military to protect Taiwan and "related positions and territories of that area in friendly hands." Two months later, Eisenhower threatened to use nuclear weapons against China if necessary. In April, the bombardment stopped. Pressure from the **Soviet Union** as well as **Third World** nations, none of which wanted to see the crisis turn into something much worse, played a significant part in China's decision to end the shelling.

In 1958, when Chiang again used Quemoy and Matsu to launch guerrilla operations against the mainland, Communist China renewed the shelling of the islands. Mao may also have wanted to use the show of force to challenge the **Soviet Union** for supremacy within the communist world. As before, the Eisenhower administration sought to keep the communists guessing as to whether it would defend Quemoy and Matsu and issued statements that it would use nuclear weapons if necessary. Furthermore, Eisenhower ordered the U.S. 7th Fleet to the Taiwan Strait. It appears the threat to use nuclear weapons, combined with a lack of Soviet support for the shelling and Nationalist victories over the communists in air battles, convinced the Chinese Communists in October to end the shelling. But in a policy that would last for the next 25 years, they bombarded the islands on odd-numbered days. *See also* COLD WAR; CONTAINMENT; MASSIVE RETALIATION.

QUIZ SHOW SCANDALS. During the 1950s, **television** game shows were extremely popular. One of the most watched was *Twenty One*, in which two contestants competed against each other, answering difficult questions on often obscure subjects. Because the first two shows were poorly received, the sponsor, Geritol, decided the best way to improve the show was to give the answers to contestants with the understanding that they had to act according to a script. Everything on the program was choreographed. The highest-grossing winner for a time was Herbert Stempel. When he had to compete against Charles Van Doren, a handsome Columbia University professor and son of a well-known literary critic, Mark Van Doren, Stempel was told when to lose. The men played 42 games, each winning exactly half of them. On the 43rd game, Stempel had to pretend he did not know the answer to a question whose answer he knew. When Van Doren won, the audience was elated. He became a celebrity and a regular guest on the popular *Today* television show. Angry at his loss to Van Doren, Stempel asked a federal investigator to prove the program was fraudulent. His suggestion was at first ignored.

In 1958, a notebook was found detailing the scripted playing of *Dotto*, another television game show. Within two months, *Twenty-One* was abruptly cancelled. Charles Van Doren was called before a U.S. Senate committee to testify about the rigged game shows. In

November 1959, Van Doren admitted he was given the answers prior to each show. Although he lost his position at Columbia University, he continues to write and has been an editor for some publishing houses. *See also* GOODSON-TODMAN PRODUCTIONS.

– R –

RACIAL INTEGRATION. The 1950s were one of the most important decades in **African American** history in the United States. They were the beginning of the end of segregation in public schools as well as the beginning of the **civil rights movement**. President **Dwight D. Eisenhower** was slow to enforce integration because he did not believe the federal government should be involved in enforcing it. His attitude only encouraged southerners not to abide by the **Supreme Court**'s 1954 ruling in *Brown v. Board of Education*. The president was forced to act when Arkansas Governor **Orval Faubus** would not allow black students into Little Rock's Central High School.

    Martin Luther King Jr. wrote Eisenhower in 1957, asking to have a meeting on civil rights; however, the president ignored the message. The media took notice, and *Time* put King on its cover because of his work in the civil rights movement. **J. Edgar Hoover**, director of the **Federal Bureau of Investigation (FBI)**, kept files on anyone in the civil rights movement. The FBI harassed King and monitored his travels. Nevertheless, integration continued to flourish. By the end of the 1950s, integration was being accepted by more and more people.

    College students were one group who supported civil rights on a large scale. In 1960, when four men in Greensboro, North Carolina, sat at a lunch counter and were not served, the story was carried by the media. The next day, more people sat at the same lunch counter. This **sit-in** was a form of nonviolent protest, and soon college students were using sit-ins to express their opposition to various things on their campuses.

    By the middle of the 1960s, all public places were integrated. Discrimination was not tolerated in federally funded projects, and companies would lose contracts if racial discrimination was proven. More civil rights legislation was passed in the 1950s and 1960s than in any other time in the country's history. *See also* BELAFONTE, HARRY; *BROWDER V. GAYLE*; BUNCHE, RALPH; CIVIL RIGHTS ACT OF 1957; CIVIL RIGHTS ACT OF 1960; DU BOIS, W. E. B.; EDUCATION; HAMMOND, JOHN; HARLAN, JOHN MARSHALL; MONTGOMERY BUS BOYCOTT; MUSIC; PARKS, ROSA; POWELL, ADAM CLAYTON, JR.; RANDOLPH, A. PHILIP; MARSHALL, THURGOOD; SOUTHERN CHRISTIAN LEADERSHIP CONFERENCE (SCLC); WHITE CITIZENS COUNCIL.

RADFORD, ARTHUR W. (1896–1973). Chair of Joint Chiefs of Staff 1953–57. Born in Chicago, Arthur William Radford was a graduate of the U.S. Naval Academy (1916). He served in both World Wars I and II. During the **Korean War**, he was commander in chief of the Pacific Fleet. From 1953 to 1957, he served as chair of the Joint Chiefs of Staff, succeeding Army General Omar Bradley. In 1957, Radford resigned to pursue a career in the private sector, although he continued to serve as a consultant to the Defense Department and as an advisor to President **Dwight D. Eisenhower**. During the 1960s, he advised both presidents **John F. Kennedy** and **Lyndon B. Johnson**. A staunch anticommunist, he vigorously promoted the need for a naval air station in the Far East. The naval air station at Cubi Point, in the Philippines, was named for Admiral Radford.

RAISIN IN THE SUN, A. Written by Lorraine Hansberry, in 1959 *A Raisin in the Sun* became the first drama by an **African American** woman to be performed on Broadway. Lloyd Richards, the play's director, was the first African American to direct a Broadway show. The play's title came from a poem by **Langston Hughes**. The all-black cast, starring **Sidney Poitier**, made funding difficult; however, after a year, the play was able to begin touring before opening in New York. After receiving favorable reviews, it opened in March 1959 on Broadway. Named the best play of 1959 by the New York Drama Critics' Circle, *A Raisin in the Sun* played for two years.

Hansberry focused her play on a family of five African Americans living in a run-down Chicago tenement apartment. When the father died, his life insurance policy paid $10,000. Always wanting a better life for her children, the mother used the check to purchase a home in an all-white neighborhood. When the homeowners association attempted to evict the family, the family fought to remain in its new home.

Hansberry's own family had faced the same problems as the characters in her play. Her father bought a home in a hostile all-white neighborhood. She remembered the fights in the courts and the help the family received from the **National Association for the Advancement of Colored People (NAACP)**.

In 1961, *A Raisin in the Sun* became an award-winning film starring Sidney Poitier. *See also* CINEMA; THEATER.

RAND, AYN (1905–1982). Russian-born Ayn Rand began her career as a screenwriter. A strong advocate of capitalism, she believed communism was immoral. In the early 1940s, her novel *The Fountainhead* became a best seller and soon a movie. Ambitious and determined, she would not allow the movie to be filmed unless she could have input into all aspects of it. The movie was a box office hit. Rand and her writings have spawned many followers, as well as the creation of the Ayn Rand Institute to promote her ideas.

Rand called her main idea *objectivism*. She believed that the ability to reason is humans' greatest attribute. And she argued that if one followed laws and befriended like-minded people, success was assured. Rand thought the ideal man was strong, idealistic, and entrepreneurial in spirit.

Rand's novel *Atlas Shrugged* (1957) further expanded her ideas. In 1991, the Book-of-the-Month Club and the Library of Congress surveyed readers on which books influenced them the most. The Bible and *Atlas Shrugged* were the two listed most often. *See also* CINEMA; LITERATURE.

RANDOLPH, A. PHILIP (1889–1979). Labor leader Asa Philip Randolph was born in Florida. After high school, he moved to New York City, where he studied at the City College of New York and became active in the Socialist Party. In 1925, he organized the Brotherhood of Sleeping Car Porters, an **African American** labor union.

In 1941, Randolph joined with the **National Association for the Advancement of Colored People (NAACP)** and other **civil rights** activists to plan a massive march on Washington to protest discrimination in the defense industry. Following the march, President Franklin D. Roosevelt signed an order banning discrimination in any defense industry that received federal funds. By the end of World War II, African Americans accounted for 8 percent of defense industry jobs, up from 3 percent before the war.

In the 1950s, Randolph became a member of the **American Federation of Labor–Congress of Industrial Organizations (AFL-CIO)** executive committee, and in 1957 became vice president of the union.

Co-founder of *The Messenger*, a **magazine** that contained articles of importance to African Americans, he often stressed the need for more rights for black workers. In 1963, he was a major force behind the march on Washington in which **Martin Luther King Jr**. delivered his famous "I Have a Dream" speech.

During the 1940s and 1950s, Randolph was often called "the most dangerous Negro in America." His socialism moderated in his later years, but he will always be remembered for his contributions to the civil rights movement. *See also* CIVIL RIGHTS ACT OF 1957; CIVIL RIGHTS ACT OF 1960; EDUCATION; LABOR MANAGEMENT REPORTING AND DISCLOSURE ACT; RACIAL INTEGRATION.

RAYBURN, SAM (1882–1961). Speaker of the House 1940–46, 1950–53, 1956–61. Born in Tennessee but raised in Texas, Samuel Taliaferro Rayburn graduated from East Texas College (B.S., 1903) and taught school for three years. In 1906, he was elected to the Texas legislature. While in office, he studied law at the University of Texas and was admitted to the bar in 1908. In 1913, he was elected to the U.S. House of Representatives, the first of 25 consecutive terms in Congress.

A **Democrat**, in the 1930s Rayburn supported President Franklin D. Roosevelt's New Deal. He favored free trade, states' rights, and successfully introduced legislation to regulate financial markets and public utilities. After **Dwight D. Eisenhower** became president, Rayburn supported Eisenhower's policies on **civil rights** and the **Interstate Highway System**. He was concerned, however, about U.S. involvement in the **Suez Crisis**.

Beginning in 1937, Rayburn served as speaker of the House during every Democratic-controlled Congress. His influence in Congress spanned more than 50 years, and he was one of the most powerful men in Washington. Rayburn's motto was "If you want to get along, go along."

RED SCARE. In the history of the United States, there have been two Red Scares. The first was in 1917–20, and the second was in 1947–57, during the administrations of Presidents **Harry S. Truman** and **Dwight D. Eisenhower**. After the World War II, the **Soviet Union** strengthened its hold over eastern Europe. The spread of communism in various regions of the world led to a widespread fear in the United States that communism had infiltrated Washington. Actions taken by Senator **Joseph McCarthy**'s Senate Permanent Subcommittee on Investigations and by the **House Un-American Activities Committee (HUAC)**, especially in the media, resulted in many suspected communists losing their jobs. Just the accusation that someone was sympathetic toward communism could ruin a career. At the peak of the hysteria, journalist **Edward R. Murrow** criticized McCarthy on his **television** program. Public opinion began to change. When McCarthy began to accuse people in Eisenhower's administration of communist leanings, the president intervened to end McCarthy's scare tactics. *See also* ARMY-MCCARTHY HEARINGS; BLACKLIST; CINEMA; COHN, ROY.

REED, STANLEY F. (1884–1980). Associate justice of the **Supreme Court** 1938–57. Born in Kentucky, Stanley Forman Reed graduated from the University of Virginia Law School (1906). In 1910–29, he practiced law in Kentucky. In 1929–32, he was general counsel of the Federal Farm Bureau, and in 1932–35 general counsel of the Reconstruction Finance Corporation. During the 1930s, he argued cases in favor of the New Deal before the Supreme Court. Appointed by President Franklin D. Roosevelt to the Court in 1938, Reed was a moderate who often balanced split decisions among the other eight justices. His southern roots almost kept him from supporting the decision in ***Brown v. Board of Education***, but realizing the importance of the case, he made the Court's decision unanimous. He retired from the Court in 1957.

REFUGEE RELIEF ACT, 1953. The spread of communism led many East Europeans to seek visas in order to come to the United States. The Refugee Relief Act allowed emergency immigration above the regular quota. Between 1954 and 1959, over 230,000 refugees were admitted into the country, including 21,500 Hungarian refugees. *See also* HUNGARIAN REVOLUTION.

RELIGION. The number of Americans belonging to an organized religion increased after World War II. Religion seemed a way of defending "the American way of life" during the **Cold War** and the nation's fear of communism. Hollywood produced several biblical epics during the 1950s, including *The Ten Commandments*, *The Robe*, and *Ben-Hur*.

Inspirational books were also extremely popular. The Bible was a best seller in 1952–54. Religious or inspirational messages made many books best sellers, including *The Power of Positive Thinking*, *Moses*, *The Robe*, *A Man Called Peter*, and *The Prayers of Peter Marshall*. **Television** and radio aired programs featuring Billy Graham, Bishop Fulton J. Sheen, and Norman Vincent Peale, who became influential through their uplifting and evangelical messages.

President **Dwight D. Eisenhower** signed legislation to add the words "under God" to the **Pledge of Allegiance** and the motto **In God We Trust** to U.S. **currency**. *See also* CINEMA; LITERATURE.

REPUBLICAN PARTY. In the 1940s and 1950s, President **Dwight D. Eisenhower** represented a moderate Republican Party, which began to appeal to many **Democrats** in the South who were concerned about President **Harry S. Truman**'s support for integration and the **civil rights** of **African Americans**. Southern Democrats helped Eisenhower win in the **1952 election**, defeating **Adlai E. Stevenson**, the Democratic candidate. Eisenhower won a second term in the **1956 election**, again defeating Stevenson.

For many Americans, Eisenhower represented the Republican Party at its best, while Senator **Joseph McCarthy** was an example of the party at its worst. But Eisenhower's popularity did not extend to his vice president, **Richard M. Nixon**, who was the Republican candidate for president in the **1960 election**. The **economy** and the **Cold War** had taken a toll on Americans, who sought hope for the future.

They found it in the charismatic Democratic candidate, **John F. Kennedy**, who offered promise to a new generation of Americans. Nixon lost the election by a narrow margin. *See also* ADAMS, SHERMAN; ANDERSON, ROBERT B.; BENSON, EZRA TAFT; BRENNAN, WILLIAM J.; BROWNELL, HERBERT, JR.; BUCKLEY, WILLIAM F., JR.; BURNS, ARTHUR F.; BURTON, HAROLD H.; DILLON, DOUGLAS; DIRKSEN, EVERETT; DULLES, ALLEN; DULLES, JOHN FOSTER; EISENHOWER, MILTON; FLEMMING, ARTHUR; FOLSOM, MARION BAYARD; HALLECK, CHARLES A.; HERTER, CHRISTIAN A.; HUGHES, EMMET; KNOWLAND, BILL; LODGE, HENRY CABOT, JR.; LUCE, CLARE BOOTH; MCCONE, JOHN A.; MCELROY, NEIL H.; MCKAY, DOUGLAS; MARTIN, JOSEPH W., JR.; MITCHELL, JAMES P.; PRESIDENTIAL DEBATES; ROCKEFELLER, NELSON; SEATON, FREDERICK A.; STASSEN, HAROLD; STEWART, POTTER; STRAUSS, LEWIS; SUMMERFIELD, ARTHUR ELLSWORTH; TAFT, ROBERT A.; WARREN, EARL; WEEK, SINCLAIR; WHITTAKER, CHARLES E.

RHEE, SYNGMAN (1875–1965). President of South Korea 1948–60. Born in Whanghai Province, Syngman Rhee was educated at an American Methodist mission school. In 1897, he was imprisoned for activity in the Independence Club, which led protests against the Korean monarchy. In 1904, after his release, he became a Christian and moved to the United States. He continued his education, culminating with a Ph.D. in political science from Princeton University in 1910.

By the time Rhee had his doctorate, Japan had taken control of Korea. Rhee returned home hoping to help Korea win its freedom, but he was forced to leave in 1919. Although he was exiled, he gained the presidency of Korea's provisional government and was able to return as the president of South Korea after the defeat of the Japanese in 1945.

When a cease-fire was signed in 1953 to end the **Korean War**, Rhee could not abide by the agreement. He believed the division of Korea was done to appease the communists. In 1954, the **Geneva Conference** was held, but it was impossible to agree on how to reunite the two Koreas, and they remained divided along the 38th parallel. As time passed, Rhee became more powerful as president.

When South Koreans revolted against his oppression, he was forced to resign in 1960.

RICKENBACKER, EDDIE (1890–1973). A World War I flying ace, Edward Vernon Rickenbacker was born in Ohio. He was a racing car driver before serving in World War I as General John J. Pershing's chauffeur. He learned to fly during the war and shot down 26 planes. He returned to the United States as a hero and received the Congressional Medal of Honor. In 1927, he bought the Indianapolis Speedway, which he owned until 1945. In the 1930s, he became a pilot for Eastern Airlines. In 1938–53, he was chief executive of the company. Rickenbacker believed an airline should follow a simple rule: fill the seats and get passengers where they needed to go.

ROBBINS, HAROLD (1916–1997). Author Harold Robbins was born Harold Rubin in New York City. After high school graduation, he held several jobs. During World War II, he moved to Hollywood, where he worked at Universal Studios, eventually becoming a studio executive. He is best known, however, as one of the best-selling authors of the 20th century. Over a 30-year period, he sold over 750 million books. His first novel, *Never Love a Stranger*, was autobiographical. In *The Dream Merchants*, he wrote about the movie industry from the silent era to talking pictures. *A Stone for Danny Fisher* was turned into a movie, *King Creole*, starring **Elvis Presley**. *The Carpetbaggers*, an international best seller, followed a Howard Hughes–like character from New York to Hollywood.

Some critics nicknamed Robbins "the man who invented sex" because of his trashy novels. In the end, his life mimicked his books. By 1982, he had been divorced five times and wrote to support his lavish lifestyle, which was spent much of the time in a wheelchair due to a hip ailment. *See also* CINEMA; LITERATURE.

ROBBINS, JEROME (1918–1998). Born Jerome Rabinowitz in New York City, Jerome Robbins began his dance career with the Ballet Theater. In 1944, he choreographed his first production, *Fancy Free*, which received rave reviews. His first musical was *On the Town* (1945), which was followed by *Billion Dollar Baby* (1946). In 1949, he became associate artistic director for the New York City Ballet.

In 1954, after many Broadway successes as choreographer, Robbins both directed and choreographed *Peter Pan*. His choreography for *West Side Story* (1957) is used in every revival of the musical. Other musicals during the 1950s for which he did the choreography were *Call Me Madam* (1952), *The King and I* (1954), *The Pajama Game* (1956), *Silk Stockings* (1956), and *Bells Are Ringing* (1959).

Robbins continued to choreograph Broadway musicals until the 1990s. During the 1970s, *Fiddler on the Roof*, *Funny Girl*, and *Gypsy* were three of his most popular musicals, all of which were made into successful movies. *See also* CINEMA; THEATER.

ROBESON, PAUL (1989–1976). Actor and singer Paul Leroy Bustill Robeson was born in New Jersey. In 1915, he entered Rutgers University on an academic scholarship. He excelled in academics as well as athletics. In 1919, he was valedictorian of his graduation class at Rutgers. In 1923, he received a law degree from Columbia University. He then joined a law firm but left when the white secretary refused to take dictation from him.

Having been a singer while at Rutgers, Robeson turned his attention to **music** and the **theater** and to promoting African and **African American** culture and history. With his deep baritone voice, he had a brilliant career for almost four decades. He starred in the stage and **cinema** production of *Showboat*, as well as in the stage productions of *Porgy and Bess* and *Othello*. He received rave reviews for his performances.

Robeson traveled the world, making friends with leaders of many countries, including **India**'s **Jawaharlal Nehru**. He championed the common person and, in the 1950s, became active in the **civil rights movement**. Robeson, a member of the Communist Party, was called before the **House Un-American Activities Committee (HUAC)** in the 1950s and **blacklisted**, which limited his employment. He was also prevented from traveling outside the United States. In 1958, Robeson was able to leave the United States, and he performed in Europe and Australia for three years. Soon after his return to the United States, he became ill. From 1961 until his death in 1976, he remained in retirement. *See also* COLD WAR; HORNE, LENA; MCCARTHY, JOSEPH; RED SCARE.

ROCK AND ROLL. Often attributed to disc jockey Alan Freed, the term "rock and roll" referred to a genre of **music** that began in the 1950s. It combined rhythm and blues, **jazz**, and gospel. Some considered rockabilly to be the beginning of rock and roll music. At first, saxophones were important in a rock and roll song, but by the mid-1950s the guitar became the main instrument. **Elvis Presley**'s first record, "It's All Right, Mama," has been credited with being the first rock and roll song. In the South, "rocking" was an **African American** gospel term that meant something was spiritual. Some music historians believe the term had sexual connotations, as when people rocked and rolled during sexual intercourse. During the presidency of **Dwight D. Eisenhower**, adults sometimes believed rock and roll led **teenagers** to become juvenile delinquents. *See also AMERICAN BANDSTAND*; BERRY, CHUCK; MATHIS, JOHNNY; MOTOWN RECORDS; PAUL, LES.

ROCKEFELLER, NELSON (1908–1979). U.S. vice president 1974–1977. Although he was an heir to the enormous Standard Oil fortune, Nelson Aldrich Rockefeller had a very prudent upbringing. He was educated at a school with students of varied backgrounds, and while at Dartmouth College, he held jobs to earn his own spending money. After graduation in 1930, he worked in his family's companies but found he was not a business person.

Rockefeller traveled to Latin America several times in the 1930s, a period when Nazism was on the rise in Europe. He wanted to help keep Central and South America from the influence of the Axis powers, and he was given his first government position as head of the Office of Inter-American Affairs. Although Rockefeller was a **Republican**, President **Harry S. Truman** gave him his first major political position as chair of the International Development Advisory Board, whose focus was underdeveloped countries. The board was to keep communism from invading them and to help them grow economically.

In 1952, President **Dwight D. Eisenhower** used Rockefeller's expertise to reorganize the federal government. Rockefeller was responsible for the formation of the new **Department of Health, Education, and Welfare (HEW)**, of which Rockefeller became undersecretary. He served under Eisenhower for only two years but helped develop the "open skies" policy and the **Atoms for Peace** plans.

In 1956, Rockefeller left Eisenhower's administration to begin a career in elective politics. He was governor of New York from 1959 to 1973. His divorce in 1961 was not a good political move; however, it did not keep him from being reelected. After serving as governor for four terms, he resigned in 1973. He attempted to run for president in 1964, 1968, and 1972 and lost every time in the Republican primaries. In 1974, after the resignation of President **Richard M. Nixon**, Gerald R. Ford became president and chose Rockefeller as his vice president. *See also* FOREIGN POLICY; GENEVA SUMMIT CONFERENCE; SOVIET UNION, RELATIONS WITH.

ROCKWELL, NORMAN (1894–1978). Artist and illustrator Norman Percevel Rockwell was born in New York City. When he was 16 years old, he left high school to pursue a career as an artist. He received training at the Chase Art School, the National Academy of Design, and the Art Students League. His success at the Art Students League began when he was commissioned to paint four Christmas cards.

In 1916, Rockwell painted his first cover for the *Saturday Evening Post*. During the next 47 years, he painted 321 covers for the *Post*. During World War II, his **magazine** covers expressed what Americans were feeling. Based on President Franklin D. Roosevelt's 1943 address to Congress on the theme of four freedoms, Rockwell created four paintings for the *Post* called the *Four Freedoms*. These were *Freedom of Speech*, *Freedom to Worship*, *Freedom from Want*, and *Freedom from Fear*. The paintings proved extremely popular and inspirational.

In 1963, Rockwell ended his association with the *Saturday Evening Post* and began to work for *Look*, an association that lasted 10 years. During the **civil rights movement**, his covers depicted **African Americans'** struggle for equality. He continued to express his views with depictions of the war on poverty and the nation's success in the exploration of **space**.

Throughout his career, Rockwell produced over 400 paintings. He illustrated over 40 books and contributed paintings to various calendars between 1925 and 1975. Some critics have used the term "Rockwellesque," an adjective meaning an idealistic portrayal of American life. In a 2006 auction at Sotheby's, one of his paintings, *Breaking Home Ties*, sold for $15.4 million. *See also* ART.

RODGERS AND HAMMERSTEIN. During the 1950s, the most powerful team on Broadway was composer Richard Rodgers (1902–1979) and lyricist Oscar Hammerstein II (1885–1960). At one point, they had four Broadway musicals appearing simultaneously, which was unprecedented. Some of their musicals were also successful as movies, including *Carousel*, *Oklahoma*, *South Pacific*, *The King and I*, *Flower Drum Song*, and *The Sound of Music*.

Popular songs during the 1950s were often show tunes. Every year, Broadway musicals produced songs that went to the top of the charts. Broadway shows were at the height of their popularity. The **economy** was booming and the public enjoyed live **theater** productions. Some critics believed that the best musicals followed the successful Rodgers and Hammerstein formula of using recognizable characters who were witty and sang from the heart. *See also* CINEMA.

RODGERS, RICHARD. *See* RODGERS AND HAMMERSTEIN.

ROGERS, WILLIAM P. (1913–2001). Attorney general 1957–61. After the death of his mother when he was a teenager, William Pierce Rogers was raised by his grandparents. In 1938, a year after he received his law degree from Cornell University, Rogers worked with Thomas E. Dewey. Dewey and Rogers prosecuted organized crime members in New York City. When Congressman **Richard M. Nixon** asked Rogers to help examine documents provided to the **House Un-American Activities Committee** in the Alger Hiss case, Rogers advised Nixon that Hiss had lied to the committee and should be tried for perjury.

In the **1952 election**, Rogers helped **Republican** presidential nominee **Dwight D. Eisenhower** secure the delegates loyal to Senator **Robert A. Taft**. He also helped Nixon, the vice presidential candidate, with the **Checkers Speech** that saved Nixon from losing his position as Eisenhower's running mate.

In 1953, Rogers was a deputy attorney general in President **Dwight D. Eisenhower**'s administration. After the resignation of **Herbert Brownell** in 1957, Rogers succeeded him as attorney general. During his years in this position, he played a vital role in **civil rights**. Rogers was involved in the integration of Central High School and played a major role in passage of the **Civil Rights Act of 1957**. After creating the Civil Rights Division in the Department of Justice, he made it one of the most forceful parts of the government.

After Nixon lost the **1960 election**, Rogers practiced law in New York. When Nixon was elected president in 1968, Rogers became his secretary of state (1969–73). Regarding the **Vietnam War**, Nixon did not rely on Rogers for his **foreign policy** decisions but turned to Henry Kissinger, the national security advisor. In fact, Rogers was kept in the dark about the majority of policies the White House decided. Kissinger succeeded Rogers as secretary of state in 1973.

In 1986, Rogers led the investigation into the space shuttle *Challenger*'s explosion. The Rogers Commission criticized the **National Aeronautics and Space Administration (NASA)** management for negligence that led to the disaster. *See also* CIVIL RIGHTS MOVEMENT; FAUBUS, ORVAL; RACIAL INTEGRATION.

ROOSEVELT, ELEANOR (1884–1962). First lady 1933–45; **United Nations (UN)** delegate 1946–52. Anna Eleanor Roosevelt was born in New York City. After the death of her parents, she was raised by her grandmother. She was the favorite niece of President Theodore Roosevelt, and she married a distant cousin, Franklin D. Roosevelt. After their marriage, Franklin and Eleanor became members of the **Democratic Party**. During her husband's four terms as president of the United States, she was invaluable to him as an adviser. After his death, she was active in the UN. President **Harry S. Truman** appointed her as a delegate to the UN in 1946.

During the **1952 election** and **1956 election**, Roosevelt worked unsuccessfully to defeat the **Republican** candidate, **Dwight D. Eisenhower**. She did not forget his decision not to defend his friend and mentor **George C. Marshall** from the unfounded accusations about him by Senator **Joseph McCarthy**. She also disapproved of **Richard M. Nixon**, Eisenhower's running mate.

Roosevelt also thought that Eisenhower's record on **civil rights** was shameful. When the **Supreme Court** decided *Brown v. Board of Education* (1954), she was highly critical of Eisenhower's failure to immediately enforce the law. When Arkansas Governor **Orval Faubus** would not allow **African American** students to enter Central High School in Little Rock, she thought Eisenhower should have acted immediately in sending troops to uphold the law.

After Eisenhower was elected president in 1952, he wrote a token letter accepting her resignation as a UN delegate, and she was not invited to any functions at the White House while he was president. *See also* RACIAL INTEGRATION.

ROSENBERG, ETHEL (1915–1953), AND JULIUS (1918–1953). Julius Rosenberg had joined the Communist Party as a young man, and he and his wife, Ethel, were part of a spy ring in the United States. When Klaus Fuchs was convicted in **Great Britain** of giving **atomic** bomb secrets to the **Soviet Union**, the Rosenbergs were implicated. Julius worked for the U.S. Army, and David Greenglass, Ethel's brother, worked at Los Alamos, New Mexico, where the atomic bomb tests were held. Arrested in 1950, the Rosenbergs and Greenglass were tried and convicted of treason in 1951. To save his own life, Greenglass became a witness for the prosecution. Before the trial was held, the Soviet Union had exploded its first atomic bomb (1949) and the **Korean War** was intensifying. These two facts added to the country's fear of communism. The Rosenbergs were put to death in 1953. *See also* COHN, ROY; COLD WAR; EINSTEIN, ALBERT; FOREIGN POLICY.

ROSENBERG, JULIUS. *See* ROSENBERG, ETHEL, AND JULIUS.

RUDOLPH, WILMA (1940–1994). Olympic athlete Wilma Glodean Rudolph was born in Tennessee. She was stricken with polio at a young age. Her mother helped her get the medical care and exercises she needed. She was an **African American** and her local hospital only helped white patients. Her mother took her twice a week to the black medical college of Fisk University, 50 miles from their home. By age 12, Rudolph was on the road to recovery and decided to enter athletics. In high school, she was a **basketball** and track star. In

1956, she was on the Olympic track and field team and won a bronze medal in the 4x4 relay. She continued to excel in track and field, and in 1960 she won three gold medals at the Rome Olympics, the first American female athlete to do so. Her accomplishments in athletics helped break down barriers in **sports** dominated by men. *See also* WOMEN'S MOVEMENT.

– S –

ST. LAWRENCE SEAWAY. The St. Lawrence River flows from Canada to the Great Lakes of the United States. The mouth of the river begins at the Atlantic Ocean. The river flows by Montreal, Canada, and connects to Lake Ontario. As early as the late 1800s, the idea of a waterway to connect the St. Lawrence River to the Great Lakes was discussed. With such a waterway, large ships could go from the Atlantic Ocean into the Great Lakes, thus reducing the cost of shipping to the large cities of the Midwest. The problem was the land between the St. Lawrence River and the Great Lakes.

President **Harry S. Truman** tried to persuade Congress to approve construction of the St. Lawrence Seaway. Truman's plan included hydroelectric facilities, but Congress believed the cost was too great. President **Dwight D. Eisenhower** deleted the hydroelectric facilities, which cut the cost of the seaway. He presented Congress with a plan in which he stressed the importance of the waterway to the **economy** of the United States. Funding from federal, state, and private contributions and from Canada could make the waterway a reality. The legislation passed in 1954. The United States and Canada began constructing a 114-mile deep-water navigation channel. In 1959, the waterway opened. At a cost of $1 billion, it was the most expensive construction project to that date.

SALINGER, J. D. (1919–). Jerome David Salinger grew up in New York. His parents were wealthy enough to send him to a private school, which became the setting for his first novel, *Catcher in the Rye*. He left school when he was 17 and worked on a cruise line, where he was a dance partner for wealthy women. He enrolled in Columbia University but did not do well. After serving in World

War II, he wrote his first novel, which was published in 1951. *Catcher in the Rye* was criticized for its vulgar language and sexual content, and it was often banned by libraries. To this day, however, Salinger's *Catcher in the Rye* is a popular book with **teenagers** and college students.

Salinger is a very private person who writes at his home in New Hampshire. He has written other novels, including *Franny and Zooey* and *Raise High the Roof Beam. See also* LITERATURE.

SALK, JONAS (1914–1995). Jonas Edward Salk was born and educated in New York City. While in medical school, he found a cure for the flu virus. In 1939, he graduated from New York University's College of Medicine. Salk began working to develop a **polio** vaccine. For decades, polio had crippled and killed thousands of people. In the 1950s, it was one of the most feared illnesses. Whereas one could be treated for tuberculosis and get well, polio had no known cure. In 1954, Salk introduced a vaccine to prevent the dreaded disease. Tests of the vaccine proved it to be up to 80 percent effective. By the end of 1955, 7 million schoolchildren had been vaccinated. Prior to his death, Salk was working on HIV, the virus leading to AIDS. *See also* MEDICAL ADVANCES; POLIO-MYELITIS VACCINATION ACT.

SAMUELSON, PAUL A. (1915–). Economist Paul Anthony Samuelson was born in Indiana and received degrees from the University of Chicago (B.A., 1935) and Harvard University (M.A., 1936; Ph.D., 1941). While a graduate student, he already had won international fame with his economic theories. In 1940–85, he taught at the Massachusetts Institute of Technology (MIT). In his first book, *Foundations of Economic Analysis* (1947), Samuelson stated that mathematics was necessary if one wanted to understand economics. His *Economics: An Introductory Analysis* (1948) was an extremely successful economics textbook. He made the economics department at MIT one of the finest in the country.

Samuelson has been a consultant to various governmental agencies, including the U.S. Treasury (1945–52), the Bureau of the Budget (1952), and the Research Advisory Board Committee for Economic Development (1960). Since 1949, he has been a consultant to the RAND Corporation. He was also an economic advisor to President, **John F. Kennedy**. In 1958, Samuelson, part of the Committee for Economic Development, stated that the greatest economic problem facing the country for the next 20 years would be inflation. He was awarded the Nobel Prize in Economics in 1970. Perhaps more than anyone else during the second half of the 20th century, he changed the way economics was perceived. *See also* BANKING; ECONOMY.

SANDBURG, CARL (1878–1967). Born in Illinois, Carl Sandburg was the son of Swedish immigrants. He fought in the 1898 Spanish-American War, then returned to Lombard College in his hometown of Galesburg. As a journalist in Chicago, he wrote for the **magazine** *Poetry*. Many of his poems focused on the American worker. He won Pulitzer Prizes for two of his works: *Abraham Lincoln: The War Years* and *Complete Poems*. He wrote one novel, *Remembrance Rock*. Sandburg worked to help elect **John F. Kennedy** to the presidency in the **1960 election** and wrote the preface to Kennedy's book *To Turn the Tide*. *See also* LITERATURE.

SANGER, MARGARET (1883–1966). Margaret Louise Higgins Sanger was born into a working class family in a poor part of New York. She watched her mother's health fail after becoming pregnant 18 times; seven of these were miscarriages. Determined to help other women avoid her mother's medical history, Sanger trained to be a midwife and practical nurse. In 1912, she helped a doctor attend a 28-year-old woman whose desperation had led her to end a fourth pregnancy by a self-induced abortion. The doctor's advice to his patient about birth control was that she should have her husband sleep on the roof of the tenement house. Three months later, the woman died from another self-induced abortion.

Sanger pursued a way to prevent other women from having unwanted pregnancies. In 1914, she published *The Woman Rebel*, which gave advice on contraceptives. In 1916, she opened a birth control clinic in New York, for which she was arrested and jailed for a month. After her release, she continued as an advocate for birth control. She founded the National Birth Control League in 1917 and opened another birth control clinic in New York in 1923. In the late

1940s, the National Birth Control League became the Planned Parenthood Federation of America.

Sanger was responsible for the first oral contraceptive. With the help of Gregory Pincus, a biologist, a **birth control pill** was approved by the Federal Drug Administration (FDA) in 1956. Women now had a way to prevent unwanted pregnancies. Sanger traveled to many countries to lecture on birth control during the 1960s. Some people believe the birth control pill contributed to the beginning of the sexual revolution of the 1960s.

In 1965, the case of *Griswold v. Connecticut* came before the **Supreme Court**. The executive director of the Planned Parenthood League of Connecticut and the medical director had been convicted for illegally providing counseling and medical advice to married couples. With Justice **William O. Douglas** writing the majority opinion, the Court decided that a state could not ban the use of contraceptives. Douglas stated that the legislation was a violation of privacy in a marriage. The case was a major decision in the history of birth control in which Margaret Sanger had been involved since almost the beginning of the 20th century. *See also* MEDICAL ADVANCES; WOMEN'S MOVEMENT.

SCHINE, G. DAVID (1927–1996). A center of controversy during the **Army-McCarthy Hearings**, Gerard David Schine was born into a wealthy New York City family, and as a young man, he wrote an eight-page booklet titled "Definition of Communism," which he placed in the many hotels owned by his family. The booklet came to the attention of Senator **Joseph McCarthy**'s chief counsel, **Roy Cohn**. Cohn hired Schine, who in 1952–53 was an unpaid consultant for the Senate Permanent Subcommittee on Investigations, which McCarthy chaired. In 1954, during the **Korean War**, Schine was drafted into the army. Cohn attempted to intervene by making Schine a permanent member of the committee, thus keeping him from being drafted. When his plan failed, Cohn tried to intimidate the secretary of the army, Robert Stevens, by saying he would "wreck the army" if his demands for Schine were not met. Cohn's actions led to the Army-McCarthy Hearings. The U.S. Army accused Cohn and McCarthy of using improper tactics in Schine's behalf. McCarthy and

Cohn responded that the army was trying to halt their investigation of communists. For two months, **television** stations carried the hearings, during which McCarthy's power was slowly eroded as 20 million viewers watched the proceedings.

By 1971, Schine had become a business executive involved in movies, hotels, and **music**. He was the executive producer of the 1971 Academy Award–winning movie *The French Connection*. In 1996, he, his wife, and their son were killed when their private plane, piloted by their son, crashed shortly after takeoff from the Burbank, California, airport. *See also* HOUSE UN-AMERICAN ACTIVITIES COMMITTEE (HUAC); RED SCARE.

SCHULZ, CHARLES M. *See PEANUTS.*

SCIENCE FICTION. Space travel, radiation from **atomic** bomb tests, communism, and the fear of the **Soviet Union** were four reasons science fiction became a popular genre in books, movies, and **magazines** in the 1950s. Writers' imaginations ran wild as they conjured up giant creatures caused by the radiation from atomic bombs. Many people reported sightings of unidentified flying objects (UFOs) in the 1940s and 1950s. The story of a UFO that crashed in 1948 in Roswell, New Mexico, stirred the imagination of writers of science fiction. To this day, people still question whether a flying saucer was retrieved at Roswell.

In movies, monsters from other planets hid on space ships without the crew knowing, then terrorized communities when the space ships returned to Earth. Communism was presented in the form of monsters overtaking humans' minds so that everyone conformed to one way of thinking, as many did under communism.

Television followed movies with science fiction shows. One very popular series was *The Twilight Zone* (1959–64), hosted by the series creator, Rod Serling. The characters in each episode found themselves in supernatural or surreal situations.

Writers such as **Isaac Asimov**, Ray Bradbury, Arthur C. Clarke, Robert A. Heinlein, and Neville Shute were just a handful of authors whose books had a science fiction theme. Asimov and Bradbury were two of many authors who crossed the line from author to screenwriter. Bradbury, for example, wrote the script for the movie *It Came from Outer Space* (1953). *See also* CINEMA; COLD WAR; LITERATURE.

SEATON, FRED A. (1909–1974). Secretary of the interior 1956–61. Born in Washington, D.C., Frederick Andrew Seaton was educated in Kansas. His father was the owner of a group of newspapers. Seaton worked for **Republican** presidential candidate Alf Landon in 1936. Moving to Nebraska, he was active in his father's newspaper group. Seaton was appointed to the U.S. Senate by Nebraska's governor to fill the position of Senator Kenneth S. Wherry, who had died in office. He worked for Republican presidential candidate **Dwight David Eisenhower** in the **1952 election**. Seaton was appointed assistant secretary of defense in 1953. In 1956, he was named secretary of the interior, a position he held for the remainder of Eisenhower's second term. During his term as secretary, **Alaska** and **Hawaii** were admitted to statehood. After Eisenhower left office, Seaton returned to head newspapers in Nebraska and Kansas. *See also* ELECTION, 1956.

SEEGER, PETE (1919–). A singer, songwriter, and political activist, Peter Seeger was born in New York and attended Harvard University. His love of **music** was inherited from his parents, both faculty members of the Julliard School of Music. In the 1940s, he sang with Woody Guthrie and later co-founded the **Weavers**. During World War II and until 1950, he was a member of the Communist Party. During the **Cold War**, Seeger was called to testify before the **House Un-American Activities Committee (HUAC).** He refused to answer questions on the basis of the Fifth Amendment. He spent one year in prison.

Seeger's music and political activism were important in the 1960s when he opposed the **Vietnam War**. College students embraced his music and his ideas. He was also active in the **civil rights movement**. When the Vietnam War ended, Seeger became involved in many causes, but the environment became his main focus.

Among the most well-known songs he wrote are *Where Have All the Flowers Gone*, *If I Had a Hammer*, *Turn, Turn, Turn*, and especially *We Shall Overcome*. *See also* BLACKLIST; COHN, ROY; MCCARTHY, JOSEPH; RED SCARE.

SEUSS, DR. (THEODORE SEUSS GEISEL) (1904–1991). Author of some of the most popular children's books, Theodore Seuss Geisel was born in Massachusetts. He graduated from Dartmouth College in 1925 and did graduate work at Oxford University. He began his career writing amusing articles for various publications, sometimes including his own humorous illustrations. He wrote his first children's book in 1936, *And to Think That I Saw It on Mulberry Street*. Writing under the name Dr. Seuss, he had a long and successful career. Dr. Seuss wrote some of the most beloved children's books, with their catchy rhymes and comical characters illustrated by Seuss. *The Cat in the Hat, Green Eggs and Ham, Horton Hears a Who!*, and *How the Grinch Stole Christmas* are only a few of his many books. A number of his stories were made into popular animated **television** productions. *How the Grinch Stole Christmas* is still shown yearly. Although he was not a doctor, he added the title to his name to appease his father, who had hoped he would earn a doctorate while at Oxford University. *See also* LITERATURE.

SHAH OF IRAN. *See* PAHLAVI, MOHAMMAD REZA.

SIT-IN. During the **civil rights movement**, one form of protest used by **African Americans** was to occupy seats in an establishment that was not racially integrated. Labor unions were the first to use sit-ins, employing the tactic in the 1930s during strikes. In 1960, four African American men sat-in at a lunch counter at a Woolworth's department store in Greensboro, North Carolina. They were not served, and more African Americans returned the next day to continue the sit-in, thus preventing other potential customers from being seated. Newspapers carried the story and soon many college students, white and black, were holding sit-ins. The 1960s brought more protests in the form of sit-ins, march-ins, and lie-ins as a way to express social protest. *See also* RACIAL INTEGRATION.

SKELTON, RED (1913–1997). Comedian and actor Red Skelton, born Richard Bernard Skelton, was one of the comic geniuses of the 20th century. The son of a former circus clown, Skelton left home when he was 10 to appear in vaudeville shows. By the age of 17, he was married to a vaudeville partner. He entertained audiences on

Broadway, on radio, and in films. In 1951, he was given a contract to star on **television**. *The Red Skelton Show* (1951–71) was always in the top 20 of the most popular television programs. Skelton's ability to ad lib and to pantomime made him a huge success. In his spare time, he painted pictures of clowns, which were highly prized by lovers of **art**; one sold for about $80,000. *See also* CINEMA.

SKINNER, B. F. (1904–1990). Born in Pennsylvania, Burrhus Frederic Skinner wanted to be a writer. In 1926, he received his B.A. in English literature from Hamilton College in New York. Unsuccessful in his attempts to have his writings published, he studied psychology at Harvard University. Skinner received his Ph.D. in 1931 and remained at Harvard as a researcher. He taught later at the University of Minnesota and at Indiana University, where he served as chair of the Psychology Department (1946–47). In 1948, he returned to Harvard, where he spent the rest of his career.

His most famous research used the "Skinner Box," in which animals were presented with various stimuli so Skinner could watch their responses. Rewards of food were given to animals that performed an expected task. He believed this research carried over to humans, especially in **education**, where good performance was reinforced with rewards.

Skinner's books include *The Behavior of Organisms*, *Walden II*, *Science and Human Behavior*, and *Schedules of Reinforcement*. *The Technologies of Teaching* is still referred to for educational instruction methods although it was published in the 1960s.

SLANG. The **space** race, **television**, communism, and the **atomic** bomb affected the English language during the 1950s and 1960s. **Teenagers**, in particular, created new terms. The space race produced the word "blast," which meant a good time. If you were wise and knew what was happening, you were "in orbit," and a reliable person was "earthbound." Your "pad" was your home. And to be on "cloud 9" was to be happy.

On the popular television program *77 Sunset Strip*, the character Kookie, played by Edd Byrnes, was "cool," which meant something was extra special. "Crazy" meant good. Something negative was "bad news." If you asked too many questions, you might be asked,

"Are you writing a book?" Bothering someone meant you were "bugging" them. "Dig?" was a way to ask if you understood, and if you did not understand, you might be "cruisin' for a bruisin'." TV westerns popularized the phrase "meanwhile back at the ranch," which got a speaker back to the subject.

If you asked for "bread," you wanted money, and "threads" were clothes. The popularity of cars produced many slang expressions. A "classy chassis" meant a great body. The "horn" was the telephone and "souped up" referred to a fast car. And if you were going "to make out," you were going "to watch the submarine races."

Parents definitely were not "hip" or "cool" or "with it." If asked to do a job, a teenager might answer with "no sweat," which meant it was not a problem. And when leaving, the phrase was "See you later, alligator."

SLOAN, ALFRED P., JR. (1875–1966). President of General Motors 1937–56. Alfred Pritchard Sloan, Jr., who was born in Connecticut, was an 1892 graduate of the Massachusetts Institute of Technology (MIT). Sloan's first job was with a company that made roller bearings, which were used in **automobiles**. When the company began to flounder, Sloan's father and a business partner purchased the company, making Sloan manager. Sloan was able to sell the company to General Motors. Made vice president in charge of operations, he soon was president. Sloan produced a new car model each year. He also created five companies within General Motors, each making a different car, so consumers could work up from a Chevrolet to a Cadillac. A generous philanthropist, he contributed millions to MIT and cancer research, and he created the Alfred P. Sloan Foundation, which funds programs in **science**, economics, technology, **education**, and national issues. Sloan wrote the standard text on company management, *My Years at General Motors. See also* ECONOMY; TECHNOLOGICAL INNOVATIONS.

SMITH, WALTER BEDELL (1895–1961). CIA director 1950–53. A native of Indianapolis, Walter Bedell Smith briefly attended Butler University. He began his military service as a private in the Indiana National Guard. He served in both world wars, eventually reaching the rank of general, and he was General **Dwight D. Eisenhower**'s chief of staff during the North Africa campaign in World War II. Smith was U.S. ambassador to the **Soviet Union** in 1946–49. In 1950, President **Harry S. Truman** appointed him director of the Central Intelligence Agency (CIA). President Eisenhower appointed him undersecretary of state in 1953, and he was a delegate to the **Geneva Conference** in 1954. Having been ambassador to the Soviet Union, Smith had a knowledge of Soviet politics that was invaluable to Eisenhower. *See also* FOREIGN POLICY; KHRUSHCHEV, NIKITA.

SOCIAL SECURITY. During the **1952 election**, **Republican** candidate **Dwight D. Eisenhower** stated that the federal government needed to play a major role in Social Security, the program begun by Franklin D. Roosevelt in 1935. Soon after taking office, Eisenhower asked Senator **Robert A. Taft**, a distinguished conservative, if he would support expanding Social Security. Taft willingly approved, and by August 1954 Eisenhower signed into law the **Agricultural Act of 1954**. The law brought Social Security coverage to 3.6 million farm operators and 2.1 farm workers. The Social Security Amendments Act, signed four days later, brought Social Security coverage to about 5 million professionals. With these acts, retirement benefits were included, as well as increased support for disabled Americans and increased monthly benefit payments. The president believed these changes brought peace of mind and more security to Americans as they aged.

SOUTHEAST ASIA TREATY ORGANIZATION (SEATO). The purpose of the Southeast Asia Treaty Organization, formed in 1954, was to stop communism from spreading into Southeast Asian countries. SEATO was a way for the United States to remain in the region, rather than simply a way to prevent communism from spreading throughout the region. **France** was fighting to keep its colony of Vietnam from falling into communist hands. President **Dwight D. Eisenhower** believed that should Vietnam fall, so would other Southeast Asian countries, like a row of dominoes. As it turned out, the United States became the major player in the **Vietnam War**. SEATO disbanded in 1977. The original members of SEATO were Australia, France, **Great Britain**, New Zealand, Pakistan, Thailand, and the United States. *See also* DOMINO THEORY; FOREIGN POLICY.

SOUTHERN CHRISTIAN LEADERSHIP CONFERENCE (SCLC). Led by **Martin Luther King Jr.**, the Southern Christian Leadership Conference (SCLC) was formed in 1957. That same year, King asked President **Dwight D. Eisenhower** to hold a conference on **civil rights**; however, the president ignored King's proposal. Believing that the **National Association for the Advancement of Colored People (NAACP)** was not effective enough, a number of black churches and ministers had formed the SCLC. Due to the group's protests, which were covered by the media, the Civil Rights Acts of 1964 and 1965 were passed during the administration of President **Lyndon B. Johnson**.

SOUTHERN MANIFESTO. In response to the **Supreme Court**'s 1954 decision in *Brown v. Board of Education*, the Southern Manifesto was drawn up in 1956 and signed by 96 members of the U.S. Congress from southern states. The document questioned the desegregation of public schools. The Constitution, they argued, did not mention **education**; thus, they disputed the Supreme Court's decision. Members of the U.S. House of Representatives from Texas were the largest group of southern congressmen who refused to sign the document. The Senate majority leader, **Lyndon B. Johnson**, was not asked to sign it. The Supreme Court's decision was upheld and schools were integrated. *See also* RACIAL INTEGRATION.

SOVIET UNION, RELATIONS WITH. During World War II, General **Dwight D. Eisenhower** and his counterparts in the Soviet Union (Union of Soviet Socialist Republics) fought to defeat the Nazis. When the war ended, **Germany** was divided into two parts, with the Soviet Union governing East Germany while the United States, **Great Britain**, and **France** presided over West Germany. The Soviet Union added East Germany to its other communist strongholds, and the **Cold War** was officially begun between the United States and **Joseph Stalin**'s Soviet Union.

Eisenhower was elected president of the United States in 1952. Stalin died the next year. When **Nikita Khrushchev** became the Soviet leader in 1957, he and Eisenhower had a contentious relationship. Khrushchev continued his hold on the communist bloc countries. The spread of communism throughout the world was one of Eisenhower's greatest fears. Although Eisenhower kept his promise to bring an end

to the **Korean War**, North Korea became a communist nation. South
Korea, however, remained free.

In 1955, Eisenhower proposed his "open skies" policy to Khrushchev, by which the United States and Soviet Union would open their
airspace to one another so they could monitor military strengths and
verify compliance with disarmament agreements. The Soviet leader
quickly rejected the idea. He viewed open access to his military sites
from aerial reconnaissance as spying.

In 1956, the Soviet Union crushed the **Hungarian Revolution**.
The United States could not help the Hungarian people in their fight
for freedom from communism because the **Suez Crisis** took priority
in Eisenhower's view. President **Gamal Abdel Nasser** had control
of the Suez Canal and asked the Soviet Union for aid. The fear of
communism spreading into the Middle East was a constant worry
throughout the crisis.

In 1957, the Soviet Union launched the satellite *Sputnik*, and the
space race began. The United States began its own space program
with former German rocket scientist **Wernher von Braun** as head
of the program. **Education** in the United States focused more on **science** and math.

In 1959, Eisenhower and Khrushchev met in Washington, D.C.
The encounter went well, and a meeting was planned for the following year. In 1960, however, one of the U.S. covert surveillance
spy planes was shot down over the Soviet Union, causing the **U-2
Incident**. Eisenhower claimed he was unaware of these secret flights.
When the president finally admitted that he knew about the secret
surveillance flights, Khrushchev appeared at the **United Nations**
to voice his rage, even removing his shoe and banging it on a desk.
After Eisenhower left office, President **John F. Kennedy** had a more
serious problem with Khrushchev when Soviet missiles were sighted
in **Cuba**. **Fidel Castro**, the communist leader of Cuba, had turned to
the Soviet Union after the **Bay of Pigs** invasion staged by the United
States. *See also* FOREIGN POLICY.

SPACE. The space race of the 1950s was one of the most important
developments during the presidency of **Dwight D. Eisenhower**. The
United States was stunned in 1957 by the **Soviet Union**'s launching
the satellite *Sputnik*, thereby beginning the space race. Russian cos-

monaut **Yuri Gagarin** (1934–1968) orbited the earth in April 1961; the following month, Alan Shepard of the United States was the first American to be sent into space. The importance of the space race carried over into **education**, with math and **science** overtaking the **arts** in school curriculums. Although the Soviet Union was the first to orbit a man around the earth, in July 1969 the United States was the first country to successfully land a man on the moon. *See also* FOREIGN POLICY; NATIONAL AERONAUTICS AND SPACE ADMINISTRATION (NASA).

SPORTS. Interest in sports intensified in the 1950s, mainly due to **television**. *Sports Illustrated*, a new **magazine**, introduced in 1954, kept sports enthusiasts apprised of the latest news and introduced little-known athletes to readers.

In 1957, the Brooklyn Dodgers moved to Los Angeles, becoming the first major league **baseball** team to be located on the West Coast. The New York Yankees dominated baseball during the 1950s, winning six of the nine World Series.

Football was another popular sport in the 1950s. The American Football League (AFL), founded in 1959, provided major cities with the opportunity to acquire a professional football team. Dallas and Denver were the first two cities to have AFL teams. The AFL included **African American** players, unheard of in the National Football League (NFL). In 1969, the AFL and NFL merged into one league, forcing the NFL to integrate. Weekly televised professional football games gained in popularity as the decade progressed, rivaling college games.

Boxing and wrestling were popular. With the increased ease of air travel, world famous boxers and wrestlers were introduced to American audiences.

Golf, a favorite sport of President **Dwight D. Eisenhower**, was popular with many Americans. In 1950, **Babe Zaharias** helped form the Ladies Professional Golf Association (LPGA), which gave women a chance to compete in a sport dominated by men.

During the **Cold War**, Americans who traveled to the 1952 and 1956 **Olympics** watched the rivalry between athletes from the United States and the **Soviet Union**. In 1960, for the first time, American television covered the Olympics.

Baseball was integrated in 1947 when Jackie Robinson was recruited by the Brooklyn Dodgers. By the end of the 1950s, African Americans and women were involved in most professional sports. Audiences judged athletes on their ability and not their place in society. Noted African American athletes included **Althea Gibson** (tennis), **Wilma Rudolph** (track and field), and **basketball** greats Elgin Baylor, Oscar Robertson, and Wilt Chamberlain.

SPUTNIK. Launched in October 1957 by the **Soviet Union**, the satellite *Sputnik* was the first spacecraft to orbit Earth. *Sputnik* orbited Earth for three months. The second *Sputnik* flight in 1957 orbited with a dog in it. This was the first space flight of a living creature. *Sputnik* began the **space** race between the United States and the Soviet Union. In 1958, the United States launched *Explorer 1*. By 1962, Canada and **Great Britain** had joined the race by launching their own satellites. That same year, Bell Laboratories had developed Telstar, the first communications satellite. *See also* TECHNOLOGICAL INNOVATIONS.

STALIN, JOSEPH (1879–1953). Soviet leader 1924–53. The 1917 Russian Revolution was the stepping stone for Stalin to eventually become the leader of the **Soviet Union**. Born in Georgia, Stalin studied to become a priest; however, he was expelled, possibly for his Marxist beliefs. When Vladimir Lenin became the head of the Soviet Union after the revolution, Stalin became part of the Politburo. In 1924, he was able to take control of the country when Lenin died.

During his many years of leadership, Stalin used brute force to keep control of his country. When he reintroduced collectivism, an idea used before and then dismissed, the peasants rose in protest. Stalin responded by killing many of the protestors and intensifying the repression.

After World War II, Stalin took control of many parts of Europe and made them part of the Soviet Union. Stalin died in 1953, soon after President **Dwight D. Eisenhower** was inaugurated. *See also* COLD WAR; KHRUSHCHEV, NIKITA.

STASSEN, HAROLD (1907–2001). Presidential candidate 1948–92. Born in Minnesota, Harold Stassen graduated from high school at the age of 14. By the age of 32, he had a law degree and was elected the youngest governor ever of Minnesota. In 1940, he gave the keynote address at the **Republican** National Convention. Many Republicans believed Stassen would one day be president. In the **1952 election**, he gave his votes to **Dwight D. Eisenhower**, which ensured Eisenhower's nomination over **Robert A. Taft** of Ohio. Stassen was governor of Minnesota four times, governor of Pennsylvania twice, a U.S. senator twice, and mayor of Philadelphia once. He ran as a Republican candidate for president nine times but never won. *See also* ELECTION, 1956; ELECTION, 1960.

STEEL INDUSTRY. After World War II, the United States was the dominant steel producer in the world. In 1959, President **Dwight D. Eisenhower** was confronted with a strike by the United Steelworkers of America (USWA), led by its new president David McDonald. The dispute was over a wage increase. McDonald watched the United Auto Workers achieve pay increases while his union did not. The steel mills were making high profits, but they were not benefiting the steelworkers. In 1959, McDonald led the union in a strike that would go on for 116 days. President Eisenhower attempted to end the strike by using the Taft-Hartley Act, which the union ignored by saying it was unconstitutional. The **Supreme Court** set a date to hear the argument between the USWA and the United States. The strike was affecting the production of **automobiles** and military equipment. For the first time in the nation's history, foreign countries exported steel to the United States. When the strike was finally settled, the workers had a wage increase that they supported. However, imported steel was found to be just as good as steel produced in America. For the American steel mills, it was the end of their dominance in the world. *See also* ECONOMY.

STEVENSON, ADLAI E. (1900–1965). Presidential candidate 1952 and 1956. Adlai Ewing Stevenson was born in California. He received his B.A. from Princeton University (1922) and his law degree from Northwestern University (1926). Stevenson practiced law in Chicago. During World War II, he served in various capacities, including special assistant to the secretary of the navy. After the war, he worked with the U.S. delegation to the **United Nations**.

In 1948, he was elected governor of Illinois. During his administration, he improved the highways, the welfare system, schools, and the police force.

Stevenson was a gifted speaker, but often his oratory was stilted. He had a quick wit, but he often spoke in terms unfamiliar to ordinary people. Some people had a difficult time relating to this intellectual candidate for president when in the **1952 election** and again in the **1956 election** Stevenson was the Democratic presidential candidate. His opposition both times was **Republican** candidate **Dwight D. Eisenhower**. Stevenson was defeated in both elections. President **John F. Kennedy** named Stevenson ambassador to the United Nations.

STEWART, JIMMY (1908–1997). James Maitland Stewart was born in Pennsylvania. A graduate of Princeton University (1932), he worked in summer stock headed by director Joshua Logan, whom Stewart had met while at the university. He performed on Broadway before going to Hollywood. Director Frank Capra cast the gangly, stammering Stewart in some of his best movies, including *Mr. Smith Goes to Washington* and *It's a Wonderful Life*. During the 1950s, Stewart made several westerns. One of director **Alfred Hitchcock**'s favorite actors, he starred in some of Hitchcock' suspense-filled films, including *Rope, Vertigo, Rear Window*, and *The Man Who Knew Too Much*. His service during World War II was used in the filming of **Strategic Air Command** (1955). In 1959, he starred in *Anatomy of a Murder*, a courtroom drama. Stewart was popular with audiences from the very beginning of his film career (1936). His effortless acting was his greatest strength. *See also* CINEMA.

STEWART, POTTER (1915–1985). Associate justice of the **Supreme Court** 1958–81. The retirement of Supreme Court justice **Harold H. Burton** led President **Dwight D. Eisenhower** to appoint Potter Stewart to the bench. Only 39, when he was appointed to the Supreme Court, Stewart was a moderate jurist who carefully thought through his decisions. His father had been a justice on the Ohio Supreme Court. Stewart stated one of the most quoted opinions in Court history in the obscenity case of *Jacobellis v. Ohio*. He said of obscenity, "I know it when I see it."

President **Richard M. Nixon** considered Stewart for the Chief Justice when **Earl Warren** resigned; however, Stewart did not want his family to endure the questioning one had to go through for the appointment. In 1985, Stewart resigned and was replaced by the first woman justice on the Supreme Court, Sandra Day O'Connor.

STRATEGIC AIR COMMAND (SAC). After World War II, the Strategic Air Command was created to provide long-range operations worldwide. From its beginning in 1946 until 1992, when it was abolished, SAC was in control of most of the country's nuclear weapons. Although President **Dwight D. Eisenhower** hoped he could negotiate with the **Soviet Union** during the **Cold War**, he also wanted to have a deterrent against attacks from the Soviets. SAC was the major deterrent. The head of SAC during the Eisenhower era was General **Curtis LeMay**. LeMay made SAC into one of the best fighting forces in the world. *See also* ATOMIC AND NUCLEAR ENERGY; FOREIGN POLICY.

STRAUSS, LEWIS L. (1896–1974). Chair of **Atomic Energy Commission** 1953–58. Lewis Lichtenstein Strauss was a wealthy businessman who began his political career during the administration of President Herbert Hoover. After World War II, he was active in the Atomic Energy Agency and became chair of the Atomic Energy Commission in 1953. He favored production of the **hydrogen bomb** while **J. Robert Oppenheimer**, one of the lead scientists who helped create the **atomic** bomb, opposed it. Strauss used his influence to undermine Oppenheimer's credibility during hearings held by Senator **Joseph McCarthy**. In 1958, President **Dwight D. Eisenhower** appointed Strauss to succeed **Sinclair Weeks** as secretary of commerce. Strauss was acting secretary for 10 months, but Congress rejected his nomination. Strauss's rejection was largely due to the way he had treated Oppenheimer. President Eisenhower appointed **Frederick Mueller** to the position and he was confirmed. *See also* TELLER, EDWARD.

SUBURBIA. After World War II, the baby boom began. Families wanted their own homes, but many could not afford them. The federal government's housing programs of the 1940s through the 1960s made houses affordable. New housing in the suburbs drew many new homeowners away from the major cities. Living outside the city gave families their own space. Levittown in New York was one of the first planned communities, with ranch-style homes. Porches were not a part of the new suburban **architecture**, and the backyard became the family's private area. The **automobile** allowed people to live outside the city and drive to work. Kansas City developer J. C. Nichols laid out housing subdivisions that included prototypes of today's shopping malls. Nichols had built the first shopping center in the United States in the 1920s, the Country Club Plaza in Kansas City. Suburban communities were often segregated, since many **African American** families could not afford to live in the suburbs, or were not welcome. A common belief in the 1950s was that if blacks moved into an area, property values would go down. In 1968, the Fair Housing Act was passed, which prohibited anyone from discriminating when selling, buying, or renting a dwelling. *See also* RACIAL INTEGRATION.

SUEZ CRISIS. After the United States backed out of plans to help Egypt build the Aswan Dam, Egyptian President **Gamal Abdel Nasser** nationalized the Suez Canal on 26 July 1956. Seeking control of the canal, **Great Britain**, **France**, and **Israel** joined to attack Egypt, sending forces in October–November 1956. Israeli forces invaded the Gaza Strip while the French and British moved ships and troops into the area. In response, Nasser ordered Egyptian forces to sink ships in the canal, which blockaded the canal; they would not be cleared until 1957. In November 1956, the **United Nations**, supported by both the **Soviet Union** and the United States, announced a settlement to the crisis. In 1957, the invading forces withdrew. The seizure of the Suez Canal made Nasser a hero in the eyes of his country and others in the Middle East. President **Dwight D. Eisenhower** lamented later that he was so immersed in the Suez Crisis, he was not able to focus on helping the Hungarians in the **Hungarian Revolution** against Soviet forces. *See also* COLD WAR; CONTAINMENT; FOREIGN POLICY.

SUKARNO, AHMED (1902–1970). President of Indonesia 1945–68. Educated in Dutch schools, Ahmed Sukarno was a bright student who spoke several languages. His greatest passion was independence for his country, which had been under Dutch rule prior to World War II. When the Japanese invaded Indonesia in 1942, Sukarno worked with them against the Dutch. After the war, Indonesia became independent and Sukarno was its first president.

During the **Cold War**, Sukarno began shifting toward communism. However, the people of Indonesia grew weary of the country's internal conflicts. Sukarno attempted to make himself the sole voice of his country, which led to his overthrow by a military coup in 1967.

SULLIVAN, ED (1902–1974). Born in New York, Edward Vincent Sullivan was educated at parochial schools in Port Chester. Sullivan's first job was with the local newspaper in 1918. In 1919, he worked for the *Hartford Post*, which folded in his first week. He returned to New York City, where he continued to work as a newspaper reporter. In 1929, he became the Broadway reporter for the *Daily Mirror*. Aside from his newspaper job, Sullivan directed radio programs, produced vaudeville shows, and organized benefits for various causes. During World War II, he raised over $500,000 through benefits he organized for the American Red Cross and the Army Emergency Relief. A pioneer in **television**, he was given his own television program in 1947, *Toast of the Town*, a variety show, which became *The Ed Sullivan Show* in 1955. Sullivan's program was immensely popular. He was able to have **Elvis Presley** and later the Beatles appear for the first time on television on his program. *The Ed Sullivan Show* ended production in 1971, three years before Sullivan died.

SUMMERFIELD, ARTHUR ELLSWORTH (1899–1972). Postmaster general 1953–61. Arthur Ellsworth Summerfield left school at the age of 13. But before he was 30, his Pure Oil Company was Michigan's largest independent oil distributor. Although he attempted earlier to run for political office, his political career actually began when he became one of the organizers of **Republican** candidate Wendell Wilkie's 1940 presidential campaign. In the **1952 election**, Summerfield was chair of the Republican National Committee and supervised presidential candidate **Dwight D. Eisenhower**'s campaign. President Eisenhower appointed Summerfield to the postmaster general's position. Summerfield standardized postal equipment and improved mail delivery. Some of his changes saved the post office money and increased the pay of postal workers. Summerfield also attempted to keep obscene materials from being distributed through the post office.

SUPREME COURT. The highest court in the United States is the Supreme Court. It is composed of nine justices, all appointed by the president and confirmed by the U.S. Senate. A justice's term is for life unless he resigns or is removed by Congress. In 1953, **Earl Warren** was appointed chief justice of the Supreme Court. In his first year as chief justice, the Court made one of its most historic decisions, in *Brown v. Board of Education* (1954), which declared segregation in the public schools unconstitutional.

During the anticommunist hysteria of the **Red Scare** and the witch hunts of Senator **Joseph McCarthy** and the **House Un-American Activities Committee (HUAC)**, a number of Americans had been unfairly treated. In *Watkins v. U.S.* (1957), the Court reversed a contempt conviction of Watkins, a labor leader. He refused to name others who had been earlier members of the Communist Party like himself. In the case of *Sweezy v. New Hampshire* (1957), the Court decided Sweezy's political associations and academic freedom had been compromised by the state of New Hampshire in its search for subversives. The decision in *Boynton v. Virginia* (1960) stated that a bus terminal was part of interstate travel; therefore, passengers could not be segregated as they traveled across state lines.

The Supreme Court justices during the administration of President **Dwight D. Eisenhower** were **Hugo L. Black, Stanley F. Reed, Felix Frankfurter, William O. Douglas, Robert H. Jackson, Harold H. Burton, Tom C. Clark, Sherman Minton, John Marshall Harlan, William J. Brennan Jr., Charles E. Whittaker**, and **Potter Stewart**. Justices Harlan, Brennan, Whittaker, and Stewart were appointed by President Eisenhower.

SYNTHETIC MATERIALS. After World War II, synthetic materials became common in consumer products. Plastic and fiberglass were used in furniture. In 1954, nylon was used in tires. Acrylic, polyester, and Dacron were all produced in the laboratories of DuPont

Industries during the 1950s. These materials were used in everything from clothing to furniture to luggage. The Dow Chemical Company introduced Saran resins and films, or PVDC. Saran Wrap was introduced in 1956. PVDC is used in packaging, since it can be processed to meet various packaging needs. The polymers in PVDC provided hygienic, long-term storage for oils, chemicals, drugs, and food products. *See* TECHNOLOGICAL INNOVATIONS.

– T –

T-SHIRT. The T-shirt was first worn under uniforms during World War II. During the 1950s, it became popular as outerwear. When **Dwight D. Eisenhower** ran for president in the **1952 election**, T-shirts saying "I Like Ike" were seen on **television**, which surprised many viewers. By 1955, T-shirts were accepted as outerwear by the public. T-shirts were used to advertise resorts in Florida as well as Disney characters, such as Davy Crockett and Mickey Mouse. Screen prints on T-shirts also began in the 1950s. **Teenagers** adopted the T-shirt, following **cinema** stars **James Dean** and **Marlon Brando**, who began the fashion trend. *See also* CLOTHING AND FASHION; FADS.

TAFT, ROBERT A. (1889–1953). U.S. senator 1939–53. The son of President William Howard Taft, Robert Alphonso Taft was born in Ohio and educated at Yale University (B.A., 1910) and Harvard University Law School (1913). He was a lawyer in Ohio until he was elected to the U.S. Senate (1939). He served in the Senate until his death from cancer in 1953.

Often called "Mr. Republican," because of his conservative views, Taft was against the New Deal of the 1930s and was one of the writers of the Taft-Hartley Act of 1947. He supported General **Douglas MacArthur** when MacArthur denounced President **Harry S. Truman**'s actions involving **China** during the **Korea War**. Taft hoped to be the presidential candidate in three different elections (1940, 1948, and 1952); however, he was never the chosen candidate. Although Taft was considered the front-runner in the **1952 election**, **Dwight D. Eisenhower** became the **Republican** candidate.

TAIWAN STRAIT CRISES. *See* QUEMOY AND MATSU CRISES.

TECHNOLOGICAL INNOVATIONS. World War II led to some of the most world-changing technological advances in history. Warfare was never the same after the dropping of the **atomic** bomb in 1945. Nuclear technology led to the **hydrogen bomb** in 1952. After World War II, when both the United States and the **Soviet Union** possessed nuclear weapons, fear of a nuclear war escalated.

Rockets used during World War II led to satellites for **space** exploration and weather satellites. Space exploration began when the Soviet Union sent up *Sputnik* in 1957. In 1958, the United States launched *Explorer 1. TIROS-1*, a weather satellite, was sent into the atmosphere in 1960. By 1962, Canada and **Great Britain** had launched satellites. That same year, Bell Laboratories had developed Telstar, the first communications satellite. Tests were performed using Telstar for telephone and television communications, as well as other purposes. Intelsat was developed in the 1960s and is still owned and used by a consortium of countries for telecommunications.

One of the greatest innovations was the transistor. Bell Laboratories discovered the transistor in 1948 and began to market it to companies in 1952. Two companies that bought the new invention were Texas Instruments and Sony. At Texas Instruments, **Jack Kilby** used the transistor to make the integrated circuit. Sony used the transistor for electronics. Sony's portable radios were very popular in the 1950s since **teenagers**, in particular, could carry them to the beach or anywhere that an electrical outlet was not available.

Bell Laboratories also produced solar cells, which turned sunlight into electricity, mainly for use in space research. Some hand-held calculators used solar cells. Solar panels were introduced to generate heat in homes and businesses.

Computers were first employed in World War II, but their use in businesses began in the 1950s. Computer languages were invented, and the integrated circuit and transistor led to smaller computers. The first computers, however, needed a room in which to house the system's many parts.

Television was invented well before 1952, when President **Dwight D. Eisenhower** was elected; however, television sets did not become a household item until after his election. With the end of both World

War II and the **Korean War**, leisure time increased and the **economy** made the television set affordable for many families. By 1960, seven out of eight homes had a television set.

The video tape recorder was invented in the 1950s. One of the people who used it to record television programs was **Desi Arnaz**. *I Love Lucy* is still on television after 50 years because Arnaz saw the possibilities of this new invention. By the end of the 1950s, color televisions were in many homes.

Music was heard on stereo systems, and long-playing records were common in households. Although radio lost much of its popularity to television in the 1950s, very high frequency (VHF) brought more radio stations to listeners.

In 1951, direct long-distance dialing began, followed in 1952 by area codes. The princess phone, in a curved design, was introduced in a variety of colors. It was smaller and more contemporary-looking then a plain black phone. It became very popular in the 1950s.

DuPont Chemical Company introduced nylon before World War II. After the war, DuPont introduced Saran Wrap to keep foods fresh. Chemical companies began to discover other **synthetic materials**. By the end of the 1950s, fabrics, carpets, and clothing were made of synthetic materials.

Microwaves used in World War II led to the microwave oven, introduced after the war. In 1954, Swanson Foods introduced the TV dinner. One could eat at a small folding table, referred to as a TV table, just the right size for the small, precooked, frozen dinner for one.

Copies of documents were no longer reproduced on mimeograph machines one had to turn with a crank. Xerox introduced a machine that could copy a document or a newspaper article with the push of a button. Polaroid introduced a camera that could take instant pictures.

From leisure time pursuits, to household goods, to improvements in the work place, to space exploration, the 1950s were truly a decade of dramatic changes in America and in the world. *See also* ANDERSON, ROBERT B.; VON NEUMANN, JOHN.

TEENAGERS. After World War II, the U.S. **economy** was robust and salaries provided money for families to enjoy time together. Many parents, having lived through the Great Depression and two wars, wanted their children to enjoy growing up, and teenagers benefited from the prosperity.

Some teenagers owned their first car. They began to frequent drive-in restaurants, which became a hangout or gathering place for many after school. The juke box had the most popular songs, and many teens danced to the **music**. Slow **dances** were popular, but as the 1950s progressed, new dances were introduced, such as *The Twist*, which was done with a partner but without physical contact.

Transistor radios allowed teens to listen to their favorite music at the beach or anywhere an electrical outlet was unavailable. The record business became highly profitable for stores and singers. Disc jockeys played records, many influencing teens more than their parents. Teens became a formidable group in the economy.

Teen idols were singers or movie actors over whom many teenage girls swooned. Many teenage boys copied their clothing, mannerisms, and hair styles. **Television** brought these teen idols into many homes, especially through *American Bandstand*. One young singer, Ricky Nelson, was introduced on his family's weekly television program. Some of the other popular singers who became teen idols were Frankie Avalon, Bobby Darin, Fabian, Paul Anka, Buddy Holly, and **Elvis Presley**. **James Dean** and **Marlon Brando** brought a new style to teenagers: the **T-shirt** as an outer garment. Penny loafers were the popular shoe, with a penny housed in the top of the shoe.

Teenage girls followed the styles they saw in *Seventeen* worn by ingénues like Tuesday Weld and Sandra Dee. Pony tails were the popular hair-do of the 1950s. Clothing included petticoats, socks rolled down, sweaters with a cloth collar called a peter pan collar, and flat shoes. Pierced ears were not common among "good girls." Dancing was done in one's stocking feet or in one's socks, leading to the term "sock hops."

In the 1950s, many teens, especially boys, began to smoke. **Cinema** stars helped to lure teenagers to cigarettes, since many were often smokers. Movies changed as the mores of the country changed. Topics never before discussed, such as sex, began to unfold on the big screen. A car and a drive-in movie might lead to intimacy, something "good girls" did not do.

Some parents believed teenagers were causing problems within their communities because of too much leisure time. Juvenile delinquency was increasingly seen as a threat. Many parents, school officials, and law enforcement agencies believed that music and movies negatively influenced teens. They regarded Elvis Presley's gyrations vulgar, and in his appearance on **Ed Sullivan**'s popular television show, he was never shown below the waist. However, if any one person influenced teens in the 1950s, it was Elvis Presley. *See also* CLOTHING AND FASHION; FADS; HAIRSTYLES.

TELEVISION. Television replaced radio as the most popular form of home entertainment in the 1950s. Many popular radio programs and stars moved to television. Movies, a staple of family entertainment, suddenly lost much of their audience. People stayed home to watch their favorite programs. Live performances by great singers or actors and sporting events were on the small screen. By 1960, seven out of eight homes had a television set.

Television transformed the lives of most Americans. In 1954, Swanson's Foods introduced the "TV dinner" to the addicted television audience. Now viewers could heat a fully cooked meal in minutes and enjoy it on a small folding table without missing their favorite programs.

The period from about 1949 to 1960 has often been referred to as the Golden Age of Television. Many high-quality programs aired during these years, written by some of the best writers of the time, including Paddy Chayefsky, Reginald Rose, and J. P. Miller. *Marty*, *Twelve Angry Men*, and *Days of Wine and Roses* were written specifically for television audiences, and all three later became popular movies. By the end of the 1950s, *The Twilight Zone* and *Alfred Hitchcock Presents* were well-written, weekly productions. Broadway plays were broadcast live for television audiences.

I Love Lucy, formerly the popular radio program *My Favorite Husband*, starring **Lucille Ball**, became one of television's most beloved shows. However, the new medium was not available throughout the country, which led some television stars to maintain their radio programs, including **Jack Benny**, Burns and Allen, and the cast of *Our Miss Brooks*.

Television programs of the 1950s were often family-oriented, with a moral somewhere within the storyline. A programming code of ethics was instituted in 1952. Some of the most popular family-oriented programs were *Father Knows Best, Leave It to Beaver, The Donna Reed Show, The Loretta Young Show, Ozzie and Harriet,* and Art Linkletter's afternoon program, *People Are Funny.*

Public educational television began in the 1950s. The first public station was KUHT in Houston, Texas. Problems plagued the station from the beginning because it did not have funding from commercials; however, private funding from the Ford Foundation and the Carnegie Commission kept KUHT on the air. Educational television was saved when Congress passed the Public Broadcasting Act of 1967. Many colleges and universities funded their own televised closed-circuit programs.

Children were targeted on Saturday mornings. Often television programs had a gimmick to entice children to continue watching their programs. *Commando Cody: Sky Marshal of the Universe,* for example, offered a decoder ring available for a nominal cost. These items, of course, did not work as well as on the programs, but they were money-making propositions. Some of the other long-running Saturday morning programs were *The Lone Ranger, Kukla, Fran, and Ollie, Sky King, Rin Tin Tin,* and *Lassie.* In 1956, *Howdy Doody,* originally a popular afternoon program (1948–55), moved to Saturday morning. Western movie stars Roy Rogers and Gene Autrey moved from the movie screen to weekly Saturday morning slots. For preschool children, shows such as *Ding Dong School* and *Captain Kangaroo* were fun and often educational. By the end of the 1950s, half-hour programs for children were the norm.

In 1954, cartoonist **Walt Disney** moved to the small screen with his weekly program *Disneyland.* By 1961, the introduction of color television led to *Walt Disney's Wonderful World of Color.* The program featured many of Disney's popular animated characters, but also some of the finest nature programs, often using time-lapse photography. Disney's Davy Crockett series (1954–55) was not only well received but helped sell countless coonskin caps. In 1955, Disney scored another hit show with the *Mickey Mouse Club* (1955–59). The weekday variety show's stars were talented **teenagers**, called Mouseketeers, who wore mouse ears. The *Mickey Mouse Club* had a theme for each day of the week, and of course, mouse ears became a popular children's product.

Two morning talk shows with news and guests were *Today* and *The Arthur Godfrey Show*. Entertainer **Arthur Godfrey** had an incredible rapport with his audience, but he did not have the staying power of *Today*, which is still televised.

Soap operas moved from radio to television. The companies that sponsored the radio programs were unsure if women would find time to watch their television counterparts, but by the end of the decade, televised soap operas were more popular than the ones on the radio. *As the World Turns*, one of the longest-running soap operas, began in the 1950s and is still popular today.

Weekly television news programs began on the Continental Broadcasting Company in 1938. In the 1950s, news programs became very important. On *Person to Person*, journalist **Edward R. Murrow** interviewed famous people in their homes. Murrow also became the producer of *See It Now*, on which he lambasted Senator **Joseph McCarthy** for his witch hunts. *Today* covered the 1952 national conventions between presidential candidates **Dwight D. Eisenhower** and **Adlai E. Stevenson**. Other live news programs of the 1950s were *Face the Nation*, *Douglas Edwards with the News*, the *Huntley-Brinkley Report*, and *Meet the Press*.

Until the **Quiz Show Scandals**, many of the most popular programs were game shows. Many were from **Goodson-Todman Productions**. Ralph Edwards also produced popular shows, including *Truth or Consequences*, but his track record did not compare with Goodson-Todman. On *Queen for a Day*, after women who were in financial need told their tragic stories, the audience voted for who would win the various items she needed. People competed on *Beat the Clock* by doing a silly task against a clock counting down a set amount of seconds. (Actor **James Dean** began his career by trying out stunts before they were given to a contestant, but he was so proficient that he lost his job.) The *Price is Right* has been a popular game show since 1957. Groucho Marx had a very popular show called *You Bet Your Life*. Game shows are still popular today.

Evening variety shows brought families together as they gathered around the television to see skits done by **Milton Berle**, **Sid Caesar and Imogene Coca**, **Jackie Gleason**, **Red Skelton**, Jimmy Durante, **Jack Benny**, and Tennessee Ernie Ford. **Ed Sullivan**'s weekly variety program was able to acquire some of the biggest stars, often making their first television appearance. **Elvis Presley** made his first appearance on network television to loud applause and the screams of teenage girls. *The Tonight Show* had an unusually talented group of comedians with Steve Allen as its host. Many of the program's comedians went on to star in their own television programs, including Don Knotts, Tom Poston, and the Smothers Brothers. *The Tonight Show*'s adult format fit late-night viewers.

By the end of the 1950s, there were programs for all ages and all genres, including westerns (*Gunsmoke* and *Have Gun, Will Travel*), courtroom dramas (*Perry Mason*), detective stories (*Dragnet*), **sports** (*Gillette Cavalcade of Sports*), **theater** (*Philco TV Playhouse*), and **music** (*Your Hit Parade*). On *77 Sunset Strip*, a character named Kookie, played by Edd Byrnes, was always combing his 1950s hairstyle and using the latest **slang**. His mannerisms represented the coolest of the cool teenagers of the 1950s. *See also* CINEMA.

TELLER, EDWARD (1908–2003). Hungarian-born Edward Teller was one of the chief scientists who created the **atomic** bomb in the Manhattan Project headed by **J. Robert Oppenheimer** during World War II. He was also instrumental in the development of the **hydrogen bomb**. When Oppenheimer opposed development of the more powerful bomb, Teller raised questions about him. The information was enough to warrant Oppenheimer's testifying in front of the **House Un-American Activities Committee (HUAC)** in 1953. Oppenheimer was stripped of his security clearance and was declared a security risk.

Teller followed his work on nuclear weapons with a career as a professor at the University of California at Berkeley and at Stanford University. Scientists and supporters of Oppenheimer were angry with Teller. Shunned by former colleagues, he turned to work with conservative thinkers who were in favor of nuclear weapons. He was a hawk to the very end. *See also* COLD WAR; MCCARTHY, JOSEPH; RED SCARE.

THEATER. The 1950s were a mixture of some of the most successful musicals ever produced and plays with messages reflecting the decade's concerns. Most of these—especially the more popular ones — had a long Broadway run, although they may have been tried out first in smaller cities around the country. **Richard Rodgers and Oscar Hammerstein II** wrote some of the most notable Broadway musicals of the 1950s. Their collaboration produced *Oklahoma!*, *Carousel*, *The King and I*, *Flower Drum Song*, *South Pacific*, *State Fair*, and *The Sound of Music*, every one of which was turned into a successful movie.

In 1957, composer **Leonard Bernstein** introduced his hit musical *West Side Story*, which brought the audience a view of **teenage** gangs in New York. The play was different from anything audiences had ever seen on Broadway.

In 1959, *Once Upon a Mattress* introduced Carol Burnett to the public; she would become one of the most popular **television** entertainers of all time. **Mary Martin** opened in *Peter Pan*, in which she flew across the stage, suspended by wires. Martin and **Ethel Merman** were two of the most popular musical stars of the 1950s. **Jerome Robbins** was considered one of the most influential choreographers of the decade.

Two popular plays incorporated national security concerns into their plots. Cole Porter's *Silk Stockings* told the story of a Soviet economic mission to the United States during the **Cold War** and its attempt to buy needed agricultural equipment. *The Pajama Game* was set in a pajama factory where the workers wanted a raise in pay or they would strike. Striking labor unions in the United States were a problem most presidents had to worry about, and President **Dwight D. Eisenhower** was no exception. **Arthur Miller**'s *The Crucible*, set in the Salem witch trials of the 1600s, was based on Senator **Joseph McCarthy**'s interrogations of supposed communists, who sometimes lost everything because of his actions. *See also* BERLIN, IRVING; GERSHWIN, IRA, AND GEORGE GESHWIN.

THIRD WORLD COUNTRIES. During the presidency of **Dwight D. Eisenhower**, it was common to use the term "third world" in reference to nations that had gained their independence in 1946–60 and were usually underdeveloped. This was in contrast to the advanced (Western) voters of the "first world" and the "second world" of the Soviet bloc. Third world countries, however, were important during the **Cold War**. Many sought to remain "nonaligned" because they were generally neutral, but the United States and the **Soviet Union** each sought their allegiance. Some of the more important third world countries during Eisenhower's presidency were Egypt, **India**, Indonesia, and Nigeria. *See also* CONTAINMENT; FOREIGN POLICY.

THOMPSON, LLEWELLYN E., JR. (1904–1972). Ambassador to the **Soviet Union** 1957–62 and 1966–69. Born in Colorado, Llewellyn E. Thompson Jr. graduated from the University of Colorado (B.A., 1928) and in 1929 joined the foreign service. Fluent in Russian, Thompson was a consul in Moscow (1940–44) and deputy assistant secretary of state for European affairs (1949).

During the presidency of **Dwight D. Eisenhower**, Thompson performed his greatest services to promote peace. As ambassador to the Soviet Union, in 1959 he negotiated a meeting between Premier **Nikita Khrushchev** and Eisenhower in the United States. Plans for another meeting in 1960 in Paris between the two leaders were dashed when an American spy plane was shot down over Soviet territory and the pilot was captured.

Thompson continued to serve as ambassador to Moscow during the Cuban Missile Crisis in 1962 then left the position. President **Lyndon B. Johnson** appointed Thompson to his second ambassadorial tour in the Soviet Union. The **Vietnam War** hindered Thompson's ability to carry out his duties. He resigned from his position in Moscow in 1972 and returned to the United States, where he was a consultant in foreign affairs. *See also* CUBA, RELATIONS WITH; POWERS, FRANCIS GARY; U-2 INCIDENT.

TITO, JOSIP BROZ (1892–1980). President of Yugoslavia 1953–80. Josip Broz Tito was born in Croatia. He took part in the Russian Revolution in 1917 and served in World War I. After the war, he returned to Croatia, where he joined the Communist Party of Yugoslavia. He worked his way up in the party, which actively fought the Nazis during World War II. In 1943, he was named president of the National Committee of the Liberation of Yugoslavia and also marshal of Yugoslavia. In 1953, he was named president.

One of the few leaders politically strong enough to stand up to **Joseph Stalin**, Tito protested the **Soviet Union**'s invasion of Hungary and its use of force to end the 1956 **Hungarian Revolution**. He was on friendly terms with the nations of the Middle East and most of the **third world** and was a leader of the nonaligned group. Yugoslavia was also an active member of the **United Nations**.

In 1957, Tito was invited to meet with President **Dwight D. Eisenhower**, but many Americans were angry that a communist leader would be allowed to come into the country. The Veterans of Foreign Wars and the American Legion believed the visit would be an insult to Hungarians and others fighting communism. Congress pressured Eisenhower to reconsider the invitation. After Tito stated he would not visit, the president held a press conference. He stressed the importance of meeting all heads of states because he believed these face-to-face meetings led to better foreign relations.

In 1974, Tito was named president for life. However, he created a rotating, collective leadership program in his country. *See also* FOREIGN POLICY.

TONIGHT SHOW. **Television** changed the lives of people in the 1950s, and *The Tonight Show* changed late-night viewing. Introduced by the National Broadcasting Company (NBC) in 1953, *The Tonight Show* was a local program in New York. When it became a national program with Steve Allen as the host, the program ran until after midnight. Allen's late-night talk/variety show was a welcome relief from the stress of the day. The regular performers, some of whom went on to have their own television shows and appear in movies, were quirky and funny. From 1962 until 1992, Johnny Carson was the host of *The Tonight Show*, which continues to be popular under Jay Leno. However, it has competition from numerous other late-night programs.

TOYS AND GAMES. Besides the very popular **Barbie Doll**, some of the toys and games of the 1950s were Mr. Potato Head, the Pez dispenser, Matchbox cars, Play-doh, Tonka trucks, and ant farms. With the latter, one could watch real ants live and move through a two-sided plastic container.

The Wham-O Company produced some of the most unique and popular toys of the 1950s, many of which are still popular today. In 1959, when **Hawaii** became the 50th state, Wham-O introduced the Hula Hoop. Flying saucers were the idea for Frisbees. The company also created the Super Ball, Magic Sand, and Silly String.

Lionel toy trains, which had been a favorite among children for half a century, lost favor in the 1950s. Travel by car and plane rose while train travel dwindled. The company attempted to make a train set to appeal specifically to girls; however, it was a failure.

TRANSISTOR. *See* KILBY, JACK; TECHNOLOGICAL INNOVATIONS.

TRUJILLO, RAFAEL (1891–1961). Leader of Dominican Republic 1930–1961. Born in the Dominican Republic, which was occupied by the United States, Rafael Leonidas Trujillo Molina joined the Dominican National Guard, becoming its head in 1924. In 1930, during a revolt, in which Trujillo was not involved, the president of the country was ousted. Trujillo became the new president and quickly used his new office to flex his muscle. In short time, the Dominican Republic had a dictator; to utter a word against him meant death. Trujillo modernized the country and allowed the immigration of persecuted people from other countries, especially during the Nazi regime.

During the administration of President **Dwight D. Eisenhower**, Trujillo began to lose international support, including that of the United States. The Eisenhower administration feared the Dominican Republic might turn to communism, as **Cuba** did under **Fidel Castro**. In 1960, the **Central Intelligence Agency (CIA)** helped plan the assassination of Trujillo, which was carried out in 1961. For a time, the Dominican Republic was unstable. Between 1961 and 1966, the Dominican Republic had three leaders. The United States and the International Monetary Fund have provided the country with economic aid. *See also* COLD WAR; CONTAINMENT; FOREIGN POLICY.

TRUMAN, HARRY S. (1884–1972). U.S. president 1945–53. Born on a farm in Missouri, Harry S. Truman was too poor to afford a college **education**. In 1917, he joined the National Guard, serving in **France** during World War I. After the war, Truman ran a clothing store; however, the business was unsuccessful. With the help of an army friend, a nephew of political boss Tom Pendergast, Truman ran for district judge in 1922 and won. He lost his 1924 reelection bid, but again with the help of his friend, in 1926 he was elected chief judge of Jackson County.

In 1934, Pendergast helped Truman become one of Missouri's two U.S. senators. In 1939, Pendergast was arrested for tax evasion, which also left Truman's reputation in question. Unable to finance another run for the Senate, Truman traveled around the state, seeking support. He was reelected in 1940.

During World War II, Truman was chair of the Special Committee to Investigate the National Defense Program. Truman's committee exposed corporations that were grossly overcharging the federal government. In 1944, President Franklin D. Roosevelt chose Truman as his running mate.

On the death of Roosevelt in 1945, Truman became president. His greatest challenge was to defeat Japan to end World War II. His decision to drop the **atomic** bomb on the Japanese cities of Hiroshima and Nagasaki was highly criticized. Truman, however, believed his decision saved the lives of many in the military by bringing the war to a quick end.

Although the underdog, Truman was reelected president in 1948. He was unable to secure the **civil rights** legislation he promoted within the United States. In Europe, however, the **Marshall Plan**, which gave food and hope to Europeans devastated by the war, was an economic success. The **Korean War**, the firing of General **Douglas MacArthur**, and the investigations led by Senator **Joseph McCarthy** weakened Truman. He decided not to seek reelection in 1952. **Dwight D. Eisenhower**, the **Republican** presidential candidate in the **1952 election**, promised to end the Korean War by going to Korea. The glowing reputation of Eisenhower during World War II and his campaign of hope for an end to the Korean War led to his victory against his **Democratic** opponent, **Adlai E. Stevenson**.

TUBMAN, WILLIAM V. S. (1895–1971). President of Liberia 1944–71. The son of a Liberian minister and an American mother, William Vacanarat Shadrach Tubman was born in Liberia. His father was in the Liberian army, which Tubman joined while in his teens. He became an officer and studied law with a tutor. The president of Liberia was impressed with Tubman and helped him become a senator of the

True Whig Party, the only political party in Liberia. In 1943, Tubman was elected president of the country. During World War II, Liberia allowed the Allies to have bases in the country.

Liberia's economy depended on its iron ore, which brought European and American investors to the country. Under Tubman's leadership, women and Liberian-born landowners were able to vote for the first time. In 1955, an attempt on his life was thwarted.

Liberia was pro-Western and helped keep stability in West Africa. Tubman helped Liberia attain a position in the world that attracted billions of dollars in investments from the United States during the 1950s. The resulting rubber and iron ore industries were among the largest in the world. Liberia's close relationship with the United States during the administrations of Presidents **Dwight D. Eisenhower**, **John F. Kennedy**, and **Lyndon B. Johnson** was lost after the death of President Tubman. *See also* COLD WAR; CONTAINMENT; FOREIGN POLICY.

TWENTY-SECOND AMENDMENT TO THE U.S. CONSTITUTION. When the Constitutional Convention met in 1787, the delegates discussed limiting the president to two terms. Although this idea was not written into the constitution, no president served more than two terms until Franklin D. Roosevelt, who was elected to four terms. In 1951, Congress decided to add an amendment stating that the term limit for a president was two terms. In addition, if a president held office for more than two years, he could only run for one more term.

TWENTY-THIRD AMENDMENT TO THE U.S. CONSTITUTION. When the District of Columbia became the center of government in the United States, it was not considered a state; thus, citizens of the District did not vote in national elections. They could not vote for the president of the United States. For many years, the citizens lobbied for the rights given to other Americans. In 1961, an amendment to the Constitution was passed giving the citizens of the District of Columbia the right to vote in national elections. With a population in 1960 larger than some of the states, Congress stated the District of Columbia could have the same number of electoral votes as the smallest state in the United States.

– U –

U-2 INCIDENT, 1960. In 1959, the U.S. ambassador to the **Soviet Union, Llewellyn E. Thompson**, invited Premier **Nikita Khrushchev** to meet with President **Dwight D. Eisenhower** in Washington, D.C. The September meeting was a success and Thompson planned a follow-up summit in Paris the next year. His plan was dashed when the Soviet Union brought down an American U-2 spy plane over the Soviet Union and captured the pilot, **Francis Gary Powers**. The incident was extremely embarrassing to the United States, and President Eisenhower denied any knowledge of the surveillance flights over Soviet territory. Some historians believe Khrushchev did want to meet with Eisenhower even though the spy plane had been shot down. But after Eisenhower finally admitted he was aware of the flights, Khrushchev showed his anger at a meeting of the **United Nations** by banging his shoe on a desk. The flights were ended but were replaced by satellites that reported back from **space**. *See also* GATES, THOMAS S.; FOREIGN POLICY.

UNEMPLOYMENT. In 1950, the U.S. unemployment rate was 5.3 percent. In 1960, it increased to nearly 5.7 percent. It was one of the reasons **Democratic** presidential candidate **John F. Kennedy** defeated **Republican** presidential candidate **Richard M. Nixon** in the **1960 election**.

The 1950s were a decade of change in the workplace. **Technological innovations** and developments such as the **Soviet Union**'s satellite *Sputnik* meant Americans had to be educated and trained for the changes. Many in Congress wanted President **Dwight D. Eisenhower** to support legislation that would provide jobs, training, and aid to depressed areas; however, the president would not approve a bill to do so. Recessions in 1953–54 and 1957–58 affected companies, which had to lay off workers. Senator **Paul H. Douglas** of Illinois tried to help depressed areas and also to improve workers' skills through legislation. When Kennedy became president in 1961, Douglas resubmitted his legislation to help needy areas. Kennedy already had his own ideas to reduce unemployment. The Manpower Development and Training Act of 1962 was passed with overwhelming support of Congress and signed by Kennedy.

The act funded programs to increase employment through training. *See also* ECONOMY.

UNITED FRUIT COMPANY. The United Fruit Company owned much of the land in **Guatemala**, making huge profits from the bananas, cocoa, and sugar cane raised there. In 1951, after Jacobo Arbenz Guzman won the presidency, he decided to nationalize much of the land owned by American companies, including the United Fruit Company. Not only did President **Dwight D. Eisenhower** fear that Guatemala would become a communist country, but many companies in the United States would be severely hurt economically. The **Central Intelligence Agency (CIA)** launched a covert operation that deposed Arbenz. The new pro-Western government meant American businesses could operate as they did prior to Arbenz's presidency. *See also* DULLES, ALLEN; DULLES, JOHN FOSTER; ECONOMY; FOREIGN POLICY.

UNITED NATIONS (UN). President **Dwight D. Eisenhower** used the United Nations (UN) to publicize his concerns about **atomic and nuclear energy** and nuclear weapons. His famous **Atoms for Peace** speech was delivered at the UN in the first year of his presidency, in December 1953. During his two terms in office, the United States and the **Soviet Union** allowed the UN to solve the **Congo Crisis**. The United States did not involve the UN in **Guatemala**, **Lebanon**, or the **Vietnam War**. But the United Nations played a major role in settling the **Suez Crisis**. *See also* FOREIGN POLICY.

U.S. AIR FORCE ACADEMY. The separation of the U.S. Army and Air Force after World War II provided the need for a military academy for future U.S. Air Force officers. In 1954, President **Dwight D. Eisenhower** signed legislation to begin construction of the academy. Colorado Springs, Colorado, was selected as the site. The first class, admitted in 1955, was housed and educated at Lowry Air Force Base in Denver. In 1958, 1,145 cadets moved to the site in Colorado Springs.

USS *NAUTILUS*. The U.S. Congress authorized the construction of the first nuclear submarine, the USS *Nautilus*, in 1951. In 1954, First Lady **Mamie Eisenhower** broke the traditional bottle of champagne across the hull of the new ship. With the ability to run under nuclear propulsion, the *Nautilus* could submerge and travel faster and farther than any submarine before it. In 1958, the *Nautilus* made history by crossing the North Pole while being totally submerged the whole time. The USS *Nautilus* was decommissioned in 1980. *See also* ANDERSON, ROBERT B.; ATOMIC AND NUCLEAR ENERGY; TECHNOLOGICAL INNOVATIONS.

– V –

VIETNAM WAR (1963–1973). U.S. involvement in Vietnam began when **France** attempted to retake control of Vietnam after World War II. However, **Ho Chi Minh**, communist leader of the Viet Minh, fought to maintain independence from France. In 1954, the French government agreed to a settlement with North Vietnam, following the defeat of French forces at **Dien Bien Phu** a year earlier. President **Dwight D. Eisenhower** saw the communist control of Vietnam as a problem, believing other countries in the region would fall to communism one after another, "like dominoes." As early as February 1954, however, Eisenhower warned that the United States would not get involved in Vietnam's foreign affairs.

In July 1954, the **Geneva Convention** divided Vietnam into two parts: North Vietnam and South Vietnam, pending national elections. When South Vietnam refused to hold the elections, the North increased its support for the Vietminh fighting against the Saigon government. The United States had advisors in Vietnam since the early 1950s, but President Eisenhower did not send American troops. In 1961, however, President **John F. Kennedy** sent support troops to South Vietnam. In 1964, after the North Vietnamese military forces attacked U.S. destroyers in the Gulf of Tonkin, President **Lyndon B. Johnson** sent more troops and the war escalated.

Young people were being drafted in large numbers to provide troops for the war. Protests developed on college campuses and many Americans were weary of the war. In 1968, Johnson announced he would not run for another term, opening the way for **Richard M. Nixon** to win the election with his promise to end the war. In 1969, President Nixon began to withdraw American troops. By 1975, all of

Vietnam was under the communists' control. *See also* COLD WAR; CONTAINMENT; DOMINO THEORY; FOREIGN POLICY.

VINSON, FRED M. (1890–1953). Chief Justice of the **Supreme Court** 1945–53. Frederick Moore Vinson was born in Kentucky. He received his B.A. from Centre College in Kentucky in 1909 as well as his legal degree in 1911. Soon after graduation, he became the city attorney of Louisa, his hometown in Kentucky.

In 1924, Vinson was elected to the U.S. House of Representatives, where he served four terms in 1924–29 and 1931–38. A **Democrat**, Vinson gained a reputation as a fiscal expert and a supporter of labor. He served as associate justice of the U.S. Court of Appeals in 1938–43. President **Harry S. Truman** appointed Vinson as his secretary of the treasury in 1945. When Harlan F. Stone, the sitting chief justice, died, Truman appointed Vinson to become the new chief justice.

Many legal historians believe Vinson was more in favor of the government's rights than the people's rights. In cases involving **African Americans**, Vinson usually voted against them. He died in 1953, and thus did not help to decide the 1954 case of ***Brown v. Board of Education***, the Supreme Court's landmark decision against segregation in **education**.

VOCAL GROUPS AND VOCALISTS. With the transistor radio and its ability to be carried wherever a listener wished to travel, **music** was available everywhere to everyone, especially **teenagers**. The 1950s were the years of **rock and roll** and **Elvis Presley** as well as the introduction of many **African American** singers and vocal groups. Teenagers were more interested in the music than in the skin color of the singer. One of the most popular groups in the 1950s was the Platters, all African Americans. Their records were at the top of the charts.

The Andrew Sisters, who were probably the most famous and most popular women's vocal group of the 1940s, saw their popularity continue into the early 1950s. The McGuire Sisters began as a group in 1949 and stayed together until the late 1960s. But it was during the 1950s that women's vocal groups became especially popular. The Chantels, Martha and the Vandellas, the Blossoms, the Joytones, the Deltairs, and the Bobbettes often had records at the top of the charts.

These vocal groups opened the doors to many more popular women singers, including the Shirelles, the Chiffons, the Ronettes, the Crystals, and the most famous of them all, the Supremes. The majority of the women's vocal groups of the 1950s were African American, for this was one area where they could perform and not be restricted due to their race. **Berry Gordy** introduced African American singers to white teenage audiences via the radio, and *American Bandstand* did the same on **television**.

Johnny Mathis and Sam Cooke had voices that were smooth and pleasant. Their songs were especially popular at sock hops or teen parties. **Pat Boone**, Rosemary Clooney, **Doris Day**, Patti Page, Teresa Brewer, and Perry Como were other popular vocalists. *See also* WEAVERS, THE.

VON BRAUN, WERNHER (1912–1977). German-born Wernher von Braun became interested in **space** exploration after reading **science fiction** books by Jules Verne and H. G. Wells. In 1934, he received his Ph.D. in physics from the University of Berlin. Von Braun was the person most responsible for the development of the V-2 rocket **Germany** used against the Allies during World War II. After World War II, he and about 500 of his best scientists surrendered to the Allies with plans to continue their work on space research.

During the presidency of **Dwight D. Eisenhower**, von Braun was the most famous space scientist in the United States. He helped develop **intercontinental ballistic missiles (ICBMs)** and **intermediate-range ballistic missiles (IRBMs)**. After the **Soviet Union** launched the satellite *Sputnik*, von Braun and his team worked on launching an American into space. Von Braun served as director of the **Marshall Space Flight Center** (1960–72). He resigned after President **Richard M. Nixon** reduced the space budget in 1972. He worked in the private sector until 1977, when he died of cancer.

Some Americans questioned having a former Nazi scientist work for the United States, but without von Braun's expertise, the United States would not have succeeded as quickly in the space race with the Soviet Union. *See also* TECHNOLOGICAL INNOVATIONS.

VON NEUMANN, JOHN (1903–1957). Mathematician John von Neumann was born in Budapest and educated at European universities.

He received his Ph.D. from the University of Budapest in 1928. Von Neumann's reputation in quantum mechanics and set theory led to an invitation to teach at Princeton University. He became an American citizen in 1937. Princeton University offered him a position with the Institute of Advanced Studies, and he remained there for the rest of his life.

During World War II, von Neumann worked on building the **atomic** and **hydrogen bombs**. After the war, he concentrated on programming and storing information in **computers**. His expertise in nuclear weapons, however, remained of vital importance to the military, for whom he continued to act as an advisor.

In 1954, von Neumann was appointed to the **Atomic Energy Commission** after President **Dwight D. Eisenhower** announced a major advance in missile development: the **intercontinental ballistic missile (ICBM)**. After successful tests in the Pacific, the budget for producing ICBMs, followed by production of **intermediate range missiles (IRBMs)**, was quickly adopted.

Not long after receiving the Medal of Freedom from President Eisenhower for his work on national defense projects, the noted scientist passed away from cancer. *See also* TECHNOLOGICAL INNOVATIONS.

– W –

WARREN, EARL (1891–1974). Chief justice of the **Supreme Court** 1953–69. Born in California, Earl Warren received his law degree from the University of California (1914). His political career began in Alameda County, where he served in the district attorney's office. He worked his way up the political ladder to become the state attorney general of California (1938–42). He was governor of his home state for three terms (1943–53) and was **Republican** presidential candidate Thomas E. Dewey's running mate in the 1948 election. They lost to **Democratic** candidates **Harry S. Truman** and Alben W. Barkley. In the **1952 election**, Warren lost his bid for the Republican presidential nomination to **Dwight D. Eisenhower**. In 1953, upon the death of Supreme Court Chief Justice **Fred M. Vinson**, Eisenhower appointed Warren the new chief justice.

Warren aligned himself with the liberal justices who in 1954 decided one of the most important **civil rights** cases in the country's history, *Brown v. Board of Education*. During the years that followed, the Warren Court decided cases that sought equal justice in criminal cases. In the decision of *Mapp v. Ohio* (1961), the Court ruled that law officers must present a warrant in order to obtain evidence legally. In the 1963 case of *Gideon v. Wainwright*, the Court stated that anyone unable to afford a lawyer must receive defense counsel. The 1966 landmark decision in *Miranda v. Arizona* led to the "Miranda warning": when people are arrested, they must be told that anything they say can be used against them and that they will be given legal aid if they are unable to afford it.

After the assassination of President **John F. Kennedy**, Earl Warren headed the Warren Commission, which included Gerald R. Ford and **Allen Dulles**. President **Lyndon B. Johnson** created the commission to investigate all aspects of President Kennedy's assassination. After 10 months of work, the Warren Commission concluded that it was the work of one person, Lee Harvey Oswald, acting alone. *See also* CIVIL RIGHTS ACT OF 1957; CIVIL RIGHTS ACT OF 1960; CIVIL RIGHTS MOVEMENT; HARLAN, JOHN MARSHALL; RACIAL INTEGRATION.

WARREN, ROBERT PENN (1905–1989). Author Robert Penn Warren was born in Kentucky. His home was filled with books, for his mother was a schoolteacher and his father loved poetry. He hoped to go to Annapolis, but an accident leaving him blind in one eye ended that dream. He entered Vanderbilt as an engineering student but found that his interest was writing. After graduating from Vanderbilt (B.A., 1925), he continued his education at the University of California, Berkeley (M.A., 1927). He was a Rhodes Scholar at Oxford, where he met some of the greatest writers of the time, including **Ernest Hemingway**.

Warren held several academic positions but completed his career as a professor of English at Yale University (1962–73). Although he did not live in the South for much of his life, his southern background was obvious in many of his poems and novels. His most well-known work is the novel *All the King's Men*, based on the life of Governor Huey Long of Louisiana; the book soon was adapted into a major movie. Warren won a Pulitzer Prize three times, for *All the King's Men* (1947), *Promises: Poems 1954–1956* (1958), and *Now and Then* (1979). In 1986, Robert Penn Warren was named the first poet laureate of the United States. *See also* CINEMA; LITERATURE.

WARSAW PACT. After West **Germany** was admitted to the **North Atlantic Treaty Organization (NATO)** in 1955, the **Soviet Union** established the Warsaw Treaty of Friendship, Cooperation, and Mutual Assistance, more commonly known as the Warsaw Pact. The pact gave the Soviet Union a firmer hold on its satellite countries. East Germany was a member of the Warsaw Pact, along with Poland, Hungary, Albania, Czechoslovakia, Bulgaria, and Romania. In July 1991, after the Berlin Wall was demolished and the Soviet Union released its stranglehold on its satellites, the Warsaw Pact was dissolved. *See also* COLD WAR; CONTAINMENT; HUNGARIAN REVOLUTION.

WATERS, ETHEL (1896–1977). Film and **television** star Ethel Waters was born out of wedlock. Her mother was a rape victim and Waters had to be self-reliant at a young age. She began to sing in amateur-night performances and in 1921 received a contract with the Black Swan label. **Irving Berlin** heard her sing at the Cotton Club and signed her for his revue *As Thousands Cheer*. She was the first **African American** to sing on a coast-to-coast radio program. Waters's career continued with appearances on Broadway and finally on television and in movies. She appeared in the movie *Pinky* and later in *The Sound and the Fury*. She was the first African American to star in a national television series, *Beulah* (1950–52). Deeply religious, Waters spent her later years touring with evangelist Billy Graham. *See also* CINEMA.

WAYNE, JOHN (1907–1979). Actor John Wayne was born Marion Robert Morrison in Iowa but raised in California. He attended the University of Southern California on a **football** scholarship in 1925–27. His summer job as a prop man was his introduction to the director who would make him a star: **John Ford**. Wayne appeared in numerous low-budget westerns, but his role in Ford's 1939 film *Stagecoach* catapulted him to stardom. He starred in more than 20 movies directed by Ford, including *The Quiet Man*, *She Wore a Yellow Ribbon*, and *The Searchers*.

A staunch political conservative, Wayne did not serve during World War II, but he starred in numerous patriotic movies for the war effort. His patriotism was reflected in his directorial debut film, *The Alamo*, which was followed by *The Green Berets* about the **Vietnam War**. However, neither of these films was a box office hit.

During the **Red Scare** of the 1950s, Wayne was a member of the Motion Picture Alliance for the Preservation of American Ideals. Members ran an anticommunist newspaper, and many testified before the **House Un-American Activities Committee (HUAC)**, naming alleged communists in Hollywood. The members of the alliance saw themselves as patriotic, but lives were destroyed as numerous people were **blacklisted**.

No other actor starred in more movies than Wayne, who was a popular box office draw for four decades (1940s–1970s) and a cultural icon. John Wayne is still considered by some to exemplify the true American. *See also* CINEMA; COHN, ROY; MCCARTHY, JOSEPH.

WEAVERS, THE. The Weavers are the group widely regarded as beginning the modern folk **music** movement in the United States. The three men and one woman who made up the group did not appear together until 1948; before that, all had been singing or writing on their own. The most famous member of the group was **Pete Seeger**, whose leftist political beliefs came to haunt him and the group in the 1950s when fear of communism swept the country. Seeger was called to testify before the **House Un-American Activities Committee**. In 1952, the group parted ways. The problems associated with Seeger's supposed communist leanings and the group's "subversive" songs made their appearances impossible. Radio stations would not play their music, and stores would not sell their recordings.

In 1955, the Weavers, already famous for their recordings of "Kisses Sweeter than Wine" and "Wimoweh," performed in two sold-out concerts at Carnegie Hall. Their appearance brought renewed success to the group. The tape of their concert was sold to a fledgling record company, Vanguard Records, which signed a contract with the Weavers and helped renew an interest in folk music, especially on college campuses. The Weavers were the forerunners of such groups as the Kingston Trio, the Limeliters, and Peter, Paul and Mary. Their songs also inspired Bob Dylan. *See also* BLACKLIST; COHN, ROY; COLD WAR; MCCARTHY, JOSEPH; RED SCARE.

WEEKS, SINCLAIR (1893–1972). Secretary of commerce 1953–58. Born in Massachusetts and educated at Harvard University, Charles Sinclair Weeks served in World War I, after which he worked on the manufacturing of metal products. He entered local politics in Newton, Massachusetts, and became a member of the **Republican** National Committee in 1941, serving on the committee until his appointment as secretary of commerce by President **Dwight D. Eisenhower**. When Weeks left office to reenter private business, Eisenhower thanked him for his help on several important projects, including the **Interstate Highway System** and the **St. Lawrence Seaway**. *See also* ECONOMY.

WHITE CITIZENS COUNCIL (WCC). In 1954, in response to the **Supreme Court**'s decision in *Brown v. Board of Education*, which led to the desegregation of public schools, several whites in Mississippi formed the White Citizens Council (WCC). Unlike the Ku Klux Klan, the WCC met openly. Believing in white supremacy, the WCC used economic pressures against those who accepted or advocated integration. As the years passed and integration was widely accepted, the WCC disbanded as their influence was no longer tolerated.

WHITE, PAUL DUDLEY (1886–1973). Personal physician to President **Dwight D. Eisenhower**. Educated at Harvard University and a specialist in cardiology, Paul Dudley White wrote a well-received book in 1931, *Heart Disease*. Using an electrocardiogram in diagnosing heart disease was of the utmost importance to him, along with prevention of the disease through diet and exercise. He treated the president when Eisenhower had a heart attack, and he showed that one need not be inhibited from most activities because of the illness.

WHITMAN, ANN (1908–1991). Private secretary to President **Dwight D. Eisenhower**. Ann Whitman was born in Ohio. Her husband was a top public relations official for the **United Fruit Company**. Whitman got her job as Eisenhower's private secretary by taking dictation for the **Republican** presidential candidate in the **1952 election**. She began working in the White House when Eisenhower began his first term in 1953. Whitman was Eisenhower's private secretary for 20 years. She kept his personal files while he was in office and managed his correspondence. After Eisenhower left office and retired to Gettysburg, Pennsylvania, Whitman continued as his secretary.

WHITTAKER, CHARLES E. (1901–1973). Associate justice of the **Supreme Court** 1957–62. Born into a poor Kansas farm family, Charles Evans Whittaker left school when he was only 16 to help his family. Through tutoring, he qualified for admission to the Kansas City School of Law. He practiced law for about 30 years. Whittaker was president of the Missouri Bar Association when **Herbert Brownell**, U.S. attorney general for President **Dwight D. Eisenhower**, was seeking a nominee for the U.S. District Court in Missouri and chose Whittaker. When Associate Justice **Stanley F. Reed** retired from the Supreme Court, Eisenhower appointed Whittaker to succeed him.

Although he was a conservative judge, Whittaker was an advocate of **civil rights**, as shown in the case of *Gomillion v. Lightfoot*. In 1960, the city boundaries of Tuskegee, Alabama, were redrawn in order to inhibit **African Americans** from voting. The Court's unanimous decision made the boundaries illegal. The Fourteenth Amendment had been upheld by the Supreme Court.

Finding the stress of the court more than he could handle, Whittaker resigned in 1962. He continued his legal career on the staff of General Motors.

WILDER, THORNTON (1897–1975). Thornton Niven Wilder was born in Madison, Wisconsin, and educated at Yale University (B.A., 1920). He served in both world wars. In 1927, he received a Pulitzer Prize for his novel *The Bridge at San Luis Rey*. He also won Pulitzer Prizes for two of his plays: *Our Town* and *The Skin of Our Teeth*. His novel *The Matchmaker* was made into the popular Broadway musical *Hello Dolly!* Wilder published many novels and plays, and he wrote the screenplay for **Alfred Hitchcock**'s movie *Shadow of a Doubt*. *See also* CINEMA; LITERATURE; THEATER.

WILLIAMS, ESTHER (1921–). During the 1950s, Esther Williams was called America's mermaid. Born in Los Angeles, California, she attended Los Angeles City College. By her teen years, she was a champion swimmer. In 1942, she debuted in her first movie. But it was through 1950s film musicals in which she did incredible feats as a swimmer that she became a star. Her underwater ballet routines were beautiful. In the 1960s, when she realized her box office popularity was waning, she used her expertise as a swimmer to launch a line of swimsuits and to begin a business building and designing swimming pools. Some of her most popular musicals during the 1950s were *Neptune's Daughter*, *Bathing Beauty*, and *Million Dollar Mermaid*. *See also* CINEMA.

WILLIAMS, TENNESSEE (1911–1983). Born Thomas Lanier Williams in Mississippi, author Tennessee Williams wrote some of America's finest plays, many of which became popular movies. Often set in the South, his plays dealt with themes of sexual anxiety and tensions within families. His play *The Glass Menagerie* was a success on Broadway, followed by *A Streetcar Named Desire*, in which **Marlon Brando** gained acclaim for his acting genius. Williams was also the screenwriter for the film version of his play *The Rose Tattoo* and for *Baby Doll*, based on another of his plays. *See also* CINEMA; THEATER.

WILLIAMS, WILLIAM CARLOS (1883–1963). Medical doctor and writer William Carlos Williams was born in New Jersey. He received his M.D. in 1906 from the University of Pennsylvania and then attended the University of Leipzig, where he specialized in pediatrics. He opened his office in New Jersey in 1910 and practiced medicine for over 40 years.

While in college, Williams met Ezra Pound and Hilda Doolittle, two poets who influenced him to write. His first published poems appeared in *Poetry Review*. His poems were about ordinary people, an unusual topic in poetry at the time. His different meters and styles influenced future poets, including **Allen Ginsberg**. Williams's *Paterson* and *Journey to Love*, both written in the 1950s, contain some of his best poetry. *Paterson* was about Paterson, New Jersey, a city in the area where he lived and worked. In 1963, his collection *Pictures* *from Brueghel* (1962) won the Pulitzer Prize for Poetry. Williams never seemed to realize how successful he was. He compared his poems unfavorably to those of **T. S. Eliot**, in particular *The Waste Land. See also* LITERATURE.

WILSON, CHARLES E. (1890–1961). Secretary of defense 1953–57. During World War I, Charles Erwin Wilson, a 1909 graduate of Carnegie Institute of Technology, designed military equipment. Prior to the war, he designed the first auto starters. He worked his way to the presidency of the Delco-Remy Company in 1939. Wilson also held the position of vice president of General Motors. During World War II, as head of General Motors, Wilson oversaw the company's enormous defense production. President **Dwight D. Eisenhower**'s appointment of Wilson to a cabinet position was controversial. He was questioned before the Senate Armed Services Committee about his large stockholdings in General Motors, which Wilson did not see as a conflict of interest, but Wilson finally decided to sell his stocks after being pressured by the committee.

Wilson ran the military and the Pentagon like a corporation. He knew little about **foreign policy** or strategies necessary to confront the threat of the **Soviet Union**. But he helped the president promote the idea of more defense for less money. Like Eisenhower, Wilson feared the growth of the **military-industrial complex**, which led to cuts in the military budget.

Wilson often made comments that were offensive. Eisenhower had to express his displeasure with Wilson when, during the **Korean War**, he called members of the National Guard "draft dodgers." His nickname for the White House was "dung hill." Probably his most quotable comment was: "What's good for the country is good for General Motors and vice versa."

WOMEN'S MOVEMENT. After World War II, many working women felt social pressure to give up their jobs and return to their homes. For some women, it was a rude awakening, for they enjoyed working and wanted to continue. However, funding for day care was gone, and veterans were replacing them in the workforce. Some women had difficulty finding jobs to support themselves. In the 1950s, if a woman wanted to work, she could be a teacher or a secretary; very few women were lucky enough to enter a man's world. Pay for women was far below men's. The argument was that a man had to support a family. Even if a woman was single or the head of a family, perhaps widowed by the war, she still received lower pay.

Women in the 1950s were pressured to be "ladies"; gloves and hats were worn, and dresses were below the knee. Modesty was the norm, and women were not to be in competition with men. Women's **clothing** became a big business, and how a woman looked was a major topic in women's **magazines**.

As the 1950s progressed, some women began to question their place in society. They did not want simply to be sexual objects. In 1963, **Betty Friedan**, a college graduate who believed a woman needed more than being a wife and mother to feel happy and worthwhile, published *The Feminine Mystique*. It sold millions of copies and led women to think about what their roles in the world really should be. Some considered *The Feminine Mystique* the beginning of the women's movement.

One of the most important development in the 1950s for women was the **birth control pill**. Finally a woman could decide when she wanted to have a child. Critics of the birth control pill believed it would allow women to be promiscuous.

A handful of women were entering politics, including playwright **Clare Booth Luce**, the first woman to hold a major diplomatic office when she was appointed ambassador to Italy in 1953. President **Dwight D. Eisenhower** appointed **Oveta Culp Hobby** that same year as the first secretary of health, education, and welfare. And **Wilma Rudolph** and **Althea Gibson** were breaking records in sports long dominated by men. **Babe Zaharias**, considered one of the greatest women athletes, helped found the Ladies Professional Golf Association (LPGA). Women did not have an opportunity before the LPGA to show their ability in the game of **golf**. Today, the LPGA hosts tournaments around the world in conjunction with other women's golf associations.

In 1961, the case of *Hoyt v. Florida* reached the U.S. **Supreme Court**. The question the Court had to decide was one of discrimination. The state of Florida exempted women from jury duty. Hoyt, on trial for murdering her husband, was convicted by an all-male jury. The Court upheld the Florida jury's decision, stating the composition of the jury was not biased against Hoyt. A number of states shared the view that a woman's place was in the home and not on a jury. That view would not change until the 1970s. *See also* ANN LANDERS AND DEAR ABBY; BALL, AND DESI ARNAZ, LUCILLE; CARSON, RACHEL; MEAD, MARGARET; METALIOUS, GRACE; MONROE, MARILYN; ROOSEVELT, ELEANOR; SANGER, MARGARET.

WOUK, HERMAN (1915–). Author Herman Wouk was born in New York City. He graduated from Columbia University (1934), where he had edited a humorous college **magazine**. Wouk served in World War II. His experiences during the war led to his Pulitzer Prize–winning 1951 novel *The Caine Mutiny*, which became both a play and movie. His 1955 novel *Marjorie Morningstar* and the 1962 novel *Youngblood Hawke* were not as popular. In the 1970s, Wouk wrote two more novels about wars, and both became popular mini-series on **television**: *The Winds of War* and *War and Remembrance*. *See also* CINEMA; LITERATURE.

WRIGHT, RICHARD (1906–1960). Author Richard Wright was born into poverty in Mississippi. Abandoned by his father, he and his mother moved in with his grandmother. His first story was published in a local **African American** newspaper, the *Southern Register*. While working in menial jobs, he read the works of Sinclair Lewis and other established authors.

Wright moved from Mississippi to Chicago and then to New York, working different jobs and becoming involved with the Communist Party. While in New York, he was the editor of the *Harlem Daily Worker*. After four of his stories were published in the book *Uncle Tom's Children*, Wright was awarded a Guggenheim Fellowship. After breaking his ties to the Communist Party, he moved to Paris, where he became friends with such writers as Jean-Paul Sartre and Albert Camus.

In his works, Wright tried to show African Americans as different from the stereotypes constructed by whites. Two of his most famous works are *Native Son* and *Black Boy*. He wrote fiction, nonfiction, and poetry.

Wright became a French citizen in the 1940s and traveled extensively throughout Europe, Asia, and Africa. The experiences he had during his trips greatly influenced his many novels. *See also* LITERATURE.

– Z –

ZAHARIAS, BABE (1914–1956). Champion athlete Mildred Ella Didrikson Zaharias was born in Texas. She was nicknamed "Babe" after Babe Ruth when she hit five home runs in one baseball game. Zaharias seemed to excel at anything she did, from domestic tasks such as sewing to athletic competitions such as the **Olympics**. In 1930, she played **basketball** in an Amateur Athletic Union (AAU) competition and led her team to the 1931 AAU Championship. In 1932, she entered eight AAU events and won five of them; she tied for first place in a sixth one. She also set five world records that day. In the 1932 Olympics in Los Angeles, California, she was limited to entering three events. She won two gold medals (hurdles and javelin throw) and one silver (high jump).

In 1935, Zaharias began to play the **sport** for which she would become most famous, **golf**. By 1938, she was an accomplished golfer and entered three tournaments that were not opened to women. She was teamed with a man, George Zaharias, who became her husband a year later. Although she did not make the cut, she continued to excel in golf during the 1940s.

In 1950, Zaharias and several other women formed the Ladies Professional Golf Association (LPGA). Still in existence today, the LPGA supports golf tournaments around the world. In 1950, she was the wealthiest woman in the LPGA.

In 1952, Zaharias became ill with colon cancer. She underwent surgery in 1953, and in 1954 she made a comeback, winning another LPGA championship tournament. In 20 years, she won 82 tournaments. In 1955, her cancer reappeared. She was able to compete in eight tournaments, winning two of them. In 1956, at age 42, she died of cancer.

During her short lifetime, Zaharias opened doors to other women in sports dominated by men. In 1999, she was named the woman athlete of the 20th century by the Associated Press. *See also* GIBSON, ALTHEA; RUDOLPH, WILMA.

ZHOU ENLAI (1898–1976). Premier of People's Republic of **China** (1949–76). Zhou Enlai was born in the Chinese province of Kiangsu, near Shanghai. He was educated in China, Japan, and **France**. During his time in France (1920–24), he helped found a branch of the Chinese Communist Party (CCP). In 1935, he supported **Mao Zedong**'s election as leader of the CCP. For 40 years, Zhou was a loyal supporter of Mao. In 1949, he was made premier of the People's Republic of China. He also became China's chief diplomat. In 1954, negotiating the **Geneva Conference and Accords**, Secretary of State **John Foster Dulles** refused to shake hands with Zhou.

As foreign minister, Zhou was a liaison between China and Formosa (Taiwan). During the **Quemoy and Matsu Crises** of 1955, he refrained from attacking Formosa, but he threatened to invade in 1958. President **Dwight D. Eisenhower** sent American sailors to Formosa to defend the island from the Chinese Communists, which ended the hostilities.

During the 1960s Cultural Revolution, Zhou, a moderate, was criticized by radicals. Yet he remained in his position as premier. In 1972, when President **Richard M. Nixon** made his historic trip to China, Zhou Enlai welcomed him to Beijing. Diagnosed with cancer in 1972, Zhou died four years later.

Appendix I

PRESIDENT EISENHOWER AND HIS ADMINISTRATION, 1953–1961

Presidential Election Results:

Year		Popular Votes	Electoral Votes
1952	**Dwight D. Eisenhower**	**33,936,234**	**442**
	Adlai E. Stevenson	27,314,992	89
1956	**Dwight D. Eisenhower**	**35,590,472**	**457**
	Adlai E. Stevenson	26,031,322	73
	Walter B. Jones		1

Vice-President: Richard M. Nixon (1953–61)

Cabinet

Secretary of State
John Foster Dulles (1953–59)
Christian A. Herter (1959–61)

Secretary of the Treasury
George M. Humphrey (1953–57)
Robert B. Anderson (1957–61)

Secretary of Defense
Charles E. Wilson (1953–57)
Neil H. McElroy (1957–59)
Thomas S. Gates (1960–61)

Attorney General
Herbert Brownell Jr. (1953–57)
William P. Rogers (1957–61)

Postmaster General
Arthur E. Summerfield (1953–61)

Secretary of the Interior
Douglas McKay (1953–56)
Frederick A. Seaton (1956–61)

Secretary of Agriculture
Ezra Taft Benson (1953–61)

Secretary of Commerce
Sinclair Weeks (1953–58)
Lewis L. Strauss (1958–59)*
Frederick H. Mueller (1959–60)

Secretary of Labor
Martin P. Durkin (1953)
James P. Mitchell (1953–61)

Secretary of Health, Education, and Welfare
Oveta Culp Hobby (1953–55)
Marion B. Folsom (1955–58)
Arthur S. Flemming (1958–61)

*Not confirmed by the Senate

Appendix II

CONSTITUTIONAL AMENDMENTS

Twenty-second Amendment

Passed by Congress on 21 March 1947. Ratified on 27 February 1951.

Section 1. No person shall be elected to the office of President more than twice, and no person who has held the office of President, or acted as President, for more than two years of a term to which some other person was elected President shall be elected to the office of the President more than once. But this article shall not apply to any person holding the office of President when this article was proposed by Congress, and shall not prevent any person who may be holding the office of President, or acting as President, during the term within which this article becomes operative from holding the office of President or acting as President during the remainder of such term.

Section 2. This article shall be inoperative unless it shall have been ratified as an amendment to the Constitution by the legislatures of three-fourths of the several States within seven years from the date of its submission to the States by the Congress.

Twenty-third Amendment

Passed by Congress on 17 June 1960. Ratified on 29 March 1961.

Section 1. The District constituting the seat of Government of the United States shall appoint in such manner as the Congress may direct: A number of electors of President and Vice President equal to the whole number of Senators and Representatives in Congress to which the District would be entitled if it were a State, but in no event more than the least populous State; they shall be in addition to those appointed by the States, but they shall be considered, for the purposes of the election of President and Vice-President, to be electors appointed by a State; and they shall meet in the District and perform such duties as provided by the twelfth article of amendment.

Section 2. The Congress shall have power to enforce this article by appropriate legislation.

Selected Bibliography

CONTENTS

INTRODUCTION

The changes in America during the 1950s created a wealth of subject matter for both academic and popular writers. Often referred to as the "happy days," the Eisenhower era was far different from the depictions on television shows of that decade. David Halberstam, author of *The 50s*, has written the most comprehensive portrait of the decade. *American Society Since 1945* and *American High: The Years of Confidence, 1945–1960*, by William L. O'Neill, are other overviews of the decade. For a basic survey of the Eisenhower presidency, see Charles C. Hamilton's *Holding the Line: The Eisenhower Era, 1952–1961* and *The Presidency of Dwight D. Eisenhower* by Chester J. Pach and Elmo Richardson. No historian has covered Eisenhower's life and presidency more thoroughly than Stephen E. Ambrose. Based on personal interviews with the former president and extensive archival research, Ambrose's two volumes are the definitive biography of President Eisenhower. Simply titled *Eisenhower*, Ambrose has divided the president's life into the years before and after he served as president: *Eisenhower, Vol.1: Soldier, General of the Army, President-Elect, 1890–1952* and *Eisenhower, Vol. 2: The President*.

Mandate for Change, 1953–1956 and *Waging Peace, 1956–1961*, Eisenhower's memoirs, provide readers with the president's view of the 1950s from the Oval Office. Another primary source is Sherman Adam's *First-Hand Report: The Inside Story of the Eisenhower Administration*.

For readers interested in Mamie Eisenhower, see Marilyn Irvin Holt's *Mamie Doud Eisenhower: The General's First Lady*, Margaret Truman's *First Ladies*, and Gil Troy's *Mr. and Mrs. President: From the Trumans to the Clintons*.

The Cold War was the overriding foreign policy problem during the Eisenhower presidency. Two excellent overviews are Walter LaFeber's *America, Russia, and the Cold War, 1945–2002* and Stephen E. Ambrose and Douglas G. Brinkley's *Rise to Globalism: American Foreign Policy Since 1938*. See also Steven M. Gillon and Diane B. Kunz's *America During the Cold War*. Harold Brands's *Warriors: Eisenhower's Generation and American Foreign Policy*, David Allan Mayers's *Cracking the Monolith: U.S. Policy Against the Sino-Soviet Alliance, 1949–1955*, and Andrea Wenger's *Living with Peril: Eisenhower, Kennedy, and Nuclear Weapons*.

The most comprehensive study of the origins of the Korean War is Bruce Cummings's two-volume work, *The Origins of the Korean War, Vol. 1: Liberation and the Emergence of Separate Regimes, 1945–1947* and *The Origins of the Korean War, Vol. 2: The Roaring of the Cataract, 1947–1950*. The best overview of the diplomacy of the conflict is William Stueck's *The Korean War: An International History*. Other important sources are Joseph C. Goulden's *Korea, the Untold Story*, Burton I. Kaufman's *The Korean War: Challenges in Crisis, Credibility, and Command*, Rosemary Foot's *The Wrong War: American Policy and the Dimensions of the Korean Conflict, 1950–1953*, and Akira Iriye's *The Cold War in Asia: A Historical Introduction*.

For books dealing with other regions affected by the Cold War, consult Bruce Robellet Kuniholm's *The Origins of the Cold War in the Near East: Great Power Conflict and Diplomacy in Iran, Turkey, and Greece*, Salim Yaqub's *Containing Arab Nationalism: The Eisenhower Doctrine and the Middle East*, Victor S. Kaufman's *Confronting Communism: U.S. and Brit-*

ish Policies Towards China, and Burton I. Kaufman's *The Oil Cartel Case: A Documentary Study of Antitrust Activity in the Cold War*. A useful tool covering the chronology of the Cold War is *The A to Z of the Cold War* by Simon Davis and Joseph Smith.

On the Central Intelligence Agency (CIA) see Peter Grose's *Gentleman Spy: The Life of Allen Dulles*, a biography of the man who headed the agency during the 1950s. A more comprehensive overview is David M. Barrett's *The CIA and Congress: The Untold Story from Truman to Kennedy*. Philip Tubman's *Secret Empire: Eisenhower, the CIA, and the Hidden Story of America's Space Espionage* explains the aerial reconnaissance used to spy on the Soviet Union, including the downing of the U-2 plane over Soviet territory. See also Stephen E. Ambrose's *Ike's Spies: Eisenhower and the Espionage Establishment*.

Many books have been written on Senator Joseph McCarthy and the Red Scare of the 1950s. In *Naming Names*, Victor S. Navasky surprises readers with the names of not only famous entertainers in the 1950s blacklisted during the Red Scare but also entertainers who provided McCarthy with the names of their colleagues. Invaluable sources for understanding the mentality of Americans during the 1950s are *Nightmare in Red: The McCarthy Era in Perspective* by Richard M. Fried, and Robert Griffith's *The Politics of Fear: Joseph R. McCarthy and the Senate*. Richard A. Reuss and JoAnne C. Reuss's *American Folk Music and Left-Wing Politics, 1927–1957* introduces readers to the problems faced by musicians in the McCarthy era.

Vital for understanding the civil rights movement of the 1950s are *Parting the Waters: America in the King Years, 1954–1963* by Taylor Branch and *Simple Justice: The History of Brown v. Board of Education and Black America's Struggle for Equality* by Richard Kluger. Another major work is *Voices of Freedom: An Oral History of the Civil Rights Movement from the 1950s Through the 1980s*, edited by Henry Hampton and Steve Fayer, in which the editors compiled first-person accounts of the fight for equality.

Important biographies of Richard M. Nixon, John Foster Dulles, Harry S. Truman, and Douglas MacArthur include Stephen E. Ambrose's *Nixon: The Education of a Politician, 1913– 1962*, Richard H. Immerman's two books on Dulles, *John Foster Dulles and the Diplomacy of the Cold War* and *John Foster Dulles: Piety, Pragmatism, and Power in U.S. Foreign Policy*, and D. Clayton James's *The Years of MacArthur: Triumph and Disaster 1945–1964*. On MacArthur, consult also William Manchester's best-selling *American Caesar: Douglas MacArthur, 1880–1964*.

Changes in postwar America affected cities, businesses, education, and family life. See Marty Jezer's *The Dark Ages: Life in the U.S. 1945–1960*, Pete Daniel's *Lost Revolutions: The South in the 1950s*, and Diane Ravitch's *The Troubled Crusade: American Education, 1945–1980*. For purely nostalgic

264 • SELECTED BIBLIOGRAPHY

purposes, see *The Complete Directory to Prime Time TV Shows, 1946–Present* by Tim Brooks and Earle Marsh, and *Raised on Radio*, in which Gerald Nachman recalls radio's golden age.

Historians are becoming increasingly interested in the changes in the 1950s that led to the women's movement of the 1960s and 1970s. Joan Meyerowitz's *Not June Clever: Women and Gender in Postwar America, 1945–60* dispels the myths of women in the 1950s as depicted on televisions programs of that decade. In *Higher Education for Women in Postwar America, 1945–1965*, Linda Eisenmann looks at the progress women made in education beginning in the 1920s and continuing through the 1950s that set the stage for the changes that ultimately became the feminist movement. Wini Breines, a sociologist, questions the "happy days" of the 1950s in *Young, White, and Miserable: Growing Up Female in the Fifties*. Breines focuses on the darker side of the 1950s when women were concerned about the bomb, McCarthyism, and the lack of opportunity for educated women. In 1963, Betty Freidan published *The Feminine Mystique*, which exposed the barriers educated women faced in the 1950s.

The Eisenhower Library in Abilene, Kansas, is the primary resource for researchers. The National Archives and the Library of Congress in Washington, D.C., also house papers pertinent to the Eisenhower era and the 1950s. The website www.presidency.ucsb.edu/dwight_eisenhower.php offers a chronology of major events in the Eisenhower presidency. It is an invaluable website for researchers. The Miller Center of Public Affairs at the University of Virginia houses many of the president's papers, speeches, diaries, and correspondence; for information on Eisenhower materials, go to http://millercenter .org/academic/americanpresident/eisenhower. For an overview of the decade, consult http://kclibrary.nhmccd.edu/decade50.html. Two excellent websites for women's history are www.feminist.com and www.mtsu.edu/~kmiddlet/ history/women/time/wh-50s.html.

BIBLIOGRAPHIES, DICTIONARIES, AND ENCYCLOPEDIAS

Charters, Ann, ed. *The Beats: Literary Bohemians in Postwar American.* 2 vols. Detroit, Mich.: Gale, 1983.

Commire, Anne, ed. *Historic World Leaders.* 5 vols.. Detroit: Gale, 1994.

Concise Dictionary of American Biography. 4th ed. New York: Charles Scribner's Sons, 1990.

Current Biography, 1951–1961.

Daniel, Clifton, ed. *Chronicle of the 20th Century.* Mount Kisko, N.Y.: Chronicle, 1987.

Dictionary of American Biography. 18 vols. New York: American Council of Learned Societies and Charles Scribner's Sons, 1946.

Findling, John E. *Dictionary of American Diplomatic History*. Westport, Conn.: Greenwood, 1980.

Finkelman, Paul, and Peter Wallenstein, eds. *The Encyclopedia of American Political History*. Washington, D.C.: CQ Press, 2001.

Grossman, Mark. *Encyclopedia of the United States Cabinet*. 3 vols. Santa Barbara, Calif.: ABC-CLIO, 2000.

Harte, Barbara, and Carolyn Riley, eds. *200 Contemporary Authors*. Detroit, Mich.: Gale, 1969.

Hurwitz, Howard L. *An Encyclopedic Dictionary of American History*. 2nd ed. New York: Washington Square, 1970.

Kohn, George Childs, ed. *Dictionary of Historic Documents*. New York: Facts On File, 2003.

Kunitz, Stanley J., and Howard Haycraft, eds. *Twentieth Century Authors: A Biographical Dictionary of Modern Literature*. New York: H. H. Wilson, 1942.

Morris, Richard B., ed. *Encyclopedia of American History*. 2nd ed. New York: Harper and Row, 1961.

Nolan, Cathal J. *Notable U. S. Ambassadors Since 1775: A Biographical Dictionary*. Westport, Conn.: Greenwood, 1997.

Notable Names in the American Theatre. Clifton, N.J.: James T. White, 1976.

Olson, James Stuart. *Dictionary of United States Economic History*. Westport, Conn.: Greenwood, 1992.

Parry, Melanie, ed. *Chambers Biographical Dictionary*. New York: Larousse Kingfisher Chambers, 1997.

Ware, Susan, ed. *Notable American Women: A Biographical Dictionary Completing the Twentieth Century*. Cambridge, Mass.: Harvard University Press, 2004.

Who Was Who Among North American Authors, 1921–1939. 2 vols. Detroit, Mich: Gale, 1976.

Who's Who in 20th Century America. New Providence, N.J.: Marquis Who's Who, 2000.

Wieczynski, Joseph L., ed. *The Modern Encyclopedia of Russian and Soviet History*. Gulf Breeze, Fla.: Academic International, 1980.

GENERAL SURVEYS

Brinkley, Alan, and Davis Dyer, eds. *The Reader's Companion to the American Presidency*. Boston: Houghton Mifflin, 2000.

Diggins, John P. *The Proud Decades: America in War and Peace, 1941–1960*. New York: Norton, 1988.

Friedman, Robert, ed. *The Life Millenium: The 100 Most Important Events and People of the Past 1,000 Years*. New York: Life Books, 1998.

Geisst, Charles R. *Wall Street: A History*. New York: Oxford University Press, 1997.

Griffith, Robert, ed. *Major Problems in American History Since 1945: Documents and Essays*. Lexington, Mass.: D.C. Heath, 1992.

Grun, Bernard. *The Timetables of History*. New York: Simon and Schuster, 1991.

Henretta, James A., David Brody, and Lynn Dumenil. *America: A Concise History, Vol. 2, Since 1865*. 3rd ed. Boston: Bedford/St. Martin's, 2006.

Hodgson, Gordon. *America in Our Time: From World War II to Nixon—What Happened and Why*. Princeton, N.J.: Princeton University Press, 2005.

Hughes, Jonathan, and Louis B. Cain. *American Economic History*. 4th ed. New York: HarperCollins, 1994.

Isaacson, Walter. *Einstein: His Life and Universe*. New York: Simon and Schuster, 2007.

Kellerman, Barbara. *The Political Presidency: Practice of Leadership*. New York: Oxford University Press, 1984.

Lichtenstein, Nelson, ed. *Political Profiles: The Johnson Years*. New York: Facts On File, 1976.

———. *Political Profiles: The Kennedy Years*. New York: Facts On File, 1976.

Murphy, Robert. *Diplomat Among Warriors*. Garden City, N.Y.: Doubleday, 1964.

O'Brien, Steven. *American Political Leaders: From Colonial Times to the Present*. Santa Barbara, Calif.: ABC-CLIO, 1991.

Patterson, James T. *America in the Twentieth Century: A History*. New York: Harcourt Brace Jovanovich, 1983.

———. *Grand Expectations: The United States, 1945–1974*. New York: Oxford University Press, 1996.

Pauletta, Lu Ann, and Fred L. Worth. *The World Almanac of Presidential Facts*. New York: World Almanac, 1988.

Post, Robert C., ed. *Every Four Years*. Washington, D.C.: Smithsonian Exposition Books, 1980.

Seligman, Joel. *The Transformation of Wall Street: A History of the Securities and Exchange Commission and Modern Corporate Finance*. 3rd ed. New York: Aspen, 2003.

Skidmore, Max J. *Presidential Performance: A Comprehensive Review*. Jefferson, N.C.: McFarland, 2004.

Tindall, George Brown, and David Emory Shi. *America: A Narrative History.* 4th ed. New York: Norton, 1997.

Whitney, David C. *The American Presidents: Biographies of the Chief Executives from Washington Through Carter.* 4th ed. Garden City, N.Y.: Doubleday, 1978.

Wilson, Robert A., ed. *Character Above All: Ten Presidents from FDR to George Bush.* New York: Simon and Schuster, 1995.

Yergin, Daniel. *The Prize: The Epic Quest for Oil, Money, and Power.* New York: Simon and Schuster, 1992.

Chesbrough, Henry. "Why Bad Things Happen to Good Technology: New Ideas Take You Only So Far" *Wall Street Journal,* 28–29 April 2007, R11.

Douthat, Ralph. "They Made America." *Atlantic Monthly,* December 2006, 60–78.

Gordon, John Steele. "10 Moments That Made American Business." *American Heritage,* February/March 2007, 23–29.

———. "50/50: The 50 Biggest Changes in the Last 50 Years." *American Heritage,* June/July 2004, 22–24.

Mark, Gary. "Castro's Illness Reminds Cubans Longtime Dictator Isn't Forever." *Salt Lake Tribune,* 2 August 2006, A1.

Nelson, Daniel. "What Happened to Organized Labor?" *American Heritage,* July/August 1999, 81–88.

DWIGHT D. EISENHOWER

Adams, Sherman. *First-Hand Report: The Inside Story of the Eisenhower Administration.* London: Hutchinson, 1962.

Alexander, Charles C. *Holding the Line: The Eisenhower Era, 1952–1961.* Bloomington: Indiana University Press, 1975.

Allen, Craig. *Eisenhower and the Mass Media: Peace, Prosperity, and Primetime TV.* Chapel Hill: University of North Carolina Press, 1993.

Ambrose, Stephen E. *Eisenhower, Vol. 1: Soldier, General of the Army, President-Elect, 1890–1952.* New York: Simon and Schuster, 1983.

———. *Eisenhower, Vol. 2: The President.* New York: Simon and Schuster, 1984.

———. *Ike's Spies: Eisenhower and the Espionage Establishment.* Jackson: University Press of Mississippi, Banner Books, 1999.

Bischof, Gunter, and Stephen E. Ambrose, eds. *Eisenhower: A Centenary Assessment.* Baton Rouge: Louisiana State University Press, 1995.

Bowie, Robert R., and Richard Immerman. *Waging Peace: How Eisenhower Shaped an Enduring Cold War Strategy*. New York: Oxford University Press, 2000.

Brendon, Piers. *Ike: His Life and Times*. New York: Harper and Row, 1986.

Burk, Robert F. *Dwight D. Eisenhower: Hero and Politician*. Boston: Twayne, 1986.

Chernus, Ira. *Apocalypse Management: Eisenhower and the Discourse of National Insecurity*. Stanford, Calif.: Stanford University Press, 2008.

———. *Eisenhower's Atoms for Peace*. College Station: Texas A&M University Press, 2002.

Cook, Blanche Wiesen. *The Declassified Eisenhower: A Divided Legacy of Peace and Political Warfare*. New York: Penguin, 1984.

Degregorio, William A. *The Complete Book of U.S. Presidents*. New York: Gramercy Books, 2001.

Divine, Robert A. *Eisenhower and the Cold War*. New York: Oxford University Press, 1981.

Eisenhower, Dwight D. *The White House Years, Vol. 1: Mandate for Change, 1953–1956*. Garden City, N.Y.: Doubleday, 1963.

———. *The White House Years, Vol. 2: Waging Peace, 1956–1961*. Garden City, N.Y.: Doubleday, 1965.

Geelhoed, E. Bruce. *Eisenhower, Macmillan, and Allied Unity, 1957–1961*. New York: Palgrave Macmillan, 2003.

Greenstein, Fred I. *The Hidden-Hand Presidency: Eisenhower as Leader*. New York: Basic Books, 1982.

Holt, Marilyn Irvin. *Mamie Doud Eisenhower: The General's First Lady*. Lawrence: University Press of Kansas, 2007.

Kinnard, Douglas. *President Eisenhower and Strategy Management: A Study in Defense Politics*. Lexington: University Press of Kentucky, 1977.

Lee, R. Alton. *Dwight D. Eisenhower: Soldier and Statesman*. Chicago: Nelson-Hall, 1981.

Lyon, Peter. *Eisenhower: Portrait of the Hero*. Boston: Little, Brown, 1974.

Melanson, Richard A., and David Mayers, eds. *Reevaluating Eisenhower: American Foreign Policy in the 1950s*. Urbana: University of Illinois Press, 1987.

Neal, Steve. *The Eisenhowers*. Lawrence: University Press of Kansas, 1984.

Nelson, Michael, ed. *The Presidency: A History of the Office of the President of the United States from 1789 to the Present*. New York: Smithmark, 1996.

Osgood, Kenneth Alan. *Total Cold War: Eisenhower's Secret Propaganda Battle at Home and Abroad*. Lawrence: University Press of Kansas, 2006.

Pach, Chester J., and Elmo Richardson. *The Presidency of Dwight D. Eisenhower*. Lawrence: University Press of Kansas, 1991.

Perret, Geoffrey. *Eisenhower*. New York: Random House, 1999.
Peterson, Trudy Huskamp. *Agricultural Exports, Farm Income, and the Eisenhower Administration*. Lincoln: University of Nebraska Press, 1979.
Rabe, Stephen G. *Eisenhower and Latin America: The Foreign Policy of Anticommunism*. Chapel Hill: University of North Carolina Press, 1988.
Reichard, Gary W. *The Reaffirmation of Republicanism: Eisenhower and the Eighty-third Congress*. Knoxville: University of Tennessee Press, 1975.
Troy, Gil. *Mr. and Mrs. President: From the Trumans to the Clintons*. Lawrence: University Press of Kansas, 2000.
Truman, Margaret. *First Ladies*. New York: Random House, 1995.
Wicker, Tom. *Dwight D. Eisenhower*. New York: Times Books, 2002.
Wukovits, John F. *Eisenhower*. New York: Palgrave Macmillan, 2006.
Brinkley, Douglas. "Eisenhower the Dove." *American Heritage*, September 2001, 58–65.

HARRY S. TRUMAN

Hamby, Alonzo L. *Man of the People: A Life of Harry S. Truman*. New York: Oxford University Press, 1995.
McCoy, Donald R. *The Presidency of Harry S. Truman*. Lawrence: University Press of Kansas, 1984.
McCullough, David. *Truman*. New York: Simon and Schuster, 1992.
Miller, Merle. *Plain Speaking: An Oral Biography of Harry S. Truman*. New York: Berkley Books, 1974.
Pemberton, William E. *Harry S. Truman: Fair Dealer and Cold Warrior*. Boston: Twayne, 1989.
Pierpaoli, Paul G. *Truman and Korea: The Political Culture of the Early Cold War*. Columbia: University of Missouri Press, 1999.
Wynn, Neil A. *Historical Dictionary of the Roosevelt-Truman Era*. Lanham, Md.: Scarecrow Press, 2008.

RICHARD M. NIXON

Aitken, Jonathan. *Nixon: A Life*. Washington, D.C.: Regnery, 1993.
Ambrose, Stephen E. *Nixon: The Education of a Politician, 1913–1962*. New York: Simon and Schuster, 1987.
Brodie, Fawn McKay. *Richard Nixon: The Shaping of His Character*. New York: Norton, 1981.

Mazo, Earl, and Stephen Hess. *Nixon: A Political Portrait.* New York: Harper and Row, 1967.

Nadel, Laurie. *The Great Stream of History: A Biography of Richard M. Nixon.* New York: Atheneum, 1991.

Nixon, Richard. *The Memoirs of Richard Nixon.* 2 vols. New York: Warner, 1978.

Spear, Joseph C. *Presidents and the Press: The Nixon Legacy.* Cambridge, Mass.: MIT Press, 1984.

JOHN FOSTER DULLES

Beal, John Robinson. *John Foster Dulles: 1888–1959.* New York: Harper, 1959.

Berding, Andrew Henry Thomas. *Dulles on Diplomacy.* Princeton, N.J.: Van Nostrand, 1965.

Drummond, Roscoe. *Duel at the Brink: John Foster Dulles' Command of American Power.* Garden City, N.Y.: Doubleday, 1960.

Finer, Herman. *Dulles over Suez: The Theory and Practice of His Diplomacy.* Chicago: Quadrangle Books, 1964.

Goold-Adams, Richard John Morton. *John Foster Dulles: A Reappraisal.* New York: Appleton-Century-Crofts, 1962.

Heller, Deane Fons, and David Heller. *John Foster Dulles: Soldier for Peace.* New York: Holt, Rinehart and Winston, 1960.

Hoopes, Townsend. *The Devil and John Foster Dulles.* Boston: Little, Brown, 1973.

Immerman, Richard H. *John Foster Dulles and the Diplomacy of the Cold War.* Princeton, N.J.: Princeton University Press, 1990.

——. *John Foster Dulles: Piety, Pragmatism, and Power in U.S. Foreign Policy.* Wilmington, Del.: Scholarly Resources, 1999.

Marks, Frederick W., III. *Power and Peace: The Diplomacy of John Foster Dulles.* Westport, Conn.: Praeger, 1993.

Mosley, Leonard. *Dulles: A Biography of Eleanor, Allen, and John Foster Dulles and Their Family Network.* New York: Dial, 1978.

Pruessen, Ronald W. *John Foster Dulles: The Road to Power.* New York: Free Press, 1982.

DOUGLAS MACARTHUR

Considine, Bob. *General Douglas MacArthur.* Greenwich, Conn.: Fawcett, 1964.

Higgins, Trumball. *Korea and the Fall of MacArthur.* New York: Oxford University Press, 1970.

James, D. Clayton. *The Years of MacArthur: Triumph and Disaster 1945–1964.* Boston: Houghton Mifflin, 1985.

Leary, William M., ed. *MacArthur and the American Century: A Reader.* Lincoln: University of Nebraska Press, 2001.

Manchester, William. *American Caesar: Douglas MacArthur, 1880–1964.* Boston: Little, Brown, 1978.

Perret, Geoffrey. *Old Soldiers Never Die: The Life of Douglas MacArthur.* New York: Random House, 1996.

Rovere, Richard H., and Arthur Schlesinger, Jr. *General MacArthur and President Truman: The Struggle for Control of American Foreign Policy.* New Brunswick, N.J.: Transaction, 1992.

———. *The MacArthur Controversy and American Foreign Policy.* New York: Noonday, 1965.

Smith, Robert. *MacArthur in Korea: The Naked Emperor.* New York: Simon and Schuster, 1982.

Wainstock, Dennis. *Truman, MacArthur, and the Korean War.* Westport, Conn.: Greenwood, 1999.

FOREIGN RELATIONS

Accinelli, Robert. *Crisis and Commitment: United States Policy Towards Taiwan, 1950–1955.* Chapel Hill: University of North Carolina Press, 1996.

Ashton, Nigel John. *Eisenhower, Macmillan, and the Problem of Nasser: Anglo-American Relations and Arab Nationalism, 1955–59.* Basingstoke, N.Y.: Macmillan, St. Martin's, 1996.

Beschloss, Michael R. *Mayday: Eisenhower, Khrushchev, and the U-2 Affair.* New York: Harper and Row, 1986.

Bill, James A. *The Eagle and the Lion: The Tragedy of American-Iranian Relations.* New Haven, Conn.: Yale University Press, 1988.

Blaufarb, Douglas S. *The Counterinsurgency Era: U.S. Doctrine and Performance, 1950– to the Present.* New York: Free Press, 1977.

Brands, H. W. *Cold Warriors: Eisenhower's Generation and American Foreign Policy.* New York: Columbia University Press, 1988.

Chang, Gordon H. *Friends and Enemies: The United States, China, and the Soviet Union, 1948–1972.* Stanford, Calif.: Stanford University Press, 1990.

Citino, Nathan J. *From Arab Nationalism to OPEC: Eisenhower, King Saud, and the Making of U.S.-Saudi Relations.* Bloomington: Indiana University Press, 2002.

Dethloff, Henry C., and C. Joseph Pusateri, eds. *American Business History: Case Studies*. Arlington Heights, Ill.: Harlan Davidson, 1987.

Geelhoed, E. Bruce, and Anthony O. Edmonds. *Eisenhower, Macmillan, and Allied Unity, 1957–1961*. New York: Palgrave Macmillan, 2003.

Hahn, Peter L. *Caught in the Middle East: U.S. Policy Toward the Arab-Israeli Conflict, 1945–1961*. Chapel Hill: University of North Carolina Press, 2004.

———. *Discord or Partnership? British and American Policy Toward Egypt, 1942–1956*. Portland, Ore.: Frank Cass, 1988.

Hahn, Peter L., and Mary Ann Heiss, eds. *Empire and Revolution: The United States and the Third World Since 1945*. Columbus: Ohio State University Press, 2001.

Hahn, Peter L. *National Security Concerns in U.S. Policy Toward Egypt, 1949–1956*. Boulder, Colo.: Westview, 2003.

———. *The United States, Great Britain, and Egypt, 1945–1956: Strategy and and Diplomacy in the Early Cold War*. Chapel Hill: University of North Carolina Press, 1991.

Hogan, Michael J., ed. *America in the World: The Historiography of American Foreign Relations Since 1941*. New York: Cambridge University Press, 1995.

Jones, Howard. *Crucible of Power: A History of Foreign Relations from 1897*. 2nd ed. Lanham, Md.: Rowan and Littlefield, 2008.

Kahn, E. J., Jr. *The China Hands: America's Foreign Service Officers and What Befell Them*. New York: Viking, 1975.

Kaplan, Lawrence S. *A Community of Interests: NATO and the Military Assistance Program, 1948–1951*. Washington, D.C.: Office of the Secretary of Defense, Historical Office, 1980.

Kaufman, Burton I. *The Arab Middle East and the United States: Inter-Arab Rivalry and Superpower Diplomacy*. New York: Twayne, 1996.

Kaufman, Joyce P. *A Concise History of U.S. Foreign Policy*. Lanham, Md.: Rowan and Littlefield, 2006.

Kaufman, Victor Scott, *Confronting Communism: U.S. and British Policies Toward China*. Columbia: University of Missouri Press, 2001.

Kennan, George F. *Around the Cragged Hill: A Personal and Political Philosophy*. New York: Norton, 1993.

Kusnitz, Leonard A. *Public Opinion and Foreign Policy: America's China Policy, 1949–1979*. Westport, Conn: Greenwood, 1984.

Lenczowski, George. *American Presidents and the Middle East*. Durham, N.C.: Duke University Press, 1990.

Lucas, Scott. *Freedom's War: The US Crusade Against the Soviet Union, 1945–56*. Manchester, UK: Manchester University Press, 1999.

Macmillan, Harold. *Pointing the Way, 1959–1961*. New York: Harper and Row, 1972.

———. *Riding the Storm, 1956–1959*. New York: Harper and Row, 1971.

Martel, Gordon, ed. *American Foreign Relations Reconsidered, 1890–1993*. New York: Routledge, 1994.

Mayers, David Allan. *Cracking the Monolith: U.S. Policy Against the Sino-Soviet Alliance, 1949–1955*. Baton Rouge: Louisiana State University Press, 1986.

Miscamble, Wilson D. *George F. Kennan and the Making of American Foreign Policy, 1947–1950*. Princeton, N. J.: Princeton University Press, 1992.

Morgenthau, Hans Joachim. *A New Foreign Policy for the United States*. New York: Praeger, 1969.

Nash, Philip. *The Other Missiles of October: Eisenhower, Kennedy, and the Jupiters, 1957–1963*. Chapel Hill: University of North Carolina Press, 1997.

Ninkovich, Frank. *Modernity and Power: A History of the Domino Theory in the Twentieth Century*. Chicago: University of Chicago Press, 1994.

Pastor, Robert A. *Congress and the Politics of U.S. Foreign Economic Policy, 1929– 1976*. Berkeley: University of California Press, 1980.

Paterson, Thomas G., J. Garry Clifford, and Kenneth J. Hagan. *American Foreign Relations: A History*. Lexington, Mass.: D.C. Heath, 1995.

Rabe, Stephen G. *The Road to OPEC: United States Relations with Venezuela, 1919– 1976*. Austin: University of Texas Press, 1982.

Schoenbaum, David. *The United States and the State of Israel*. New York: Oxford University Press, 1993.

Schulzinger, Robert D. *U.S. Diplomacy Since 1900*. 5th ed. New York: Oxford University Press, 2002.

Stephanson, Anders. *Kennan and the Art of Foreign Policy*. Cambridge, Mass: Harvard University Press, 1989.

Stevenson, Richard W. *The Rise and Fall of Détente: Relaxations of Tension in U.S.–Soviet Relations, 1953–84*. London: Macmillan, 1985.

Welch, Richard E. *Response to Revolution: The United States and the Cuban Revolution, 1959–1961*. Chapel Hill: University of North Carolina Press, 1985.

Wenger, Andreas. *Living with Peril: Eisenhower, Kennedy, and Nuclear Weapons*. Lanham, Md.: Rowan and Littlefield, 1997.

Yaqub, Salim. *Containing Arab Nationalism: The Eisenhower Doctrine and the Middle East*. Chapel Hill: University of North Carolina Press, 2004.

Wallechinsky, David. "Parade's Annual List of the World's 10 Worst Dictators." *Parade*, 22 January 2006, 4–6.

COLD WAR

Ambrose, Stephen E., and Douglas G. Brinkley. *Rise to Globalism: American Foreign Policy Since 1938.* 8th ed. New York: Penguin, 1997.

Borstelmann, Thomas. *The Cold War and the Color Line: American Race Relations in The Global Arena.* Cambridge, Mass.: Harvard University Press, 2001.

Cooper, Chester L. *In the Shadows of History: Fifty Years Behind the Scenes of Cold War Diplomacy.* Amherst, N.Y.: Prometheus Books, 2005.

Davis, Simon, and Joseph Smith. *The A to Z of the Cold War.* Lanham, Md.: Scarecrow, 2005.

Divine, Robert A. *Eisenhower and the Cold War.* New York: Oxford University Press, 1981.

Doenecke, Justus D. *Not to the Swift: The Old Isolationists in the Cold War Era.* Lewisburg, Penn.: Bucknell University Press, 1979.

Dudziak, Mary L. *Cold War Civil Rights: Race and Image of American Democracy.* Princeton, N.J.: Princeton University Press, 2002.

Gallicchio, Marc S. *The Cold War Begins in Asia: American East Asian Policy and the Fall of the Japanese Empire.* New York: Columbia University Press, 1988.

Gillon, Steven M., and Diane B. Kunz. *America During the Cold War.* Fort Worth, Tex.: Harcourt Brace Jovanovich, 1993.

Hill, Kenneth L. *Cold War Chronology: Soviet-American Relations, 1945–1991.* Washington: CQ Press, 1993.

Hixson, Walter L. *George F. Kennan: Cold War Iconoclast.* New York: Columbia University Press, 1989.

Kaufman, Burton Ira. *The Oil Cartel Case: A Documentary Study of Antitrust Activity in the Cold War.* Westport, Conn.: Greenwood, 1978.

Kuniholm, Bruce Robellet. *The Origins of the Cold War in the Near East: Great Power Conflict and Diplomacy in Iran, Turkey, and Greece.* Princeton, N.J.: Princeton University Press, 1980.

LaFeber, Walter. *America, Russia, and the Cold War, 1945–2002.* 9th ed. Boston: McGraw-Hill, 2002.

Lansford, Tom. *Historical Dictionary of U.S. Diplomacy Since the Cold War.* Lanham, Md.: Scarecrow, 2007.

Lee, Steven Hugh. *Outposts of Empire: Korea, Vietnam, and the Origins of the Cold War in Asia, 1949–1954.* Montreal: McGill-Queen's University Press, 1995.

Leffler, Melvyn P. *For the Soul of Mankind: The United States, the Soviet Union, and the Cold War.* New York: Hill and Wang, 2007.

Lippmann, Walter. *The Cold War: A Study in U.S. Foreign Policy.* New York: Harper and Row, 1972.

McCormick, Thomas J. *America's Half-Century: United States Foreign Policy in the Cold War.* Baltimore, Md.: Johns Hopkins University Press, 1989.

Pollard, Robert A. *Economic Security and the Origins of the Cold War, 1945–1959.* New York: Columbia University Press, 1985.

West, Nigel. *Historical Dictionary of Cold War Counterintelligence.* Lanham, Md.: Scarecrow, 2007.

Woods, Randall B., and Howard Jones. *Dawning of the Cold War: The United States' Quest for Order.* Chicago: Ivan R. Dee, 1994.

Xiaobing Li, and Hongshan Li, eds. *China and the United States: A New Cold War History.* Lanham, Md.: University Press of America, 1998.

Khrushchev, Sergei. "The Cold War Through the Looking Glass." *American Heritage,* October 1999, 34–50.

KOREAN WAR

Alexander, Bevin. *Korea: The First War We Lost.* New York: Hippocrene, 1968.

Billings-Yun, Melanie. *Decision Against War: Eisenhower and Dien Bien Phu, 1954.* New York: Columbia University Press, 1988.

Cohen, Warren I., and Akira Iriye, eds. *The Great Powers in East Asia, 1953–1960.* New York: Columbia University Press, 1990.

Condit, Doris M. *History of the Office of the Secretary of Defense, Vol. 2: The Test of War, 1950–1953.* Washington, D.C.: Government Printing Office, 1988.

Cummings, Bruce. *The Origins of the Korean War, Vol. 1: Liberation and the Emergence of Separate Regimes, 1945–1947.* Princeton, N.J.: Princeton University Press, 1981.

———. *The Origins of the Korean War, Vol. 2: The Roaring of the Cataract, 1947–1950.* Princeton, N.J.: Princeton University Press, 1990.

Edwards, Paul M. *The A to Z of the Korean War.* Lanham, Md.: Scarecrow, 2005.

———. *The Korean War: A Historical Dictionary.* Lanham, Md.: Scarecrow, 2003.

Foot, Rosemary. *A Substitute for Victory: The Politics of Peacemaking at the Korean Armistice Talks.* Ithaca, N.Y.: Cornell University Press, 1990.

———. *The Wrong War: American Policy and the Dimensions of the Korean Conflict, 1950–1953.* Ithaca, N.Y.: Cornell University Press, 1985.

Goulden, Joseph C. *Korea, the Untold Story*. New York: Times Books, 1982.

Hastings, Max. *The Korean War*. New York: Touchstone, 1988.

Iriye, Akira. *The Cold War in Asia: A Historical Introduction*. Englewood Cliffs, N.J.: Prentice-Hall, 1974.

Kaufman, Burton I., *The Korean War: Challenges in Crisis, Credibility, and Command*. New York: Knopf, 1986.

Stueck, William W. *The Korean War: An International History*. Princeton, N.J.: Princeton University Press, 1995.

——. *Rethinking the Korean War: A New Diplomatic and Strategic History*. Princeton, N.J.: Princeton University Press, 2002.

Weintraub, Stanley. "How to Remember the Forgotten War." *American Heritage*, May/June 2000, 100–106.

VIETNAM WAR

Anderson, David L. *Trapped by Success: The Eisenhower Administration and Vietnam, 1953–1961*. New York: Columbia University Press, 1991.

Herring, George C. *America's Longest War: The United States and Vietnam, 1950–1975*. 4th ed. New York: McGraw-Hill, 2002.

Karnow, Stanley. *Vietnam: A History*. New York: Viking, 1983.

Kolko, Gabriel. *Anatomy of a War: Vietnam, the United States, and the Modern Historical Experience*. New York: Pantheon, 1987.

Logevall, Fredrik. *The Origins of the Vietnam War*. New York: Longman, 2001.

Moise, Edwin E. *The A to Z of the Vietnam War*. Lanham, Md.: Scarecrow, 2005.

——. *Historical Dictionary of the Vietnam War*. Lanham, Md.: Scarecrow, 2002.

CENTRAL INTELLIGENCE AGENCY

Barrett, David M. *The CIA and Congress: The Untold Story from Truman to Kennedy*. Lawrence: University Press of Kansas, 2005.

Grose, Peter. *Gentleman Spy: The Life of Allen Dulles*. Boston: Houghton Mifflin, 1994.

Jeffreys-Jones, Rhodri. *The CIA and American Democracy*. New Haven, Conn.: Yale University Press, 1989.

Olmsted, Kathryn. *Lapdog or Rogue Elephant? CIA Controversies from 1947 to 2004*. Westport, Conn.: Greenwood, 2005.

Ranelagh, John. *The Agency: The Rise and Decline of the CIA*. New York: Simon and Schuster, 1986.

Taubman, Philip. *Secret Empire: Eisenhower, the CIA, and the Hidden Story of America's Space Espionage*. New York: Simon and Schuster, 2003.

Theoharis, Athan, ed. *The Central Intelligence Agency: Security Under Scrutiny*. Westport, Conn.: Greenwood, 2006.

RED SCARE AND MCCARTHYISM

Bayley, Edwin R. *Joe McCarthy and the Press*. New York: Pantheon, 1982.

Broadwater, Jeff. *Eisenhower and the Anti-Communist Crusade*. Chapel Hill: University of North Carolina Press, 1992.

Fried, Richard, M. *Nightmare in Red: the McCarthy Era in Perspective*. New York: Oxford University Press, 1990.

Hajdu, David. *The Ten-Cent Plague: The Great Comic-Book Scare and How It Changed America*. New York: Farrar, Straus and Giroux, 2008.

Griffith, Robert. *The Politics of Fear: Joseph R. McCarthy and the Senate*. 2nd ed. Amherst: University of Massachusetts Press, 1987.

Navasky, Victor S. *Naming Names*. New York: Viking, 1980.

Oshinsky, David M. *A Conspiracy So Immense: The World of Joe McCarthy*. New Brunswick, N.J.: Rutgers University Press, 1983.

Reeves, Thomas C. *The Life and Times of Joe McCarthy: A Biography*. New York: Stein and Day, 1982.

Reuss, Richard A., and JoAnne C. Reuss. *American Folk Music and Left-Wing Politics, 1927–1957*. Lanham, Md.: Scarecrow, 2000.

Schrecker, Ellen W. *The Age of McCarthyism: A Brief History with Documents*. Boston: Bedford, 1994.

——. *McCarthyism and the Labor Movement: The Role of the State*. New Brunswick, N.J.: Rutgers University Press, 1992.

——. *Many Are the Crimes: McCarthyism in America*. Princeton, N.J.: Princeton University Press, 1998.

Slide, Anthony. *Actors on Red Alert*. Lanham, Md.: Scarecrow, 1999.

Theoharis, Athan. *Chasing Spies: How the FBI Failed in Counterintelligence but Promoted the Politics of McCarthyism in the Cold War Years*. Chicago: Ivan R. Dee, 2002.

——. *Seeds of Repression: Harry S. Truman and the Origins of McCarthyism*. Chicago: Quadrangle, 1971.

"The Graphic Menace: The Cold War–Era Assault on Comic Book Culture, Revisited." *Wired,* March 2008, 82.

Menard, Louis. "The Horror: Congress Investigates the Comics." *New Yorker,* 31 March 2008, 124–28.

Powers, Ron. "Penny Dreadfuls: A History of America's Midcentury War Against the Comics Industry." *New York Times Book Review,* 23 March 2008, 10.

Trachtenberg, Jeffrey A. "The War Against Comics." *Wall Street Journal,* 14 March 2008, W2.

AFRICAN AMERICANS

Great People of the 20th Century. New York: Time Books, 1996.

Hine, Darlene Clark, ed., *Black Women in America.* 2nd ed. 3 vols. New York: Oxford University Press, 2005.

Knight, Virginia Curtin, ed. *African Biography.* 3 vols. Detroit, Mich.: UXL, 1999.

Low, W. Augustus, and Virgil A. Clift. *Encyclopedia of Black America.* New York: McGraw Hill, 1981.

Smith, Jessie Carney, ed. *Notable Black American Men.* Farmington Hills, Mich.: Gale, 1999.

———. *Black Heroes of the 20th Century.* Detroit, Mich.: Visible Ink, 1998.

CIVIL RIGHTS MOVEMENT

Branch, Taylor. *Parting the Waters: America in the King Years, 1954–1963.* New York: Simon and Schuster, 1988.

Burk, Robert Fredrick. *The Eisenhower Administration and Black Civil Rights.* Knoxville: University of Tennessee Press, 1984.

Garrow, David J. *Bearing the Cross: Martin Luther King, Jr., and the Southern Christian Leadership Conference.* New York: Morrow, 1986.

Halpern, Stephen C. *On the Limits of the Law: The Ironic Legacy of Title VI of the 1964 Civil Rights Act.* Baltimore, Md.: Johns Hopkins University Press, 1965.

Hampton, Henry, and Steve Fayer, eds. *Voices of Freedom: An Oral History of the Civil Rights Movement from the 1950s Through the 1980s.* New York: Bantam, 1990.

Higgins, Trumbull. *The Perfect Failure: Kennedy, Eisenhower, and the CIA at the Bay of Pigs.* New York: Norton, 1987.

Jones, Leon. *From Brown to Boston: Desegregation in Education 1954–1974.* Lanham, Md.: Scarecrow, 1979.

Kluger, Richard. *Simple Justice: The History of Brown v. Board of Education and Black America's Struggle for Equality.* New York: Knopf, 1975.

Luker, Ralph E. *Historical Dictionary of the Civil Rights Movement.* Lanham, Md.: Scarecrow, 1996.

Myrdal, Gunnar. *An American Dilemma: The Negro Problem and Modern Democracy.* New York: Harper and Row, 1962.

Oates, Stephen B. *Let the Trumpet Sound: The Life of Martin Luther King, Jr.* New York: Harper and Row, 1982.

O'Brien, Gail Williams. *The Color of Law: Race, Violence, and Justice in the Post-World War II South.* Chapel Hill: University of North Carolina Press, 1999.

Patterson, James T. *Brown v. Board of Education: A Civil Rights Milestone and Its Troubled Legacy.* New York: Oxford University Press, 2001.

WOMEN'S MOVEMENT

Breines, Wini. *Young, White, and Miserable: Growing Up Female in the Fifties.* Chicago: University of Chicago Press, 2001.

Eisenmann, Linda. *Higher Education for Women in Postwar America, 1945–1965.* Baltimore, Md.: Johns Hopkins University Press, 2006.

Feldstein, Ruth. *Motherhood in Black and White: Race and Sex in American Liberalism, 1930–1965.* Ithaca, N.Y.: Cornell University Press, 2000.

Harrison, Cynthia Ellen. *On Account of Sex: The Politics of Women's Issues, 1945–1968.* Berkeley, Calif.: University of California Press, 1988.

Harvey, Brett. *The Fifties: A Women's Oral History.* New York: Harper Perennial, 1994.

Rotskoff, Lori. *Love on the Rocks: Men, Women, and Alcohol in Post-World War II America.* Chapel Hill: University of North Carolina Press, 2002.

May, Elaine Tyler. *Homeward Bound: American Families in the Cold War Era.* New York: Basic Books, 1988.

Meyerowitz, Joanne, ed. *Not June Cleaver: Women and Gender in Postwar America, 1945–1960.* Philadelphia: Temple University Press, 1994.

Saari, Peggy, ed. *Prominent Women of the 20th Century.* 4 vols. New York: UXL, 1996.

POPULAR CULTURE AND SOCIETY

Brooks, Tim, and Earle Marsh. *The Complete Directory to Prime Time TV Shows, 1946–Present*. New York: Ballantine, 1988.

Cohen, Lizabeth. *A Consumer's Republic: The Politics of Mass Consumption in Postwar America*. New York: Knopf, 2003.

Daniel, Pete. *Lost Revolutions: The South in the 1950s*. Chapel Hill: University of North Carolina Press for Smithsonian National Museum of American History, Washington, D.C., 2000.

Gilbert, James Burkhart. *A Cycle of Outrage: America's Reaction to the Juvenile Delinquent in the 1950s*. New York: Oxford University Press, 1986.

Halberstam, David. *The 50s*. New York: Villard, 1993.

Heslam, David, ed. *The Rock 'n' Roll Years*. New York: Crescent, 1990.

Jackson, Kenneth T. *Crabgrass Frontier: The Suburbanization of the United States*. New York: Oxford University Press, 1985.

Jezer, Marty. *The Dark Ages: Life in the United States, 1945–1960*. Boston: South End, 1982.

Jones, Landon Y. *Great Expectations: America and the Baby Boom Generation*. New York: Coward, McCann and Geoghegan, 1980.

Luxenberg, Stan. *Roadside Empires: How the Chains Franchised America*. New York: Viking, 1985.

Nachman, Gerald. *Raised on Radio*. Berkeley: University of California Press, 2000.

O'Neill, William L. *American Society Since 1945*. Chicago: Quadrangle, 1969.

———. *American High: The Years of Confidence, 1945–1960*. New York: Free Press, 1986.

Ravitch, Diane. *The Troubled Crusade: American Education, 1945–1980*. New York: Basic Books, 1983.

Russo, Christopher, and Allen St. John. *The Mad Dog Hall of Fame: The Ultimate Top-Ten Rankings of the Best in Sports*. New York: Doubleday, 2006.

Spring, Joel. *The Sorting Machine: American Educational Policy Since 1945*. New York: Longman, 1976.

Cheever, Benjamin H. "The Gray Flannel World." *American Heritage*, February/March 2000, 92–97.

Crossen, Cynthia. "For a Time in the '50s, a Huckster Fanned Fears of Ad 'Hypnosis.' " *Wall Street Journal*, 5 November 2007, B1.

Forbes, Tim. "You Can Tell It's Mattel . . . It's Swell!" *American Heritage*, November/December 2001, 58–62.

Hine, Thomas. "The Rise and Decline of the Teenager." *American Heritage*, September 1999, 70–83.

Karras, Christy. "Howl, Allen Ginsberg's Sound and Fury: A Poem Written and Read 50 Years Ago Still Has Haunting Relevance Today." *Salt Lake Tribune*, October 2005, E1.

LeCompte, Tom. "The 18-Hole Hustle." *American Heritage*, August/September 2005, 58–67.

Lemann, Nicholas. "Tune in Yesterday: The Making of Broadcast Television." *New Yorker*, 30 April 2007, 80–83.

Martin, Douglas. "Richard Knerr, 82, Craze Creator, Dies." *New York Times*, 18 January 2008, C9.

Schoemer, Karen. "More Mr. Nice Guy: How Pat Boone Seduced a Rock Critic." *American Heritage*, February/March 2008, 29–39.

Smoler, Fredric. "Paradise Lost." *American Heritage* February/March 1998, 58–67.

Teachout, Terry. "In Jerome Robbins's Footsteps." *Wall Street Journal*, 17 August 2007, W7.

WEBSITES

www.africanamericans.com
www.coldwar.org
www.fiftiesweb.com
www.history-of-rock.com
http://kclibrary.nhmccd.edu/decade50.html
www.sechistorical.org
www.feminist.com
www.mtsu.edu/~kmiddlet/history/women/time/wh-50s.html
http://millercenter.org/academic/americanpresident/eisenhower

About the Authors

Burton Kaufman is a retired dean of the School of Interdisciplinary Studies and professor of history at Miami University, Ohio. He has also taught at the University of New Orleans, Kansas State University, and Virginia Tech, where he was head of the history department. He has written ten books on U.S. foreign policy and the American presidency, including *The Presidency of James Earl Carter, Jr.* He is presently an adjunct professor of history at the University of Utah.

Diane Kaufman received her master's degree from Kansas State University. While teaching in Kansas, she received both a state and national award for her work in economics, as well as recognition as one of the Outstanding Leaders in Elementary and Secondary Education in 1976. She has served on the board of Scholastic Books and was a reference librarian at the Manhattan Public Library, Manhattan, Kansas. At the Newman Library of Virginia Tech, she was head of conservation. She has also headed the Western College Memorial Archives at Miami University, Ohio. She is currently working on a second book for Scarecrow Press, *The Historical Dictionary of the Carter Era*.